Undergraduate Topics in Computer Science

Undergraduate Topics in Computer Science (UTiCS) delivers high-quality instructional content for undergraduates studying in all areas of computing and information science. From core foundational and theoretical material to final-year topics and applications, UTiCS books take a fresh, concise, and modern approach and are ideal for self-study or for a one- or two-semester course. The texts are all authored by established experts in their fields, reviewed by an international advisory board, and contain numerous examples and problems. Many include fully worked solutions.

For further volumes:
http://www.springer.com/series/7592

Yosi Ben-Asher

Multicore Programming Using the ParC Language

 Springer

Yosi Ben-Asher
Department of Computer Science
University of Haifa
Haifa, Israel

ISSN 1863-7310   Undergraduate Topics in Computer Science
ISBN 978-1-4471-2163-3   ISBN 978-1-4471-2164-0 (eBook)
DOI 10.1007/978-1-4471-2164-0
Springer London Heidelberg New York Dordrecht

Library of Congress Control Number: 2012940236

Preface

This book discusses principles of practical parallel programming using shared memory on multicore machines. It uses a simple yet powerful parallel dialect of C called ParC as the basic programming language. The book contains a mixture of research directions combined with elementary material and basic concepts of parallel processing. As such it is intended to serve both as a text-book for a course on shared memory programming and as a way to improve the research background of specialists working on practical implementations of parallel programming systems over multicore machines. The objective of this book is to provide a firm basis for the "delicate art" of creating efficient parallel programs. The students can exercise parallel programming using a simulation software, which is portable on PC/Unix Multicore computers. Hence no special hardware is needed in order to gain experience in parallel programming using this book. Apart from the simulator *ParC* can be directly executed on Multicore machines. In the first four chapters elementary and advance concepts of parallel programming are carefully introduced via *ParC* examples. There is a special effort to present parallel programs as partial order over a set of assignments. Partial orders thus form the basis for determining elementary concepts such as the execution time of parallel programs scheduling, atomicity and threads.

The remaining chapters cover issues in parallel operating systems and compilation techniques that are relevant for shared memory and multicore machines. This reflects our belief that knowing how a parallel system works is necessary to master parallel programming. It describes the principles of scheduling parallel programs and the way ParC's constructs are implemented. A separate chapter presents a set of ParC programs that forms a benchmark for measuring basic constants of the underlying system, e.g., the cost of creating a thread. A set of relevant compilation techniques of ParC programs is described. A special treatment is given to stack management, showing that essentially the stacks of different threads can be mapped to the regular stack of each core.

This book targets multicore machines which are now available as regular personal computers, laptops and servers. The shared memory in multicore machines is implemented using complex algorithms maintaining cache-consistency of the different cores. The hidden costs involved with the use of cache-consistency can easily damage the expected benefit of using shared memory parallel programming in multicore machines. Thus we carefully study the issue of cache consistency in multicore machines and consider several programming techniques to optimize the cache usage in ParC programs.

The usefulness of ParC stems from two sources. On the one hand, it is similar in flavor to the pseudo-languages that are used by theoreticians for describing their parallel algorithms. Indeed, parallel algorithms can be directly coded in ParC. On the other hand, sequential code segments can be easily parallelized in ParC. These two directions of coding parallel algorithms and parallelizing sequential code form the basis for developing practical parallel programs and are thus widely studied in this book. The ParC language promotes an understanding of the problems hidden in parallel code, and allows various approaches for their solutions. Though there are several popular ways of programming multicore machines such as OpenMP and Java-multithreading, we prefer ParC for learning parallel programming:

- It is significantly simpler than OpenMP and is naturally learned and used by C programmers.
- In some sense, it is more powerful than OpenMP and Java due to its extended scoping rules and support for optimizing locality of shared memory references.

As parallel hardware becomes more and more popular the demand to develop methodologies for teaching parallel programming becomes more evident. This book promotes the idea that parallel programming is best taught through the issue of **efficiency**. The claim is, that parallel programming capability is best gained through a systematic learning of programming techniques used to derive better efficient versions of parallel programs. Rather than surveying, parallel architectures, programming stiles and a verity of applications, as is the case in many of the existing books in this field.

Finally, the only motive in developing and using parallel machines and languages is to speedup performances. This calls for a highly skilled careful programmer, who can create efficient programs, which exploit all potential advantages of the parallel hardware. A parallel algorithm can be programmed in many ways, yielding different performances. Lack of experience and careless programming can easily lead to extreme situations, namely when the performances of a parallel program executed on a given parallel machine, are actually worse than its sequential version.

In this book the method used to evaluate the expected performances of programs is **analytical**. The source code of the program is analyzed via a formula to determine the execution time of a program based on derived upper and a lower bounds. Next a speedup formula is derived and is separated to the different factors that may block the program from achieving a good speedup. Following this procedure it is possible to identify bottlenecks areas in the program and correct them. We shortly consider a second method to locate limiting factors that is based on the ParC simulator. The program is executed on a simulator, and its time measurements are used to spot performance hot-spots. Two types of time statistics for a parallel execution of a program are defined. Ideal-times are execution times that reflect optimal execution of the program without any practical considerations (such as number of cores and overheads), while the Effective-times reflect limiting factors. An efficient program is obtained (using a simulator) when the gap between the ideal times and the effective times is reduced.

Acknowledgements

ParC was first developed by Yosi Ben-Asher and Marc Snir at NYU the first implementation run on the Ultra Computer at NYU. At a later stage *ParC* was implemented on the Makbilan research project led by Larry Rudolph in the Hebrew University. The compiler and simulator were written by Yosi Ben-Asher. A new run-time environment for *ParC* on the Makbilan was implemented by Dror Feitelson, Moshe Ben Ezra, and Lior Picherski. Gudy Habber modified the *ParC* simulator from SUN workstation to PC-DOS systems.

Contents

Chapter 1
Basic Concepts in Parallel Algorithms and Parallel Programming

The world of parallel processing is complex and combines many different ideas together. We first consider the question what is a parallel machine? We answer this question by presenting a model to build parallel machines. Separately, we consider the need to define what "parallel programs" are. We use partial orders to define the notion of parallel programs and show how they can be potentially executed on parallel machines.

1.1 Parallel Machines

Parallel machines can be viewed as a collection of sequential machines (processing elements or processors) that can communicate with one another. The processing elements are also called processors and correspond to a regular computer/CPU capable of executing a sequential program. Thus, from a hardware perspective, a parallel machine is a collection of independent, sequential machines/processors that are capable of communicating with one another. From a software perspective, a parallel machine executes parallel programs which, for the time being, can be regarded as a dynamic set of sequential programs (called threads) that can communicate with one another.

It follows that the most important aspect of both parallel machines and parallel programs is the ability of the processors/threads to communicate. It is this ability that glues a set of sequential-machines or a set of sequential-programs to a single coherent parallel-machine/parallel-program. Thus, from both hardware and software perspective, in order to understand what parallel machines are we need to define what we mean by "communication". Basically we first consider the question of what is communication between two entities and consider how to extend to a larger set. In general there can be two forms of communication between two processors/threads:

- Message passing where one processors sends a data that is received by the other processor.

Y. Ben-Asher, *Multicore Programming Using the ParC Language*,
Undergraduate Topics in Computer Science,
DOI 10.1007/978-1-4471-2164-0_1, © Springer-Verlag London 2012

Fig. 1.1 Example of a communication network

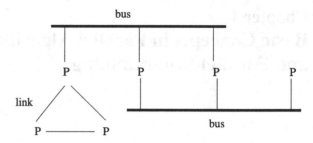

- Reading and writing to a shared memory. For example, a parallel computation between two processors using a shared memory can occur if one processor executes $t1 = read(x)$; $t2 = read(y)$; $write(x = t1 + t2)$; and the other processor executes $t1 = read(x)$; $t2 = read(y)$; $write(y = t1 - t2)$; where x, y are stored in a shared memory.

Message passing is a more basic operation than reading/writing to a shared memory. Technically we only need the two processors to be connected by a "wire" to exchange messages. Basically we can simulate shared memory by message passing. The above example of updating x and y can be simulate if the first processor hold x and executes:

$$send(x); \qquad t1 = recieve(); \qquad x = x + t1;$$

while the second processor hold y and executes

$$send(y); \qquad t2 = recieve(); \qquad y = t1 - y;$$

This is clearly only one possible way to simulate shared memory via message passing and thus our goal is first to show how to build parallel machine with message passing and then to define how shared memory can be used on top of it.

In order for processors to communicate with each other, they must be connected to each other via a communication network that can direct messages from one processor to the other. This configuration is similar to a telephone network that allows users to call each other, or to mail services that allow us to send and receive letters. The performance of the underlying communication network can definitely affect the execution time of a given program on a parallel machine. Obviously, the more the processors need to communicate with each other, the more the performance of the communication network will affect the overall execution time.

It is thus appropriate to consider several types of schematic communication networks to see how they affect performance. In general a communication network is a collection of processors that can be connected via two types of "lines":

Links connecting two processors to each other, allowing one processor to send a message to another. Only one message can pass through a link during a given time unit.

Bus is a communication line that connects several processors to each other. A bus allows one processor to broadcast a message to all the other processors that are connected to a given bus. Only one message can be broadcast on a bus at a given

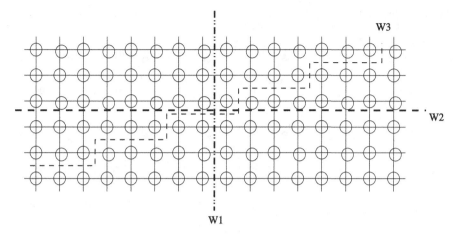

Fig. 1.2 Different ways of partitioning a communication network

time. In the case that several messages are broadcast we can assume that a special signal is generated indicating that more than one message has been broadcast.

Each processor can be connected via several buses and links but can use only one of them during a given time unit (either to send or to receive a message). Figure 1.1 depicts a possible configuration for a parallel machine using both buses and point-to-point links.

We consider three possible factors that can be used to compare and classify communication networks:

Degree is the maximal number of links/buses that connects a processor to its neighbors. The degree of each node in a communication network determines how many messages should be processed (sent/received) in every step by each node. Communication networks with smaller degrees are therefore preferable (e.g., a network with N processors and *degree* $= 4$ is preferable to a network with *degree* $= \log N$).

Latency (or diameter) is the number of links/buses through which a message sent from one processor to another may need to pass in the worst case scenario (e.g., for N processors, a latency of $\log N$ is preferable to a latency of $N - 1$).

Bandwidth is the maximal number of messages that have to pass through some links/buses if half of the processors need to exchange messages with the remaining half of the processors. In order to compute the bandwidth of a given network, we should determine the worst partition of the processors into two halves that maximizes the number of messages that have to pass through any link or a bus passing through the cut that separates these two halves. Figure 1.2 depicts three possible ways of partitioning a 16×6 grid-like network. In this case, each half $H1$, $H2$ contains 48 nodes and the bandwidth is obtained by $B = \frac{96}{\#edges\_between(H1,H2)}$. Figure 1.2 illustrates three cuts:

- $W1$ with $\#edges\_between(H1, H2) = 6$ yielding $B = 16$.
- $W1$ with $\#edges\_between(H1, H2) = 16$ yielding $B = 6$.

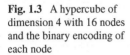

Fig. 1.3 A hypercube of dimension 4 with 16 nodes and the binary encoding of each node

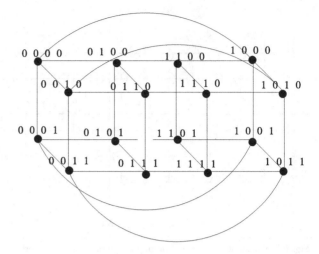

- $W1$ with #*edges_between*$(H1, H2) = 20$ yielding $B = 4.8$.

The first choice $W1$ is the "worst-possible" increasing the bandwidth to 16. Note that the minimal bandwidth will always be obtained had we used $H1$ to be all the odd elements in every row/column of the grid and $H2$ to contain all the even elements in every row/column of the grid.

Let us consider several possible types (topologies) of communication networks, assuming that there are n processors $p_1, \ldots, p_n$:

A path where p_i is connected to p_{i+1} via a link $i = 1, \ldots, n - 1$. For a path we get $degree_{path} = 2$ because each processor is connected to its two neighbors, and $latency_{path} = n - 1$ for a message sent from p_1 to p_n. For the bandwidth we get $bandwidth_{path} = n$ if we choose the first half to be $p_1, \ldots, p_{n/2}$, and the second half to be $p_{n/2+1}, \ldots, p_n$. Clearly in this case n messages have to pass through the link connecting $p_{n/2}$ and $p_{n/2+1}$.

A ring is a better arrangement because we get $degree = 2, latency = n/2, bandwidth = n$. The latency improves because each message can travel through the shortest part of the ring to its destination.

A bus yields $degree = n, latency = 1, bandwidth = n$, as it requires n steps to send n messages through a bus. Note that a bus can simulate a path by broadcasting any message, however the opposite is not true. Consider the problem of computing the AND of n inputs each stored in a different processor. A path will require at least $n/2$ steps since information must reach from both ends of the path to the processor that emits the result. Though a bus has a similar bandwidth as a path it can compute the AND of n input bits in one step since any processor that has an input bit '0' will broadcast on the bus. Thus if no signal is detected on the bus then all processors "know" that the result of the AND is true and false otherwise.

A mesh obtains $degree = 4, latency = 2 \cdot \sqrt{n}, bandwidth = \sqrt{n}$.

A mesh of buses where each row/column is a bus yields $degree = 2 \cdot \sqrt{n}, latency = 2, bandwidth = 2 \cdot \sqrt{n}$.

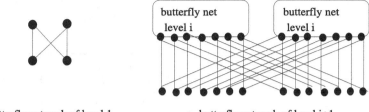

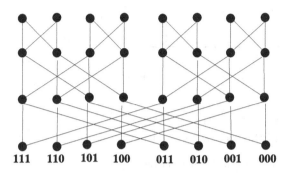

butterfly network of level 1   butterfly network of level i+1

Fig. 1.4 A recursive construction of a butterfly network

A complete binary tree improves the latency but has the worst bandwidth because all the messages from the left half and the right half of the tree must pass through the root. $degree = 3, latency = 2 \cdot \log(n), bandwidth = n$.

A hypercube (see Fig. 1.3) yields $degree = \log(n), latency = \log(n), bandwidth = const$.

A "butterfly" network (see Fig. 1.4) is an even better improvement because it gives us $degree = 2, \ latency = \log(n), \ bandwidth = const$.

Using the notion of communication networks we can now define a parallel machine as follows:

- A parallel machine is formed using any communication network.
- Some (at least two) of the nodes of this communication network are processors (denoted by P_i), while another subset (at least one) of the nodes are memory modules (denoted by M_i). For simplicity we can assume that each memory module has the same range of addresses.
- Each processor can read/write to any memory module by sending a read/write message to that module.
- A parallel program is formed by executing a dynamic set of sequential programs on some of the processors where each sequential program is enhanced by send/receive instructions to the nodes containing memory modules.

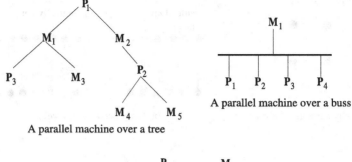

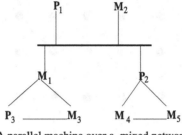

Fig. 1.5 Different ways of constructing a shared memory machine

Fig. 1.6 Using distinct addresses to create a shared memory

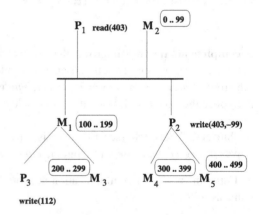

- The fact that each processor can read/write to any memory module implies that the collection of all memory modules form a "shared memory" common to all the processors.

As Fig. 1.5 illustrates, a shared memory machine can be created in several ways.

We can assign a different range of addresses to each memory module of a parallel machine thus allowing the set of sequential programs executed by the processors to communicate via regular load/store (read/write) operations as depicted in Fig. 1.6. In this case each *read(addr)*, *write(add, val)* is simulated by messages sent to the appropriate memory module. Based on this abstraction we can further simplify the notion of a parallel machine and view it as a set of processors that can access a shared memory via a communication network. Though the internal structure of the this network will affect the access times to the shared memory, we can still approximate its operation by a single read/write operation. The access time of each processor to this shared memory operation can be estimated as follows:

- Assume we have a parallel machine with n processors and n memory modules.
- We assume that each step of the parallel machine involves n read/write operations where each processor is accessing a different memory module. Thus, we ignore "bad cases" where all or many processors access the same memory module in parallel. This assumption is based on a theoretical result where by hashing the memory addresses (i.e., accessing cell i is translated to address $hash_f(i)$) we can evenly distribute the load on each memory module (with high probability over a random selection of $f()$).
- The access time of a processor to any memory module can be approximated by *latency + bandwidth* since some read/write messages can be delayed through a link/bus on the selected cut of the bandwidth and then need to travel along the path selected for the latency.

This is of course an estimation to what can happen in a communication network when all the processors attempt to access the shared memory modules. Note that in Fig. 1.6 if $P3$ needs to access $M3$ it can be completed in one link while an access of $P3$ to $M5$ will take at least 5 links. Moreover, there can be bottlenecks if all processors attempt to fetch data from $M5$. Thus, the above formula is an estimation only.

Another aspect of parallel machines is the way in which all of the processors are synchronized. As described in Fig. 1.7, a shared memory machine can be either:

Synchronous Such that all processors execute commands in steps using a common clock.

Asynchronous Such that each processor has its own clock and therefore executes threads at its own rate.

As a result, the execution of a parallel program can be either synchronous or asynchronous. In other words, all threads (programs running at each processor) are executed step-by-step or in an arbitrary order. Clearly, asynchronous machines are easier to build and are more scalable (i.e., can be extended to have more processors) than synchronous ones because the latter require a common clock that has to trigger many processors very quickly, a difficult goal to realize.

1.2 Basic Concepts of Parallel Programs

Here we consider the problem of defining parallel programs in terms of syntax and semantics. We seek to do so without using the notion of parallel machines. Parallel

Fig. 1.7 Synchronous and asynchronous shared memory machines

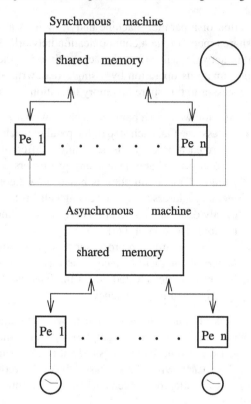

programs are thus represented as abstract entities unrelated to possible execution by a parallel machine. Note that a parallel program can be executed by a sequential machine. Thus, parallel programs are separate entities independent of their execution. We thus reject the common manner of defining parallel programs as programs that generate threads/processes which can be executed concurrently by a parallel machine. Instead, we describe parallel programs as a generalization of sequential programs. In our definition, a parallel program is a set of sequential programs out of which, upon execution, one program is non-deterministically selected.

In this section we present several models to describe the syntax and semantics of parallel programs and their execution. The basic concepts that are presented include:

- Parallel programs
- Threads
- Execution order
- Scheduling
- Execution of parallel programs
- Execution graph induced by a parallel program

1.2.1 Partial Orders as Basic Parallel Programs

Let a partial order P over a set of elements $S = \{a_1, \ldots, a_n\}$ be a consistent set of relations $r_k : a_i < a_j$. The term "consistent" implies that we cannot show any transitive applications of the order relations such that $a_i < a_j$ and $a_j < a_i$ where i is not necessarily different than j. For example, $a_1 < a_2, a_2 < a_3, a_3 < a_1$ is not a partial order because we can show that $a_1 < a_3$ yet $a_3 < a_1$. We say that two elements are not comparable (denoted as $a_i \| a_j$) if we cannot prove by transitive applications of the P's order relations that $a_i < a_j$ or $a_j < a_i$. A partial order P is a "total order" if it does not have two elements that are incomparable. We say that a total order P' is a "completion" of a partial order P if: both orders have the same set of elements and if every $a_i < a_j \in P$ is consistent with P'. If those two conditions hold, then either $a_i < a_j$ is consistent with P or $a_i \| a_j$ is consistent with P.

Basically, we argue that parallel programs are partial orders over a set of assignments to a shared memory. Thus a parallel program contains a set of assignments and order relations. For example the following is a parallel program:

$$
\begin{aligned}
&parallel\ program\ PP: \\
&assignments: \\
&a_1: \quad a = 0; \\
&a_2: \quad c = 0; \\
&a_3: \quad a = c + 1; \\
&a_4: \quad c = a + 1; \\
&order\ relations: \\
&a_1 < a_3; \\
&a_2 < a_4;
\end{aligned}
$$

In this way we have specified parallel programs without using the notion of parallel machines. The execution of such a program can now be defined as:

1. For a given program P compute the set of all possible completions of P to total orders $P'_1, \ldots, P'_k$.
2. Arbitrarily choose one such P'_i and execute its assignments as a sequential program.

For example, for the above program we have the following ways of completion P to a total order (using ';' instead of $<$):

$$
\begin{aligned}
P'_1: &\quad a_1; a_2; a_3; a_4; \quad Longrightarrow \quad a = 1, c = 2 \\
P'_2: &\quad a_1; a_2; a_4; a_3; \quad Longrightarrow \quad a = 2, c = 1 \\
P'_3: &\quad a_1; a_3; a_2; a_4; \quad Longrightarrow \quad a = undef, c = undef
\end{aligned}
$$

Note that there can be several possible outputs for executing a parallel program depending on which completion to a total order was actually selected.

Using partial orders is thus a very powerful way to describe parallel programs since we are replacing the meaning of "parallel" which we can not really comprehend due to our inherent mode of sequential thinking, by an arbitrary selection of one possible sequential program. However, there is another important aspect of programs that is still missing from this definition (*parallel − programs* ≡ *partial_order*) and that is lack of "recursive structure". A basic feature of all programming languages (and also natural languages) is that they are fully recursive, i.e., complex programs are recursively decomposed to sub-programs until elementary assignments. Even more specifically a partial order (such as PP) need not be recursively decomposable. In particular we miss the use of parentheses where a program R is decomposable to R *Longrightarrow* $\{R_1; R_2; \ldots; R_k\}$ This elementary structure is what allows us to "read" programs and "squeeze" many computations into a few lines of code. Thus we make a second step in our search for a definition of parallel programs and out of the set of all possible partial orders choose those that can be recursively decomposed using two types of parentheses: $(R_1; R_2; \ldots; R_k)$ for sequential decomposition to sub-programs and $[R_1|| R_2|| \ldots ||R_k)$ for decomposition to sub-programs that can be executed in parallel. As will be proved later this choice will significantly reduce the amount of partial orders that can be expressed as parallel programs.

Let $a_1, \ldots, a_n$ denote basic assignments to shared variables of the form $a_i \equiv v = expression$. A parallel program R is a partial order above a set of assignments defined by the following recursive grammar rules:[1]

$$R \longleftarrow a_i \quad R \longleftarrow (R; \ldots; R) \quad R \longleftarrow [R_1|| \ldots ||R_n]$$

For example, the following three terms:

$$[x = y||y = x + 1] \quad \left(x = x + 1; \left[x = x - 1||(y = y - 1; y = x)\right]y = 0\right)$$
$$(x = y; y = x)$$

are parallel programs. For example, $[x = y||y = x + 1]$ can be constructed recursively by applying the rules:

$$a_1 \longleftarrow x = y$$
$$a_2 \longleftarrow y = x + 1$$
$$R_1 \longleftarrow a_1$$
$$R_2 \longleftarrow a_2$$
$$R \longleftarrow [R_1||R_2]$$

We also use a short syntactic form where a_i is used instead of an explicit assignment. The $||$ operator stands for "incomparable" so that $[R_1|| \ldots ||R_n]$ indicates that there is no order between $R_1, \ldots, R_n$. This syntax allows us to generate a partial order which is one string so that it resembles a program. Hence, $R = (a_1; a_2)$ is equivalent to the partial order $a_1 < a_2$, while $R = [(a_1; a_2)||(a_3; a_4)]$ is the partial order $a_1 < a_2$ and $a_3 < a_4$.

As with general partial order programs P, the result of executing a "recursive" partial order program R is defined to be the result of executing some sequential program $R' = (a_1; \ldots; a_k)$ that completes the partial order of R to a total order. Each

---

[1] We assume that the reader is familiar with the notion of Context Free Grammars and derivations.

of these sequential programs is a possible "execution order" of the original parallel program. Hence, the results of executing a parallel program are not unique and are dependent on the particular execution order that actually took place. In this way we have defined the semantics of parallel programs using the semantics of sequential programs, which are well defined. For example, let $R = [t = x; ||x = y; ||y = t;]$. Then, any one of the following programs is a completion of R into a total order:

$$R'_1 = (t = x; x = y; y = t;) \qquad R'_2 = (t = x; y = t; x = y;)$$
$$R'_3 = (x = y; t = x; y = t;)$$
$$R'_4 = (x = y; y = t; t = x;) \qquad R'_5 = (y = t; t = x; x = y;)$$
$$R'_6 = (y = t; x = y; t = x;)$$

Note that this set is all the possible completions to a total order since there can be only *factorial*(3) = 6 ways to order the three statements.

Hence, in some cases, the parallel program R swaps the value of two variables, e.g., $R'_1 \equiv swap(x, y)$, but $R'_2 \equiv y = t = x$, and $R'_4 = swap(t, y)$. Thus, the only observation we can make about the semantics of R is that it does not necessarily swap two variables and, in fact, "has a bug."

Note that not every partial order can be represented as a parallel program. For example, the following partial order specified by order relations cannot be represented as a parallel program:

$$(b > a) \qquad (b > c) \qquad (d > b) \qquad (e > b) \qquad (e > s) \qquad (s > c).$$

This statement can be verified by simply testing all possible parallel programs over a, b, c, d, e, s. Intuitively, once we have ordered the path $c; b; e$ and $c; s; e$ (possibly as $e; [b||s]; c$) we cannot add the relation $d > b$ and also preserve the fact that $d||(e; s)$. Note that without d there is only one way to represent all order relations and the fact that $c||$ and $b||s$ as a parallel program which is $[c||a]; [b||s]; e$. However both possible ways of inserting d are false:

- $[c||a]; [b; d||s]; e$ does not preserve that $d||e$.
- $[c||a]; [b||s]; [e||d]$ does not preserve that $d||s$.

Thus, the above partial order does not describe a parallel program as we defined it. This is because the three grammar rules for creating parallel programs impose a recursive decomposition of any parallel programs to sub-parallel program. However, a general set of order relations need not necessarily be decomposed in such a way.

There are several missing aspects of the above definition stating that "the parallel execution of a parallel program R is **equivalent** to a sequential execution of one of R's total orders". The following is a very short discussion of these aspects:

- It is timeless. It does not allow us to relate a time to an execution because the time for executing a sequential program is its size, so the parallelism is lost.
- It is not clear that the set of possible execution orders can be generated or computed effectively. If not, then there is no guarantee that we can really understand what a parallel program does because we may not know how to generate all the sequential execution orders of a parallel program.

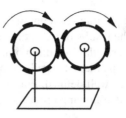

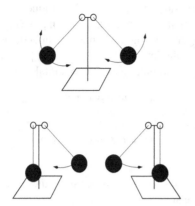

turning both weals at the same
time is not equivalent to turning
one after the other, as in a parallel
turn none of the weals will move
howeber in a sequential order

both weals will move

realising both balls is not the same as
realising them one after the other

Fig. 1.8 True parallelism

- It is not necessarily true that the parallel execution of a set of instructions is always equivalent to some sequential order. Such a situation of "true concurrency"
  is depicted in Fig. 1.8. Note that in these cases (tooth-wheels and colliding balls)
  any sequential order will result in a different outcome than the parallel execution. We remark, that of course a sequential simulation of physical systems is
  always possible but at a finer granularity, e.g., turning the two tooth-weals with
  incremental steps one after the other.
- It is not clear that it is a realistic definition. We do not know if we can actually
  build a machine that can execute any parallel program such that the result will
  always be equivalent to some sequential execution order.
- For a given parallel machine, it may be that only a partial set of execution orders
  (out of the set of all possible orders) can actually occur. For example, if we have
  a parallel machine with only one processor that executes assignments in the order
  specified by the parallel program then $a = 0; c = 0; [a = c + 1 \parallel c = a + 1]$ will
  always result in $a = 1, c = 2$ while the other order that yields $a = 2, c = 1$ will
  never occur.

  Thus it is clear that real parallel machines, due to some fixed order in which
  they are working, will not generate all possible execution orders. Unlike an ideal
  parallel machine which could give with equal probabilities all possible execution
  orders. However, a parallel program contains an error (bug) if potentially there
  is one execution order that computes wrong results of get into an infinite loop.
  It does follows that parallel machines can, due to the fixed order in which they
  operate, can hide away faulty execution orders.

  We now show that the set of all possible sequential execution orders can be generated in a systematic way. To do so, we will use rewrite rules that transform the

partial order into a sequential execution order without violating the partial order. Let R_1, R_2, R_3, R_4 be partial order programs over a set of assignment $a_1, \ldots, a_n$. Then the following rewrite rules form a complete system that can generate all possible sequential execution orders depending on the order in which we apply them:

Interleaving of two parallel programs is done by inserting one of the programs inside the other:

$$[(R_1; R_2)||R_3] \longrightarrow \begin{cases} ([R_1||R_3]; R_2) \\ (R_1; [R_2||R_3]) \end{cases}$$

Distributing of two parallel program is done by mixing the two programs as follows:

$$[(R_1; R_2)||(R_3; R_4)] \longrightarrow ([R_1||R_3]; [R_2||R_4])$$

Sequential ordering (Atomicity) of two parallel programs is done by imposing a sequential order between them:

$$[R_1||R_2] \longrightarrow \begin{cases} (R_1; R_2) \\ (R_2; R_1) \end{cases}$$

Re-ordering of two parallel programs is done as follows:

$$[R_1||R_2] \longrightarrow [R_2||R_1]$$

Adding parentheses allows us to apply the rules such that a sub-sequence of $\ldots; R_i; \ldots; R_{i+k}; \ldots$ or $\ldots ||R_i|| \ldots ||R_{i+k}|| \ldots$ is treated as one component.

$$[\ldots ||R_1||R_2|| \ldots] \longrightarrow [\ldots ||[R_1||R_2]|| \ldots]$$

$$(\ldots; R_1; R_2; \ldots) \longrightarrow (\ldots; (R_1; R_2); \ldots)$$

Consider, for example, the program $[(a; b)||(c; d)]$. This program can be rewritten as a sequential order by applying the above rules in an arbitrary way, e.g.:

$$[(a; b)||(c; d)] \longrightarrow ([a||(c; d)]; b) \longrightarrow (c; [a||d]; b) \longrightarrow (c; a; d; b).$$

Figure 1.9 demonstrates how the set of all the possible execution orders of a simple program can be obtained using the above rewrite rules. Note that some orders are generated more than once.

The following facts regarding the set of rules (Interleaving, Distributing, Ordering and Adding-parentheses) are brought here without formal proof:

- Any order of applying the rules to a given R halts.
- Applying the set of rules to a parallel program R results in a sequential program which is a completion of R to a total order. This is because, basically this process eliminates all the $||$ operators from R.
- Any legal completion of R to a total order can be obtained by applying the rules in some specific order.
- It is possible to generate all legal completions of R to a total order by backtracking process whose depth is bounded by the length of R.

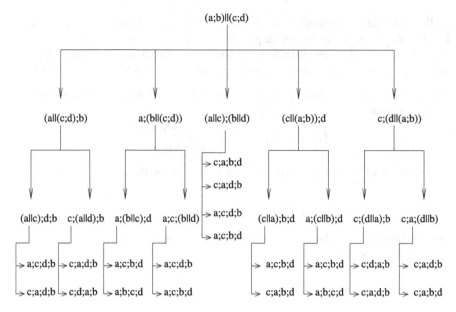

Fig. 1.9 Deriving all possible sequential execution orders of $[(a; b)||(c; d)]$

We finally indicate that the fact that each execution of a parallel program must be equivalent to some sequential order of execution follows from the fact that computer systems are built to obey the rule of **sequential ordering**. Thus, the hardware manufacturers of parallel machines have always constructed their machines in such a way that concurrency is always equivalent to a sequential order, a fact that is evident in all levels of implementation. For example, boolean gates are not sensitive to parallel signals, and parallel interrupts are stored in a table and executed sequentially. Thus, in the reality of parallel machines there should be no "true concurrency" effects.

1.3 Time Diagrams

Here we consider the first missing aspect of our definition of parallel programs and show that we can associate time with parallel execution of parallel programs. The notion of time can be introduced using time diagrams. Let a parallel execution of a program R be a time diagram which assigns a time index to every instruction of the program such that:

- The order imposed by the partial order of R is preserved.
- There are no empty steps, so that there is at least one assignment that is executed in every step.
- If the parallel program contains k occurrences of '||'s, then we require that in any time diagram there will be at least $k + 1$ assignments that are executed in parallel (though not necessarily at the same time step). Intuitively, this implies

Fig. 1.10 Parallelism/time diagram of the program $R = [t = x; ||x = y; ||y = t;]$

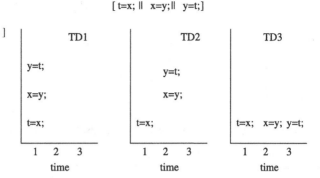

that the $[R_i || R_j]$ indicates that at least one assignment from R_i must be executed in parallel to some assignment from R_j.

For example, Fig. 1.10 describes three possible time diagrams for the program $R = [t = x; ||x = y; ||y = t;]$. Only one of these diagrams, $TD1$, is legal in that it satisfies the above conditions. $TD2$ and $TD3$ do not "preserve" the two $||$ operations of the original program. As for time, the first diagram executes the program in one step, the second in two steps and the third uses three steps. Thus, the execution time of $R = [t = x; ||x = y; ||y = t;]$ is one step because it is the only legal time diagram of R.

For a given program R, its execution time $T(R)$ is the maximal number of steps over all possible legal time diagrams of R. For example for $R = [a||b||c||d||e||f]$, the "worst" time digram is

$$T(R) = \max\big([a||b]; [c||d]; [e||f], [a||b||c||d||e||f]\big) = 3$$

as these are the only two time diagrams with 6 operations that are executed in parallel. Note that the above conditions are the weakest possible, since even for a program that contains lots of parallelism such as

$$R' = \big[(a_1; a_2; \ldots; a_n)||(b_1; b_2; \ldots; b_n)\big]$$

it only requires that there will be one time step where two operations $a_i || b_j$ are executed in parallel while the rest of the steps can contain only one assignment. We remark that had this program R' been written as

$$R' = \big[(a_1||b_1); (a_2||b_2); \ldots; (a_n||b_n)\big]$$

it would force a time digram where no parallelism is lost and each step will contain two parallel assignments $a_i||b_i$.

Clearly, any time diagram can be written as a parallel program where the $||$ operator joins assignments, not complex programs. In other words, a time diagram is a parallel program of the form:

$$\big([a||\ldots||a]; [a||\ldots||a]; \ldots \ldots [a||\ldots||a];\big).$$

For example, the three time diagrams of Fig. 1.10 can be written as

$$[t = x; ||x = y; ||y = t;] \qquad \big(t = x; [x = y; ||y = t;]\big) \qquad (t = x; x = y; y = t;).$$

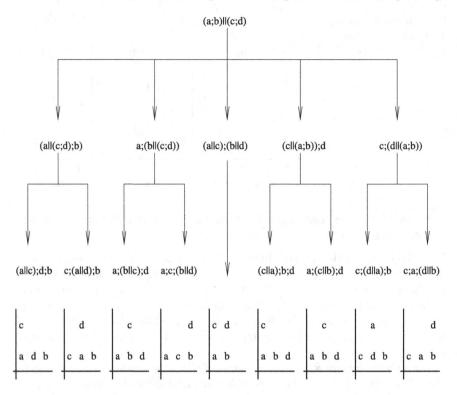

Fig. 1.11 Generating all possible time diagrams of $[(a; b)||(c; d)]$

Finally, the set of all possible time diagrams of a given program can be generated if we do not use the **sequential re-ordering** rule. In this way the $||$s are not removed and are "pushed down" so that they "operate" between assignments, not between more complex programs. This process is demonstrated in Fig. 1.11, where all legal time diagrams of $R = [(a; b)||(c; d)]$ are derived using rapid applications of the above rules.

It may be necessary to restrict the set of possible time diagrams of a program beyond what is allowed by the above three conditions. Consider, for example, the program $R' = [(a_1; a_2; a_3; a_4)||(b_1; b_2; b_3; b_4)]$ that is executed by a parallel machine with two processors. Clearly, the time diagram $TD = [(a_1||b_1)||a_2; a_3; a_4; b_2; b_3; b_4]$ is legal yet implies that some processor (out of the two) is active only in the first step. It is more likely that the parallel execution of R' by two processors will be the following:

$$TD = \big[(a_1||b_1); (a_1||b_1); (a_1||b_1); (a_1||b_1)\big].$$

Hence, in order to approximate the actual execution time of a given program we must restrict the set of all possible time diagrams of a program so that no processor will be "idle" in some step without a "reason." For example, in the program $R'' = [(a_1; a_2; a_3)||(b_1; b_2)||c_3]$ executed by three processors, there can be only one step in any legal time diagram where two processors will work. In addition, we may also wish to restrict the number of ||'s executed in the same time-step to be less equal the number of processors that are executing the program, e.g., if R'' is executed by two processors than no time step should contain more than one ||.

1.4 Execution Times of Parallel Programs

The problem of generating the set of all possible "realistic" time diagrams of a given program executed by P processors requires that we actually determine which assignments are executed by every processor. This can be done if we consider the way parallel machines really work. In reality, a parallel program is divided into threads (also known as tasks or processes), which are sequential fragments of the original program that can be executed in parallel with at least one other thread. We first describe how to divide a parallel program into threads and show that using the division of the program into threads will allow us to generate a set of time diagrams with minimal execution time.

In addition to being sequential, a thread contains instructions for spawning other threads. In this way, executing a thread will invoke other threads, which can be executed in parallel. Hence, a thread A_i is a sequential program with calls for spawning other threads:

$$A_i = a_1; a_2; \ldots; a_k; spawn(A_{j_1}, \ldots, A_{j_n}); a_{k+1}; \ldots; spawn(A_{l_1}, \ldots, A_{l_m}); \ldots$$

Partitioning a program R into a set of threads $R = A_1, \ldots, A_n$ can be used to compute a time diagram with minimal execution time. Intuitively, we start with A_1 and fill the time diagram with the sequential part of A_1 until we reach a spawning instruction. A spawning instruction $spawn(A_1, \ldots, A_k)$ allows us to fill the time diagram in parallel such that the instructions for the next step are from $A_1, \ldots, A_k$. Spawning instructions inside A_i increase the parallelism, allowing us to select more instructions for the next step. This process is repeated for all threads while preserving the three conditions of time diagrams. Consider, for example, the program $R = (a; [(b; c)||(d; e)]; f)$, with the following set of threads:

$$A_1 = a; spawn(A_2, A_3); f \qquad A_2 = b; c \qquad A_3 = d; e$$

The first step of the time diagram is to execute 'a'. Then, A_2 and A_3 become active so we can execute 'b' and 'd' for the third step, 'c', 'e' for the fourth step and finally 'f' in the fifth step, as depicted in Fig. 1.12. Clearly, such a time diagram depicts minimal execution time because anything that can be executed in parallel in the next step is executed in this step.

The division of a parallel program R into threads is performed by the following process:

Fig. 1.12 Constructing a
time diagram according to the
partition of R into threads

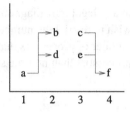

```
Let c=0 be the counter for the threads;
Let S = Ø be the set of threads generated so far;
divide(R)
R is the program;
{
Let A hold the current thread;
   A=NULL;
   c = c+1;
   while(R ≠ NULL){
   if(R ==  "(a_i; R_1)"  ){
       /* remove assignments into the current thread*/
       A = A · "a_i;";
       R = (R_1);
   } else
   if(R ==  "([R_1||R_2||...||R_k]; R')"  ){
       /* recursively generates inner threads */
       A = A · "; spawn(A_{c+1}";
       A_1=divide(R_1);
       for i=2,...,k do {
          A = A · ", A_{c+i}";
          A_i=divide(R_i);
       }
       R = (R');
       A = A · ")";
   } }
   S = S ∪ A ∪ A_1 ∪ ··· ∪ A_k;
}
```
Partitioning a program into threads

Consider, for example, the program

$$R'' = \left(a; \left[\left(b; [e||f]\right)||(c; g)||\left(d; [(h; j)||(i; k)]\right)\right]; l\right).$$

Applying the above process will divide the program into the following threads:

$$A_1 = a; spawn(A_2, A_5, A_6); l$$

$$A_2 = b; spawn(A_3, A_4)$$

$$A_3 = e$$

$$A_4 = f$$

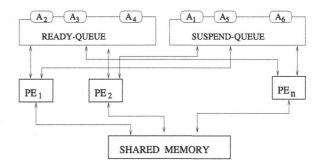

Fig. 1.13 Schematic representation of a queue machine

$$A_5 = c; g$$
$$A_6 = d; spawn(A_7, A_8)$$
$$A_7 = h; j$$
$$A_8 = i; k$$

Let P denote the number of processors of a given parallel machine. Clearly, the set of time diagrams that describes the possible executions of a parallel program by this machine must be restricted such that the maximal number of steps executed in every step is less equal P. On the other hand, the set of possible time diagrams produced by an actual machine with P processors should not include sequential time diagrams that do not use the available parallelism of the underlying machine. For example, the third time diagram (TD3) in Fig. 1.10 is not possible for a parallel machine with 2 processors, and TD2 should not be possible for a parallel machine with 3 processors. Thus, we seek to define a mechanism for computing a time diagram that does not use more than P assignments per step, but maximizes the parallelism at every step.

The proposed mechanism will use the partition of the program into threads to generate the desired time diagram in a manner similar to that described in Fig. 1.12. Ultimately, we will demonstrate that this mechanism is similar to the way in which parallel machines actually work.

The proposed mechanism is a "queue machine" (see Fig. 1.13) that uses two queues to select the next instructions: a ready queue containing all the threads that can be executed in the next step; and a suspend queue containing all the threads that have spawned new threads and are waiting for their completion/termination.

At every step, each processor of the proposed machine executes all the following steps:

1. It selects a thread A from the ready queue and executes the first instruction of that thread.
2. If the first instruction in A is an assignment, then the assignment is executed and is removed from A, and A is inserted back into the ready queue.
3. If the first instruction in A is a spawn instruction (e.g., $spawn(T_1, \ldots, T_k)$), then $T_1, \ldots, T_k$ are inserted into the ready queue, and A (minus the spawning instruction) is moved to the suspend queue.

Fig. 1.14 Stages of the execution of R'' by a queue machine with three processors

step	ready-queue	suspend-queue	time-diagram
0	A_1		
1	A_1		a
2	$A_2 A_5 A_6$	A_1	
3	$A_2 A_5 A_6$	A_1	d c a b
4	$A_7 A_8 A_3 A_4$	$A_1 A_2 A_6$	d c g a b
5	$A_2 A_7 A_8$	$A_1 \quad A_6$	d f c g e a b h
6	A_8	$A_1 \quad A_6$	d f c g e i a b h j
7	A_6		d f c g e i k a b h j
8	A_1		d f c g e i k a b h j l

4. If the instruction executed in the previous step is the last one in A, then A is terminated. Let A' be the thread that spawned A. If A is the last terminating child of A', then A' is resumed and moved from the suspend queue to the ready queue. This rule is applied recursively for all spawning "fathers" of A, e.g., if A' spawned by A'' also terminates, then we terminate A'' and so forth.

The assignments that are executed in each step form the next step in the time diagram that is constructed during the execution of the above rules by each processor.

Initially, the ready queue contains A_1. The time diagram is obtained by listing the instructions executed by the P processors of the queue machine in every step. For example, Fig. 1.14 describes the execution of

$$R'' = \left(a; \left[(b; [e||f])||(c; g)||\left(d; \left[(h; j)||(i; k)\right]\right)\right]; l\right)$$

by a queue machine with $P = 3$ processors. In the first step we have one thread in the queue, so only one instruction can be executed. A_1 spawns A_2, A_5, A_6 and is suspended; A_2 executes 'b', A_5 executes 'c', and A_6 executes 'd' (as described in step 3). Next, A_2 spawns A_3, A_4;, A_6 spawns A_7, A_8 and A_5 executes 'g' and terminates. In step 5 we have four threads in the ready queue, out of which we can choose only three: A_7 executes 'h', A_3 executes 'e' and terminates, A_4 executes

'f' and terminates while moving A_2 back to the ready queue. Next, A_2 terminates, A_7 executes 'j' and terminates, and A_8 executes 'i'. Finally, A_8 executes 'k' and terminates, and moves A_6 to the ready queue. A_6 terminates, and $A - 1$ is moved to the ready queue, where it performs the last instruction 'l';.

Different selections of the threads from the ready queue by the processors can affect the resulting time. For example, if $[[b||c]||d||e]$ is executed by two processors, then by first selecting $d||e$, we will get the TD of $[d||e], [b||c]$. However, if we first select $[[b||c]||d]$, we will get a longer TD $d; [e||b]; c$.

It is interesting to note that if we allow true parallelism, it will be possible to write a parallel program that may also produce different outputs, depending on the number of available processors. Consider, for example, the following program R:

$$x = 0; [x = x + 1; ||x = x + 1; ||x = x + 1;];$$

$$printf(\text{``executed by } \%d \text{ processors''}, 4 - x);$$

We now assume that the semantic of $z = expression1||y = expression2$ is not equivalent to one of the two orders $z = expression1; y = expression2$ or $y = expression2; z = expression1$ but is equivalent to first evaluating the expressions $temp1 = expression1||temp2 = expression2$ and then performing the updates $z = temp1||y = temp2$. In this case if the program is executed by one processor $x = 3$, the printing is correct. Next, if the program is executed by two processors $P = 2$, there will be one parallel step with two operations $[x = x + 1; ||x = x + 1;]$ that will change x from zero to 1. Thus, in this case the final value of x must be two and the output is correct. Similarly, for $P = 3$ the only possible value of x is one and the printing is correct. Obviously, R cannot determine if we are using more than three processors. However, with true parallelism, it is possible to write a parallel program that determines if the number of processors of the underlying machine is smaller than P:

$$x = 0$$
$$[x = x + 1;_1 ||x = x + 1;_2 ||\ldots ||x = x + 1;_P]$$
$$if(x > 1)printf(\text{``number of processors is smaller than } \%d\text{''}, P);$$

Even without true-parallelism it might be possible to say something about the number of processors. Let us assume that we require that when a thread is selected from the ready-queue it is done **randomly** with equal probability of selecting any thread that is ready to run. Consider the following program:

$$x = 0$$
$$\big[(t1 = x + 1; \ x = t1;) ||(t2 = x + 1; \ x = t2;) ||(t3 = x + 1; \ x = t3;)\big];$$
$$printf(\text{``executed by } \%d \text{ processors''}, 4 - x);$$

It follows that if the number of processors P is one then printing $4 - 1$, $4 - 2$ and $4 - 3$ are all possible results with equal probability. If the number of processors P is two then printing $4 - 1$ and $4 - 2$ are all possible results with equal probability (but not $4 - 3$). Finally, if the number of processors P is three then printing $4 - 1$ is the only possible result. Thus by sampling several runs of the program we can say what is the number of processors that is used with high probability.

It is incorrect programming to write code whose output may be affected by the underlying number of processors. Clearly, a correct parallel program should compute the same output regardless of the number of available processors.

1.5 Moving to a General Parallel Programming Language

In this section we extend the notion of parallel programs to include all the elements of imperative programming languages, namely *loops*, *if* statements, and function calls. The partial order used in the previous section and the time diagrams are no longer suitable for handling the complex execution of such programs. The thread model with a queue machine is also not suitable for fully depicting the way control statements such as *while − loops* are executed in parallel. Instead we use the notion of "program graphs" in order to represent the program and its execution. The different forms in which a parallel program can be executed by a given queue machine are now called **schedulings** and are obtained by moving arrows on the different nodes of a "program graph." Intuitively, the program graph corresponds to the machine code of the underlying program and the arrows correspond to the set of program-counter registers of the processors that execute the parallel program. Thus, the program graph model is designed to best approximate the actual execution of a parallel program by a parallel machine. We believe that understanding all three representations (partial orders, threads + queues-machine and program graphs) is beneficial to really understanding the way in which parallel programs are executed. We also remark that directed acyclic graphs can be used to express partial orders and vice-versa. Thus, using program graphs is in fact continuing using partial orders to express parallelism but expressed as graphs rather than a set of order relations.

The new syntax of parallel programs is based on the syntax of C and is given by the following grammar using the symbol 'S' or 'S_i' for statements:

Variables and expressions are used as they are in sequential programming languages like *Pascal* or C, and include terms such as arrays, structures and pointers. **Assignments** are basic statements of the form:

$$S \Longrightarrow identifier = expression$$

e.g., $x = x + 1$ or $A[i] = A[A[i]] * 2$.
Conditional statements of the form

$$S \Longrightarrow if (expression)\ S_1\ else\ S_2$$

e.g., $if (x \le A[x])x = x + 1\ else\ A[i] = A[A[i]]$.
Loops statements including `for`, and `while` loops can be used, with the syntax:

$$S \Longrightarrow while(expression)\ S$$

$$S \Longrightarrow for(identifier = expression_1, \ldots, expression_2)S$$

e.g., $for(i = 1 \ldots n)g = g + 1$.

Blocks of statements can be used with the syntax

$$S \implies \{ S_1; S_2; \ldots; S_n\}$$

This resembles the $(S_1; S_2; \ldots; S_n)$ syntax used for partial order programs.
Parallel blocks of statements can be used with the syntax

$$S \implies [S_1||S_2||\ldots||S_n]$$

This resembles the $[S_1||S_2||\ldots||S_n]$ syntax used for partial order programs.
Function calls and function definitions are used as in C where functions are defined by the syntax:

$$Fundef \implies identifier(parameter\ list)\ S$$

A program consists of a set of function definitions, and like C, the execution starts with $main()$.

This syntax allows us to generate threads in complex ways, using loops and recursive calls to spawn new threads. For example, in the following program each invocation of $f(x, y)$ keeps forking two new parallel invocations of $f()$ until $x = y$.

```
int g=10;
f(int x,y){
    while(x < y){
        [ f(x+1,y) || f(x,y-1) ];
        x=x+1; y=y-1; g=g+1;
    }
}
main(){
    [ f(g,g*g) || f(1,g) ];
    print g;
}
```
Complex ways to spawn threads in parallel programs.

Using the new syntax, a program can have an infinite set of time diagrams, each with a different execution time (number of steps). Consider, for example, the program

$$x = 0;\ y = 1;\ [while(x < y)x + +; ||while(x < y)y + +;]$$

Clearly, for this program we can generate a time diagram with any number of steps (including one with an infinite number of steps) depending on the number of processors (for $P \geq 2$ we get $TD = \inf$ and for $P = 1$ any value depend on the scheduling). Thus, if we are able to define a set of time diagrams associated with a given program, we must require that there are no infinite time diagrams (program halts) and that the execution time will be the maximal number of steps over all possible time diagrams of this program.

Let the execution of any parallel program be eventually equivalent to a time diagram, wherein each step contains all the assignments that were performed in parallel

Fig. 1.15 Program graph

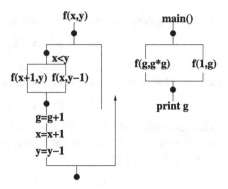

in that step. Unlike the previous case of the partial order model, the rewrite rules for general programs are complex. It is not simple to define the set of possible time diagrams that characterizes the execution of a parallel program. The solution that we use here is to represent the program as a directed graph (called the "program graph"), and then expand it to an execution graph that describes one possible execution of the program. The goal here is not to develop a formal model, but (based on the fact that we already know what threads and execution orders mean) to give some schematic representation of the execution. Such a representation will be more intuitive, and will help us study parallel programs for practical purposes, such as computing the execution time and identifying bottlenecks.

The program graph is basically an alternative way to represent restricted forms of partial orders. Each assignment or function call forms a node. The program graph is recursively constructed using the following rules.

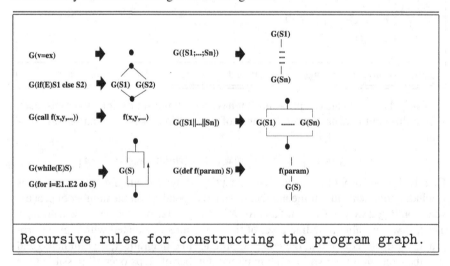

Recursive rules for constructing the program graph.

The program graph is obtained by applying those rules to every function definition in the program. For example, the program graph of the above complex program is depicted in Fig. 1.15.

The scheduling process of a set of program graphs $G_{main}, G_{f1}, \ldots, G_{fk}$ (one program graph for every function defined in the program) is a sequence of steps that moves arrows on an execution graph GE, which is built during the scheduling process. Each arrow $\overset{i}{\Longrightarrow}$ is marked by the number of a processor and points to the next instruction of p_i. The general scheduling process works as follows:

1. A set of shared variables is associated with every node. For the time being, we will ignore the issue of definition and access of shared variables and assume an intuitive understanding as to how these variables are allocated to the different nodes and how they are being accessed.
2. Initially, we have a pool of P arrows $\overset{i}{\Longrightarrow}$, one arrow for each processor.
3. The execution starts by choosing one arrow from the pool and placing it on the first node of $GE = G_{main}$.
4. In each step we "advance" the arrows on the various nodes of GE and possibly take arrows from the pool and place them on GE. The rules for advancing the arrows will be given later on, however, intuitively we do the following:

   • If an arrow points to an assignment node, it is moved to its successor in GE (only one successor is possible).
   • If an arrow points to a loop-statement or an if-statement, the arrow is moved to a node in GE which corresponds to the next statement in the suitable branch of the if-statement/loop-statement.
   • If an arrow points to a function call $f()$, we replace the current node in GE with G_f.
   • if the current node points to a spawn instruction, we return the arrow to the pool and mark the first node in each thread as ready.
   • If there is a node marked as "ready" and a "free" arrow is in the pool, we place that arrow on the marked node and remove the mark "ready" on that node. This process is repeated until there are no nodes marked as ready or until the pool of arrows is empty.
   • If an arrow points to a node which is the last node of a thread (before the tread joins its spawning thread), we do one of the following:
     – if this is the last thread to join in, we return the arrow to the pool and mark its successor as ready (allowing the spawning thread to continue to the next stage).
     – if this is not the last thread to reach the join point, we return the arrow back to the pool.

5. Since each execution graph is a partial order, then, once the execution graph is computed we can generate the time diagrams by applying the derivation rules or the queue-machine rules as described earlier.

Figure 1.16 illustrates the different cases of moving arrows on GE.

Formally, the execution time T_P of a program R by a parallel machine with P processors can be defined as follows:

1. Generate the set G of all possible execution graphs of R executed by a given input I. Note that G can be infinite and can also contain infinite execution graphs.

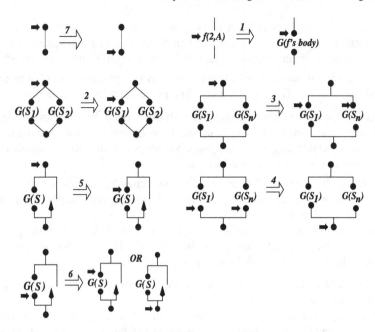

Fig. 1.16 Scheduling process of an execution graph

2. If G contains infinite execution graphs, then $T_P = \text{infinite}$.
3. Otherwise, G must be finite and we can generate the set of all time diagrams for each execution graph in G by moving arrows.
4. T_P is the maximal number of steps of a time diagram generated in the previous step.

It follows that the set of all time diagrams of a program could have been computed directly by recording the moves of the arrows at every step of the above process. Given that there are only P arrows, at any stage we perform at most P moves. However, by using this "two-phase" definition we obtain the following:

- We can still associate a partial order with every parallel program (set of all possible execution graphs).
- We associate a time to an execution not during the execution. In this way, there can be several time diagrams associated with a given execution rather than the execution determining the time as well.
- This bypasses the problem caused by recording a given execution generated with P processors and executing it as a parallel program on another machine with $P' \neq P$ processors.

Note that for a given input value there can be many possible execution graphs to a specific program run. Consider the program given in Fig. 1.17, typically the value of n, m depends on the execution order that occurs, namely how long each thread of the $[\dots || \dots]$ was executed before the other thread reset its flag. It is thus not possible

Fig. 1.17 A program whose
execution graph depends on
the scheduling order

```
int f(int x){
int n=0,m=0,a=1,b=1;
    [
        while(a)  n++;
        ||
        while(b)  m++;
        ||
        {
        a = 0;
        b = 0;
        }
    ]
    if(n+m < 1000) {
        [
            a = f(n-1);
            ||
            b = f(m-1);
        ]
        return(a+b);
} }
```

to attribute a single execution graph to this program. However, in general attributing
a single execution graph for each run of a program with a specific input is usually
possible and can be regarded as a reasonable assumption or an approximation.

Consider, for example, the program of Fig. 1.18, with two program graphs, G_f
and G_{main}. It easy to see that there is only one possible execution graph for this
program, which is depicted on the right side of Fig. 1.18. In this example, the final
value of g will be the total number of iterations executed by the program, i.e., $10 +
9 + \cdots + 1 = 50$.

Computing the execution time T_P is more complicated and requires us to follow
several scheduling processes. First, if $P \geq 10$, then all of the arrows in the execution
graph can be moved in every step and the total execution time will be 20, as there
are 10 invocations of $f()$ and another 10 steps to return from every call. This is
the longest path in the execution graph. If $P < 10$, then we should select the worst
scheduling for this graph using the following argument:

- Verify that there are no synchronization points between the threads (which is the
  case in the above example of Fig. 1.18). This is done by verifying that there is
  no active waiting where a while-loop in one thread depends on a value that is
  updated by another thread.
- Since there is no case of active waiting, the P arrows are constantly moving.
  However, this fact does not guarantee that all of the arrows can be advanced all
  the time. Estimations regarding such cases will be given later on.

```
int g=0;
f(n){
  if (n > 0)
  [ for i=1 .. n do g=g+1; || f(n-1) ]
}
main(){ f(10); }
```

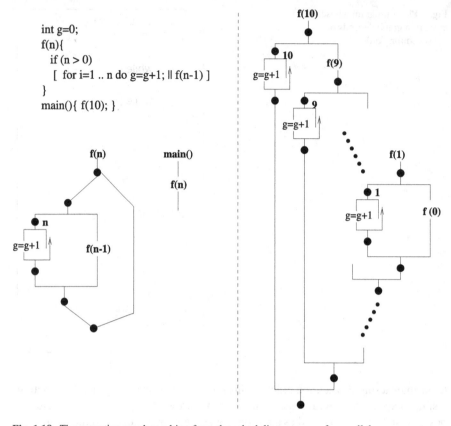

Fig. 1.18 The execution graph resulting from the scheduling process of a parallel program

The following two claims can be made:

1. For every program R, $T_p \leq T_1$. This follows from the fact that the bad scheduling of moving p arrows can always be repeated by one arrow.
2. There exists a program R for which $T_p \leq \frac{T_1}{p}$ for a given input I. Consider, for example, a parallel program that traverses an array looking for a cell that contains a given number x:

```
int flag=1;
[
    int i=0;
    while(flag && i < n/2)
    {
        if(A[i] == x) flag=0;
        else i++;
    }
||
    int j=n/2;
```

```
    while(flag && j < n)
    {
        if(A[j] == x) flag=0;
        else j++;
    }
]
```

Clearly, if $A[n/2] == x$, then $T_2 = 1$ for any bad scheduling we may choose, while for some scheduling that advances the first thread, we can obtain $T_1 = n/2$, which is significantly slower than 1.

We remark that a parallel language should contain some mechanisms to force a desired order on the execution. For example, in the divide and conquer algorithm for building a brick wall described later in this chapter, a worker should be synchronized with his neighbor so he will not start to fill the gap until his neighbor has finished building the left side of his pyramid. Note that shared variables can be used for synchronization as well. In this same example of building a brick wall, one worker can observe (read) a global variable indicating the height of the last brick placed on the left side by his neighbor. When this height is H, he knows it is time to fill the gap.

1.6 Developing Practical Parallel Algorithms

The first step towards mastering the art of practical parallel programming is to be able to develop a "practical" parallel algorithm. Let A be a parallel algorithm and R_A a possible parallel program that implements A. The following two claims justify the need to first work in algorithmic level before implementing any software:

1. We believe that if A does not incorporate certain desired features, any implementation of R_A will most likely be inefficient. Moreover, we believe that working at the algorithmic level may also improve the probability that any "reasonable" version R_A will also be efficient.
2. In some cases practical considerations, such as amount of available resources must be considered at the algorithmic level first. This is because different resource limitations can completely change the algorithm we are using.

This situation where resource constraints affect algorithm design (the first claim) is true for sequential programs as well. Consider, for example, a program that traverses a two dimensional array $a[n, n]$, possibly in column major order. Clearly, such a program is subject to many cache misses if $a[n, n]$ is stored in row major order in the memory. It is better to use an algorithm that traverses $a[n, n]$ by scanning small sub-arrays of size $p \times p$. By setting $p^2 = chache\ size$, we can always improve the cache performance regardless of the order in which $a[n, n]$ are stored in the memory.

Another example, demonstrating the second claim, is determining whether all the elements in a given array $A[n]$ are different or not (assuming all values are between 0 and $n - 1$):

- Assume that we are allowed to use only two memory cells. We need n^2 to compare each element with all the others:

```
int i,j;
for(i=0;i<n;i++)
    for(j=i+1;j<n;j++)
        if(A[i] != A[j])printf("Not all equal");
```

- Assume that we have $O(n)$ calls to use. We can solve the problem with one scan of the array:

```
int i,B[n];
for(i=0;i<n;i++) B[i]=0;
for(i=0;i<n;i++)
    if(B[A[i]] > 0)
    printf("Not all equal");
else B[A[i]]++;
```

1.6.1 Some Basic Properties of Efficient Parallel Algorithms

Our goal in this section is to present the basic features a parallel algorithm should satisfy in order to function efficiently in practice. We are particularly interested in the "scalability" of a given parallel algorithm. Scalability means that the algorithm can use any amount of parallelism that is available in the underlying parallel machine. In other words, the same algorithm can scale-up and speedup its execution time on a machine with two processors or on a machine with 100 processors. Thus, a practical parallel algorithm has two parameters: P (the number of available processors) and N (the input size, as is the case with sequential algorithms). A practical parallel algorithm is denoted by $A(P, N)$ and its execution time $T_{A(P,N)}$ depends on both parameters. For example, $T_{A(P,N)} = \frac{N^2}{P} + P^2$ is an execution time that combines the input size and the number of processors. The scalability is reflected by the fact that the execution time varies not only when the input size changes, but also when P changes. We also require that the adaptation to P should not be trivial, so an algorithm which uses only one or two processors out of the $P > 2$ possible should not be considered scalable. Thus, the execution time should be inversely proportional to P. For example, $T_{A(P,N)} = N + P$ does not scale as well with P compared to $T_{A'(P,N)} = \frac{N}{P}$, where the execution time decreases by a half every time we double P. Thus $A'(P, N)$ scales better than $A(P, N)$.

Let us demonstrate the issue of scalability with a simple problem for constructing a round wall of bricks in parallel:

Pile A wall is constructed by placing bricks one on top of the other. However, each brick should be placed on top of two adjacent bricks.

H The height of the wall in bricks.

L The length of the wall in bricks.

P The number of workers who should build the wall in parallel.

Step One brick can be placed by each worker at every time unit, provided that:

- No two bricks can be placed next to each other at the same time. In other words, adjacent bricks cannot be placed in parallel.
- A brick cannot be placed "half in the air," meaning that it can be placed only on two adjacent existing bricks or on the ground.

The sequential solution for constructing a wall will use one worker and will need $T_s = L \cdot H$ steps.

First, consider a simple greedy algorithm $A_{greedy}(P, N)$. The greedy algorithm attempts to place as many bricks as possible at every stage. In the first step we build an initial "pyramid" wherein row h contains three bricks fewer than row $h-1$, where the first row is of length $3H - 2$.  Once the initial pyramid has been built, two bricks can be added in parallel to the two ends of every row

This algorithm requires $\frac{L}{2}$ steps because in every stage $2H$ bricks are placed in parallel. This algorithm does not scale well with P because it cannot use more than $2 \cdot H$ workers and its execution time is $T_{P, N=L \cdot H} = max(\lfloor \frac{N}{P} \rfloor + 1, \frac{N}{2 \cdot H})$. Note that the $\frac{N}{P}$ term is for the case where $P < 2H$ and in this case if P does not equally divides $2H$ (e.g., $P = 2h - 8$ then 8 bricks are left for the next round which will use 8 workers to fill the remaining 8 bricks from the previous round and the $2H - 16$ bricks from this round. This is because the we can set that the remaining un-done bricks of this round will be at the top following the order of brick placement that would have occurred had we exactly $2H$ workers. The $+1$ term is due to the fact that we may need another round to complete the last bricks.

Thus, we continue to look for a better solution that can use more than $2 \cdot H$ workers. Another possibility for building a parallel algorithm is to divide the work among the P workers. Therefore, we call the following algorithm $A_{divide}(P, N)$. In this algorithm, each worker should build a local section of size $\frac{L}{P}$ in parallel. Recall that two workers cannot put on adjacent bricks at the same time. Hence, each worker will skip bricks which are shared or adjacent to the wall of another nearby worker. After completing the local section of the wall, the worker can "fill in" the gap left between his part and that of his neighbor to the left. This technique, called divide and conquer, characterizes many sequential and parallel algorithms. In our case the wall should be built in parallel time $T_p \approx \frac{L \cdot H}{P} + H$.

Since a wall section of the form: violates the second condition for putting on the bricks (the end bricks are "in the air"), a worker can build only pyramids, and the gaps between each section will be in the shape of a triangle.

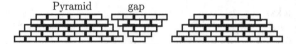

The algorithm divides the wall into sections of size $r = \frac{L}{P} - 1$, where one brick is left as a gap between every two adjacent workers. In the first stage each worker constructs a pyramid of wall height H. Each row that a worker puts down must be smaller by one brick than the previous one. The total number of bricks in a pyramid is therefore:

$$r + r - 1 + r - 2 + r - 3 + \cdots + r - (H - 1) = r \cdot H - \frac{H(H-1)}{2}$$

The total number of bricks that are needed to fill in the gap is $\frac{H(H+1)}{2}$. Therefore, the expected parallel time for a round wall with $N = L \cdot H$ bricks and P workers is:

$$T_{P,N} = r \cdot H - \frac{H(H-1)}{2} + \frac{H(H+1)}{2}$$
$$= r \cdot H + H = \left(\frac{L}{P} - 1\right)H + H = \frac{L \cdot H}{P} = \frac{N}{P}$$

This is also the optimal time possible, because every worker is constantly putting bricks down in the right places and each brick is used only once. The optimality of this algorithm can be formally derived by the following "lower bound" argument known as Brent's theorem. Brent's theorem claims that if $Ts_{A(N)}$ is the best sequential time for solving A, then $T_{A(P,N)} \geq \frac{Ts_{A(N)}}{P}$ where P is the number of processors or processing elements. Otherwise, there could have been a faster sequential algorithm than $Ts_{A(N)}$ which simulates the parallel operations of $T_{A(P,N)}$ one after the other. For example, in the case of the wall, if $T_{A(P,N)} < \frac{Ts_{A(N)} = L \cdot H}{P}$, then there would have been a "super" worker who could have constructed the wall in fewer than $L \cdot H$ steps, which is impossible according to the model.

A_{divide} is indeed optimal. However, it has the limitation that $r \geq H$. Otherwise, the worker cannot construct the pyramid to a height of H bricks (every row must be one brick smaller than its predecessor). This indicates a limitation of the value of P, $\frac{L}{P} - 1 \geq H$ yields $P \leq \frac{L}{H+1}$. Thus, only $\frac{L}{H+1}$ of the workers can be used. Recall that it is not possible to use more than $\frac{L}{2}$ workers in each step because doing so would require us to put two bricks on top of one another or place them close to each other.

A third option for an algorithm is the odd-even algorithm, denoted as $A_{odd-even}$. It uses $P \leq \frac{L}{2}$ workers, such that in every step all of the workers put down one brick. The algorithm works in $2H$ steps, such that in every even step, all of the workers put down the even bricks of the current row, and in the next odd step, they complete the row by putting down all of the odd bricks. This simple algorithm achieves the maximal number of processors with the minimal time. The algorithm can optimally use any fraction of $\frac{L}{2}$ workers. For example, consider $P = \frac{1}{3}L$. Three steps are needed to complete one row. First, $\frac{1}{3}L$ even bricks are put down. Then, in parallel the remaining $\frac{1}{6}L$ even bricks are put down in parallel with the $\frac{1}{6}L$ leftmost odd bricks. Finally, in the third step the remaining $\frac{1}{3}L$ odd bricks are put down. For example with $L = 6$ a row of 6 bricks can be constructed by two workers in three steps $t1, t2, t3$ as follows:

$t1$	$t2$	$t1$	$t3$	$t2$	$t3$

This algorithm can exploit more workers than the divide and conquer algorithm because it can use up to $\frac{L}{2}$ workers. In contrast, each worker in the divide and conquer algorithm has to build a pyramid of width H, so this approach can use at most $\frac{L}{H+1}$ workers.

Note that, in accordance with Brent's theorem, the optimality of the divide and conquer method is restricted to the range $P \leq \frac{L}{H+1}$. Perhaps in this respect the "odd-even" algorithm is better. Clearly, any algorithm will need at least H steps to construct a wall. Before drawing any final conclusions we must determine the optimality of the third odd-even algorithm.

The following induction argument can be used to show that for any P there can be no parallel algorithm that can construct a wall of size $L \times H$ faster than $2H$. Note that a lower bound of H trivially follows from the fact that a brick can be placed in row h only after row $h - 1$ contains at least one brick. Formally, the induction claims that a wall of height H with two adjacent bricks at the top cannot be constructed with fewer than $2H$ steps. For $H = 2$ it is obvious that 4 steps are needed: one brick in the first step, two at its sides, then one brick on the second row and finally, in the fourth step, an adjacent brick can be put down. Note that two adjacent bricks can be placed in row H only on top of three adjacent bricks on row $H - 1$. Assuming that the induction is true for $H - 1$, at least one other step is needed to add three adjacent bricks at height $H - 1$ and one more brick at height H. Finally, the last brick can be put down at height H.

	$2H\text{-}1$	$2H$	
$2H\text{-}2$	$2H\text{-}2$	$2H\text{-}1$	

A similar argument holds for all the other possibilities. We first put down two non adjacent bricks, then fill the gap, and place the other two bricks at height H.

1.6.2 Reducing Synchronization in Practical Parallel Algorithms

Consider the three algorithms presented in Sect. 1.6.1 A_{greedy}, A_{divide} and $A_{odd\text{-}even}$. For a given value of P number of processors where L, H are the length and height of the wall, all three algorithms can possibly achieve an optimal execution time. Moreover, while $A_{odd\text{-}even}$ can use more workers than A_{divide}, intuitively, $A_{odd\text{-}even}$ seems like the best choice. We will now show that this "intuitive" choice is not justified due to another property of these algorithm, namely, the number of synchronized steps each algorithm uses.

In the example of the wall, synchronization occurs when a worker is waiting for another worker (or all the workers) to complete his current task. In order to compare

the amount of synchronization in each algorithm we can consider the following
schematic description of each algorithm:

$A_{divide}(P = L/(H+1), N)\{$
    worker $I = 1 \ldots P$:
    build wall section i;
    if $(I < P)Inext = I + 1$;
    else $Inext = 1$;
    if $(I > 1)Iprev = I - 1$;
    else $Iprev = P$;
    signal worker $Inext$;
    await signal of $Iprev$;
    complete gap$(I, Iprev)$;
$\}$

$A_{odd\text{-}even}(P = L/2, N)\{$
    worker $I = 1 \ldots P$:
    for$(h = 1; h < H; h + +)\{$
        put brick $I \cdot 2$ row h;
        signal rest of workers;
        await signal all workers;
        put brick $I \cdot 2 - 1$ row h;
        signal rest of workers;
        await signal all workers;
    $\}$

and the last algorithm

$A_{greedy}(P = 2H, N)\{$
    worker $I = 1 \ldots P$ $(P <= 2H)$:
    if $(I <= H)myrow = I$;
    else $myrow = I/2$;
    if $(I == 1)\{$
        build initial pyramide;
        signal rest of workers;
    $\}$ else
        await signal worker 1;
    while$(not\ completed\ myrow)\{$ $/*$ about $L/2$ steps $*/$
    if $(I > H)$ put brick
        right end myrow;
    else put brick
        left end myrow;
    signal rest of workers;
    await signal all workers;
    $\}$

We can now compute two complementary properties:

- "synchronization size" as the total number of signals that needs to be received
- "granularity," which is the amount of work each worker performs between two
  consecutive synchronization steps.

Due to the large overhead possibly involved with synchronization, we should prefer
an algorithm which minimizes the synchronization size and maximizes the granularity. In order to understand the issue of granularity, we can model the signaling operation by sending a message to the processor/worker $S(P_i)$ and receiving a message
from the processor/worker $R(P_j)$. Sending a message is a non blocking operation allowing the sender to continue working without waiting for an acknowledgment that
the message was received. The receive operation is a blocking operation, causing

Fig. 1.19 Overlapping communication with useful work is beneficial

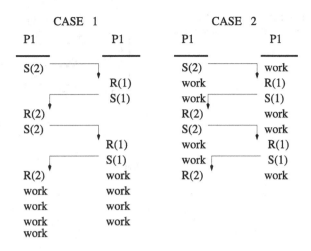

the receiver to wait until some message reaches its destination. Granularity allows the receiver to engage in useful work while waiting for a message. Figure 1.19 illustrates the effect of large-scale granularity by showing two cases of sending and receiving two messages between two processors/workers. In the first case, messages are sent and received at the beginning of the work (*granularity* $= 0$). In the second case, each worker/processor executes some useful work between the messages. In the first case, the time needed to wait for a message delays the completion time, while in the second case (*large granularity*), it overlaps with useful activity. Counting the total number of messages and the granularity is clearly a very simplified model for assessing synchronization but it is sufficient for choosing between different alternatives.

For $A_{odd\text{-}even}$ we determine that the synchronization size is $2 \cdot H \cdot P \cdot P = (L \cdot N)/2$ and the granularity is one brick. A_{greedy} has a synchronization size of $P \cdot (L/2) \cdot P = N \cdot H$ and a granularity of one brick. Thus, the better choice is A_{divide} with a synchronization size of $P = L/(H + 1)$ and a granularity of N/P.

We still must show that A_{divide} can be used for larger values of P, namely, $L/2 > P > L/(H + 1)$ in order to make the comparison between A_{divide} and $A_{odd\text{-}even}$ fair. This can be trivially demonstrated if, when $L/2 > P > L/(H + 1)$, we divide the construction of the wall into stages wherein in each stage a wall of height $H' = L/P$ is constructed in parallel by the P workers of A_{divide}. Thus, the wall is built in $max((P \cdot H)/L, 1)$ stages, increasing the synchronization size to $max((P \cdot H)/L, 1) \cdot P$. For example, assume that $L = 100$, $H = 9$ and $P = 20$; hence, the condition of $P \leq L/(H + 1)$ is not satisfied. Based on the above, we build the wall in two stages:

1. A wall of height $H' = L/P = 100/20 = 5$ is constructed using A_{divide} in optimal time.
2. The remaining wall of height $9 - 5$ is also constructed.

Note that each stage requires an all-to-all synchronization between the workers.

Fig. 1.20 Workers selecting threads from a common board

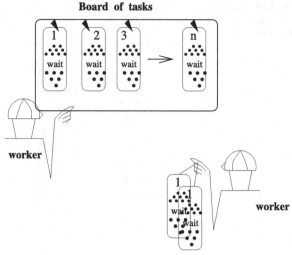

One final note regarding all-to-all synchronization is that it can be made more efficient if instead of letting each worker send and receive P messages (P^2 messages in total) we do the following:

1. We select a special worker, say worker 1 that will serve as the "master synchronizer".
2. Each worker sends a message to the master saying "I am done here". After sending this message each worker will wait for a message from the master by executing *recieve*() operation.
3. The master will wait for $P - 1$ "done" messages and then will send $P - 1$ messages to the rest of the worker that will continue the algorithm.

Synchronization can be also based on using shared memory as well, not just on message passing, as was done earlier. Using shared memory, one worker/thread can raise a flag using one shared memory cell. All of the other workers can be synchronized with this flag. By waiting for this flag to change its value *while(flag == 0)*; they can continue to work knowing that the underlying worker has raised the flag. We will learn more about this issue later on. In the example of the wall, the workers can select a thread out of a thread board (ready queue) as described in Fig. 1.20. The board of threads is analogous to the ready queue of the queue machine. Synchronization is also used to implement the queue machine described earlier.

1.6.3 Some General Methods for Implementing the Scalability of Parallel Algorithms

In this setting we have a parallel algorithm $A(P(N), N)$ which requires that the number of processors be proportional to the input size N. For example, an algorithm which finds the smallest element of an array $a[N]$, by making N^2 parallel comparisons and selecting the element which did not loose any comparison does not satisfy this condition. The problem is how to use such an algorithm with a machine with a fixed number of processors P (for any value of P).

There are three simple ways to use fewer processors and make a parallel algorithm $A(P(N), N)$ "adaptive" to a variable number of processors:

Using self simulation   We can use a new algorithm $A'(P, N) \equiv A(P(N), N)$ such that in every step each processor of $A'(P, N)$ simulates the operations of $\frac{P(N)}{P}$ processors of the original $A(P(N), N)$. Such a transformation may complicate the resulting program but essentially does not require additional overhead.

Using a virtual machine   Simulate a virtual parallel machine with $P(N)$ processors on the current machine with its P processors. Specifically, each processor can run an interpreter that simulates $P(N)/P$ processors of the virtual machine. Each of these virtual processors can execute one task of the original algorithm. In spite of its inherently non-optimality, this process is, in fact, what is implemented in parallel machines because parallel machines usually have an operating system that allows parallel programs to use any amount of parallelism.

Using sequential solutions of sub-problems   Assume that $A(P(N), N)$ computes a function $f(x_1, \ldots, x_n)$ and that $f()$ is associative or can be reconstructed such that

$$f(x_1, \ldots, x_n) = f\left(f(x_1, \ldots, x_{\frac{n}{P}}), \ldots, f(x_{\frac{n \cdot (P-1)}{P}}, \ldots, x_n)\right)$$

Each processor will sequentially compute sub-problem $y_i = f(x_{\frac{n \cdot i}{P}}, \ldots, x_{\frac{n \cdot (i+1)}{P}})$ in parallel. Thus, we are left with P partial results $y_1, \ldots y_P$ that can be computed in parallel by the original algorithm with P inputs. Theoretically, we have the following possibilities:

$$A(P(N), (x_1, \ldots, x_n) = A\left(P, \left(A_{seq}(x_1, \ldots, x_{\frac{n}{P}}), \ldots, A_{seq}(x_{\frac{n \cdot (P-1)}{P}}, \ldots, x_n)\right)\right)$$

or, even if P is sufficiently small, use only the sequential algorithm

$$A(P(N), (x_1, \ldots, x_n) = A_{seq}\left(A_{seq}(x_1, \ldots, x_{\frac{n}{P}}), \ldots, A_{seq}(x_{\frac{n \cdot (P-1)}{P}}, \ldots, x_n)\right)$$

Clearly the most efficient technique of the above three is to use sequential solutions if we can decompose the algorithm such that solutions to sub-problems can be used.

Consider, for example, the problem of computing the sum of n numbers. The parallel algorithm will use $P(n) = P/2$ processors and sum the numbers in $\log n$ steps following a binary tree of plus operations (see Fig. 1.21). Applying the third method for this algorithm yields an adaptive algorithm that:

- lets each processor compute the partial sum of $\frac{n}{P}$ numbers $y_i = \sum_{j=\frac{n \cdot i}{P}}^{\frac{n \cdot (i+1)}{P}} x_j$.
- computes the sum of $y_1, \ldots, y_P$ using the tree algorithm in $\log P$ steps.

This method yields an algorithm $\mathcal{A}(n, P)$ that computes the sum in $\frac{n}{P} + \log P$ steps. The optimality of this algorithm is demonstrated by the following argument:

Fig. 1.21 A circuit that represents the $\frac{n}{P} + \log P$ summing algorithm

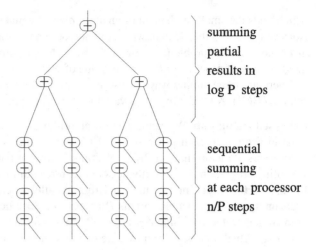

summing

partial

results in

log P steps

sequential

summing

at each processor

n/P steps

- Let us first restrict the class of possible summing algorithms to the class of algorithms that does not perform any operation other than the addition of two numbers.
- Any parallel algorithm that computes the sum of n numbers in T steps with P processors using only addition can be represented by circuit C_n of PLUS gates with depth (longest path in C) $d(C_n) = T$. For example, the circuit in Fig. 1.21 represents the above algorithm for summing n numbers. The circuit is constructed level by level, such that each addition operation to/from the shared memory $z = x + y$ is represented by an addition gate whose inputs are connected to the gates that correspond to the operations wherein x and y have been computed.
- Thus, the lower bound will follow if we can show that any circuit C_n that computes the sum of n numbers with width P (number of gates at each level) has a depth greater equal $\frac{n}{P} + \log P$.

The proof for the last claim uses a simple induction on the number of inputs n, claiming that for any $P \leq z \leq n - 1$, $d(C_z) \geq \lfloor \frac{z-1}{P} \rfloor + \log P$. It is easy to see that there is a sub-circuit in C_n which is a binary tree whose leaves include all the inputs. Hence, for $n = P$, $d(C_n) = \log P$, which is the minimal depth of that tree. In general let C_n be a suitable circuit with minimal depth, and let C'_{n-k} be the circuit obtained by replacing each gate in the first level of C_n by one of the two original inputs to this gate. Note that each gate in the first level of C has two inputs, and because there are at most P gates, we get $k \leq P$. Clearly, C'_{n-k} computes the sum of $n - k$ numbers and $d(C'_{n-k}) = d(C_n) - 1$ by the induction hypothesis:

$$d(C_n) - 1 \geq \left\lfloor \frac{n-k-1}{P} \right\rfloor + \log P \geq \left\lfloor \frac{n-P-1}{P} \right\rfloor + \log P$$

implying that

$$d(C_n) \geq \left\lfloor \frac{n-P-1}{P} \right\rfloor + \log P + \frac{P}{P} \geq \left\lfloor \frac{n-1}{P} \right\rfloor + \log P.$$

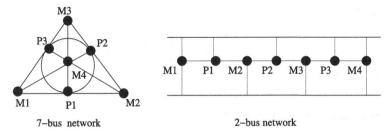

Fig. 1.22 A 7-bus parallel machine versus a 2-bus parallel machine

Clearly, for $n = P$ there is a spanning tree in C that reaches every input.

1.7 Exercises

1. Consider the two machines given in Fig. 1.22 (buses are denoted with thicker lines):
   (a) Compute the degree, latency and bandwidth for each type.
   (b) Find (if possible) a communication setting of read/write requests where the 7-bus machine has a clear advantage over the 2-bus machine. If you believe this is not true then explain why.
2. Consider the five re-write rules (Interleaving, Distributing, Sequential Ordering, Re-Ordering and adding) to generate all possible sequential execution orders of partial-order programs. Assume that apart from assignment to shared variables we also allow to add guards or conditional execution of parallel programs:

$$R \longleftarrow a_i \qquad R \longleftarrow (R; \ldots; R) \qquad R \longleftarrow [R_1 || \ldots || R_n]$$
$$R \longleftarrow if(var1 \leq var2) \qquad R$$

   - What do the following three programs do (in terms of possible execution orders)?

$$x = 0; y = 1; \left[x = y + 1 || if(x > y)y = x + 1\right]$$
$$x = 0; y = 1; \left[if(x < y)x = y + 1 || if(x > y)[x = x - 1||\right.$$
$$\left. if(x == y)(y = y - 1; \ if(x > y)x = x - 1)\right]\right]$$
$$x = 0; y = 1; \left[x = y + 1 || y = x + 1 || if(x < y)x + + || if(y < x)y + +\right]$$

   - Are the following rules sufficient to expose all possible execution orders in the case that $if(E)R$ statements are used?

   If-propagation We use a new temporary t_i and propagate the if-condition:

$$if(E)(R_1; R_2) \longrightarrow (t_i = E; if(t_i)R1; if(t_i)R2)$$
$$if(E)[R_1 || R_2] \longrightarrow (t_i = E; [if(t_i)R1||if(t_i)R2])$$

   where t_i is a new temporary allocated for this application.

Interleaving

$$[(R_1; R_2)||R_3] \longrightarrow \begin{cases} ([R_1||R_3]; R_2) \\ (R_1; [R_2||R_3]) \end{cases}$$

Distributing

$$[(R_1; R_2)||(R_3; R_4)] \longrightarrow ([R_1||R_3]; [R_2||R_4])$$

Sequential ordering (Atomicity)

$$[R_1||R_2] \longrightarrow \begin{cases} (R_1; R_2) \\ (R_2; R_1) \end{cases}$$

Re-ordering

$$[R_1||R_2] \longrightarrow [R_2||R_1]$$

Adding

$$[\ldots ||R_1||R_2||\ldots] \longrightarrow [\ldots ||[R_1||R_2]||\ldots]$$
$$(\ldots; R_1; R_2; \ldots) \longrightarrow (\ldots; (R_1; R_2); \ldots)$$

3. Let R be the program:

$(a; [(b; [[f||g]||(h; i; j)||(k; [m||l]; n)]; r)||([c||d]; e; [[p||q]||(o; x; y)])]; w)$

  (a) Write the partial order for the program $(a; [b||c]; [d||(e; f)])$ as a list of pairs.

  (b) Divide R into threads using the algorithm described earlier.

  (c) Construct a time diagram with minimal execution time for R and determine P_{max}.

  (d) Show a time diagram obtained by a queue machine with $P = 3$ processors. Is this time diagram unique? and why?

  (e) Let the "efficiency" of a time diagram be the number of "full" steps, i.e., steps where each processor executes one instruction. Clearly, a sequential execution with one processor is always efficient. Define a criterion that maximizes the efficiency of a time diagram and minimizes the execution time. Construct a time diagram for R that optimizes your criterion.

4. Consider the program

```
int g=0;
int A[N+1]={1,1,....,1};

f(int n){
    if(n > 1)
        [while(A[n] > 0)g++; || f(n-1) ];
    A[n-1] = 0;
}
f(5);
```

(a) What types of dependencies exist between the threads spawned by this program?

(b) Draw a schematic execution graph of the above program, with the first and the last calls to $f()$ completely developed, and all the middle range of calls represented by dots.

(c) What is the range of possible final values of 'g' for the best scheduling? (Hint: Consider the case of $P \geq N$ and $P = 1$).

(d) Describe in words the best scheduling for $P \leq N$ processors. Compute the execution time and the total number of steps for this scheduling.

(e) What is the minimal number of processors that guarantees that the above program will halt?

5. Consider the program

```
int g=0,n=3;

f(int x,*y){
    [
        while(x > 0)g++;  ||
        { if(x > 0)  f(*y-1,&x);  *y=x;  }
    ] }
main(){
    f(n,& n);
}
```

(a) Draw the execution graph of this program, where each call is denoted by $f(x = 3, y = \&z)$ instead of $f(3, \&z)$.

(b) Compute the number of threads, T_p, T_s and the final value of g.

6. Let P, Q be two sequential programs whose input is given by the initial values of shared variables. Are the following situations possible? (Give examples for a positive answer and an argument for a negative answer):

(a) P and Q halt (as separate programs) but $[P||Q]$ does not.

(b) P and Q do not halt (as separate programs) but $[P||Q]$ does.

(c) P halts, Q does not halt but $[P||Q]$ halts.

7. It follows that for any parallel program $T_p \leq T_1$, because any bad scheduling used to get T_p can be repeated by a single processor. The opposite claim is not necessarily true since it is not clear that the bad scheduling of one processor can always be repeated by P processors.

(a) What rule of the queue machine for scheduling might yield the above claim?

(b) Provide a simple parallel program that does not halt using one processor, but does halt when using scheduling with more than one processor.

(c) What is the phenomenon that produces the desired effect?

(d) Which of the following claims is true for a program where bad scheduling with one processor cannot be simulated by $P \geq 1$ processors:

    i. $T_1 \geq p \cdot T_p$.

    ii. $p \cdot T_1 \geq T_p$.

    iii. $\frac{T_1}{T_p} = p$.

8. Consider the relationship between the number of threads in the ready queue (R) and the number of threads in the suspend queue (S) at any given time during the execution of a parallel program:

- In what case it is likely to say that $R > S$?
- In what case it is likely to say that $R < S$?
- Which case is more likely?

1.8 Bibliographic Notes

The way parallel machines are described here differs from the common models that are based on using either point-to-point networks or buses. Basically, the way we unify buses and point-to-point communications as a hyper graph was not used. However Point-to-point multistage networks are surveyed in many works including:

- Siegel (1979) describes N cube, Omega, Shuffle exchange, and other multistage networks.
- Bermond et al. (1987) find a graph-theoretic property for equivalence of multistage networks.
- Blake and Trivedi (1989) analyze the time to failure of shuffle-exchange networks with and without an extra stage.
- In Kruskal and Snir (1983) buffered and unbuffered Banyan networks are analyzed, using the probability of a packet reaching its destination as the metric for performance.
- Mourad et al. (1991) perform a comprehensive testing of Multistage Interconnection Networks.

Interconnections between processors that are based on buses have been wildly studied in the context of the mesh of buses (Ben-Asher and Newman 2002; Iwama and Miyano 1997; Sheu and Chen 1988; Suel 1995). Combinations of multistage networks and buses were also considered. For example, Fiduccia (1992) considers the case where a bus is associated with each node in a hypercube, connecting it with all its cube neighbors. Thus nodes in a d-dimensional cube connect to $d + 1$ buses: their own bus, and those of d neighbors. It is shown that by writing to one bus and reading from another, messages can be exchanged across one or even two dimensions in a single cycle. Works on the reconfigurable mesh (Ben-Asher et al. 1991) can be regarded as a mixture of interconnection networks and buses. Using universal hashing for shared memory simulations can be tracked from Dietzfelbinger and auf der Heide (1992).

    The notion of partial orders as a way to express concurrent processes and the idea of using them to simulate time can be obtained from Ben-Asher and Farchi (1986).

The idea for the bricks wall is derived from Fox et al. (1988), where a wall of bricks is also constructed. However we derived our discussion in a different manner than in Fox et al. (1988) and use this example to discuss efficiency and time properties of parallel algorithms. Other works presenting basic concepts of parallel algorithms can be obtained from text books on parallel algorithms such as Reif (1993) or JáJá (1992). Definitions related to complexity of parallel algorithms can be found in Kruskal et al. (1990). Lower bound for addition can be derived from lower bound on parity (Beame and Astad 1987) showing an $\Omega(\log n / \log \log n)$ optimal lower bound for parity on a CRCW PRAM with polynomial processors.

References

Beame, P., Astad, J.: Optimal bounds for decision problems on the CRCW PRAM. In: Ann. Symp. Theory of Computing, pp. 83–93 (1987)

Ben-Asher, Y., Farchi, E.: Using true concurrency to model execution of parallel programs. Int. J. Parallel Program. **22**(4), 375–407 (1986)

Ben-Asher, Y., Newman, I.: Geometric approach for optimal routing on mesh with buses. In: Proceedings IEEE Seventh IEEE Symposium on Parallel and Distributed Processing, 1995, pp. 145–152. IEEE, New York (2002). ISBN 0818671955

Ben-Asher, Y., Peleg, D., Ramaswami, R., Schuster, A.: The power of reconfiguration. J. Parallel Distrib. Comput. **13**(2) (1991). Special issue on Massively Parallel Computation

Bermond, J.C., Fourneau, J.M., Jean-Marie, A.: Equivalence of multistage interconnection networks. Inf. Process. Lett. **26**(1), 45–50 (1987)

Blake, J.T., Trivedi, K.S.: Multistage interconnection network reliability. IEEE Trans. Comput. **38**(11), 1600–1604 (1989)

Dietzfelbinger, M., auf der Heide, F.: High performance universal hashing, with applications to shared memory simulations. In: Data Structures and Efficient Algorithms. Lecture Notes in Computer Science, vol. 594, pp. 250–269 (1992)

Fiduccia, C.M.: Bused hypercubes and other pin-optimal networks. IEEE Trans. Parallel Distrib. Syst. **3**(1), 14–24 (1992)

Fox, G., Johnson, M., Lyzenga, G., Otto, S., Salmon, J., Walker, D.: Solving Problems on Concurrent Processors. Vol. I: General Techniques and Regular Problems. Prentice-Hall, New York (1988)

Iwama, K., Miyano, E.: Oblivious routing algorithms on the mesh of buses. In: Parallel Processing Symposium, pp. 721–727 (1997)

JáJá, J.: An Introduction to Parallel Algorithms. Addison Wesley Longman, Redwood City (1992). ISBN 0201548569

Kruskal, C.P., Snir, M.: The performance of multistage interconnection networks for multiprocessors. IEEE Trans. Comput. **C-32**(12), 1091–1098 (1983)

Kruskal, C.P., Rudolph, L., Snir, M.: A complexity theory of efficient parallel algorithms. Theor. Comput. Sci. **71**(1), 95–132 (1990)

Mourad, A., Özden, B., Malek, M.: Comprehensive testing of multistage interconnection networks. IEEE Trans. Comput. **40**(8), 935–951 (1991)

Reif, J.H.: Synthesis of Parallel Algorithms. Morgan Kaufmann, San Francisco (1993). ISBN 155860135X

Sheu, J.-P., Chen, W.-T.: Performance analysis of multiple bus interconnection networks with hierarchical requesting model. In: Intl. Conf. Distributed Comput. Syst., pp. 138–144 (1988)

Siegel, H.J.: Interconnection networks for SIMD machines. Computer **12**(6), 57–65 (1979)

Suel, T.: Permutation routing and sorting on meshes with row and column buses. Parallel Process. Lett. **5**(1), 63–80 (1995)

Chapter 2
Principles of Shared Memory Parallel Programming Using *ParC*

This chapter introduces the basic concepts of parallel programming. It is based on the ParC language, which is an extension of the C programming language with block-oriented parallel constructs that allow the programmer to express fine-grain parallelism in a shared memory model. It can be used to express parallel algorithms, and it is also conducive for the parallelization of sequential C programs. The chapter covers several topics in shared memory programming. Each topic is presented with simple examples demonstrating its utility. The chapter supplies the basic tools and concepts needed to write parallel programs and covers these topics:

- Practical aspects of threads, the sequential "atoms" of parallel programs.
- Closed constructs to create parallelism.
- Possible bugs.
- The structure of the software environment that surrounds parallel programs.
- The extension of C scoping rules to support private variables and local memory accesses.
- The semantics of parallelism.
- The discrepancy between the limited number of physical processors and the much larger number of parallel threads used in a program.

2.1 Introduction

ParC was developed as part of a quest to make parallel programming simple namely easy to use and quick to learn. ParC is a block-oriented, shared memory, parallel version of the C programming language. ParC presents the programmer with a model of a machine in which there are many processors executing in parallel and having access to both private and shared variables.

The main feature of ParC is that the parallelism is incorporated in the block structure of the language. As such it makes the structure of a parallel program very similar to a sequential C program. This fully nested structure and the similarity to the structure of a sequential C program has the following implications:

Y. Ben-Asher, *Multicore Programming Using the ParC Language*,
Undergraduate Topics in Computer Science,
DOI 10.1007/978-1-4471-2164-0_2, © Springer-Verlag London 2012

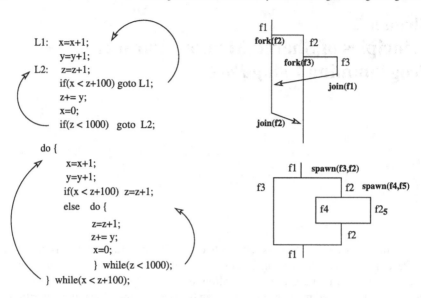

Fig. 2.1 General goto structure versus nested loops and general parallelism versus nested parallelism

- It leads to a nested structure of parallelism which, similar to sequential programming ease the task of coding parallel algorithms.
- It simplifies the task of transforming a parallel program to a sequential one and vice-versa. This is useful for debugging and gradual parallelization of sequential code (as will be discussed later).

ParC supports nesting of parallel constructs and as such it does not support arbitrary forms of parallelism. This is similar to the use of closed **while** loops instead of a general **goto** instruction. Figure 2.1 illustrates this concept showing a general goto structure versus the use of nested while-loops. This case is similar to the use of general *fork(thread)* and *join(thread)* operations that allow us to generate any graph of threads versus the use of nested parallelism. In nested parallelism a thread does not fork another thread but rather spawns children threads that must be merged eventually before the spawning thread can continue. Thus in the context of parallelism, nesting of constructs results in the use of closed parallel constructs rather than arbitrary **fork** and **join**. Similar to C's alternative loop-constructs (**for**, **do**, and **while**), ParC has several redundant parallel constructs, as well as redundant synchronization mechanisms.

ParC is accompanied by a virtual machine that virtually can execute or simulate ParC programs over a set of *P* processors. This virtual machine forms a model for executing ParC programs thus restricting the implementation of ParC to fulfill the guidelines of the virtual machine. Through this virtual machine and other assumptions, it is possible to estimate the execution time of a given program. The programmer can thus use this model to improve the performance of a given program. For this purpose, ParC includes features and constructs to control the execution of a program by the virtual machine, e.g., mapping code-segments to specific processors at run time. Another direction to improve performances that is based on the ability to define execution time of parallel programs is to restrict the program to increase or decrease the amount of code that is executed by parallel constructs versus the amount of code that is executed sequentially. This tuning is usually done after the application has been fully developed and performance analysis has indicated the problem areas.

ParC is an extension of the *C* programming language, so there is no need to review any of its standard features.

2.1.1 System Structure

The environment of ParC is composed of three parts: a pre-compiler that translates ParC code into *C*, a simulator that simulates parallel execution on a UNIX machine, and a thread system library that supports the execution of ParC programs by a shared memory machine (SMM) (see Fig. 2.2).

The parallel program is represented by a single operating system process. Regular system calls may be used in a parallel program, however care must be given if they are used in parallel mode or to their effect on the execution. For example, executing a process-fork call in a ParC program may leave the child-process in a faulty non consistent state. All I/O operations must be serialized since file descriptors are shared by all the parallel threads spawned by the program. The subject of I/O operations during the run of a parallel program is more complicated, but for the time being it is assumed not to be part of the language but is subject instead to the way the underlying file system works. For example, assume that we have k threads that open the same file, store it in a local pointer and then write their IDs $1 \ldots k$ to the file and close it. It is unclear what the file will contain. Will it be one number or a permutation of the numbers $1 \ldots k$? This in general depends on the way in which the file system handles I/O operations. On multicore machines we may assume Posix I/O semantics for multi-threaded code. A more complicated question is, what happens if one of the threads closes the file or deletes it before other threads have completed their writing? These questions are outside the scope of this chapter but in general are related to practical parallel programming.

The pre-compiler is more complicated than a preprocessor compiling ParC's constructs to system calls for generating and executing the program's code segments in parallel. The pre-compiler has to recognize the language and keep a symbol table in order to support the scoping rules and other features. In particular, the compiler can generate new temporary variables and control the memory layout of the parallel program.

All these aspects are important when building a parallel program since they can affect its execution and performance.

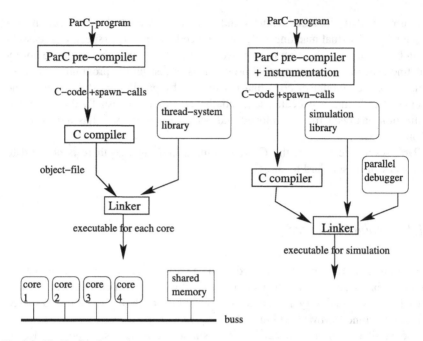

Fig. 2.2 The ParC software system

2.2 Parallel Constructs

Parallelism in parallel programs can be extracted from two sources of sequential constructs:

- loop's iterations that are executed in parallel and
- function calls and in particular recursion that are executed in parallel.

The parallel constructs in ParC are especially designed to handle both cases in an efficient and structured manner. The parallel "things" generated by ParC are called "*threads.*" Each thread is a sequential code that may be executed in parallel to other threads (as explained in the previous chapter). Each thread has its own private stack that is allocated in the shared memory when the thread is generated. The thread stack allows function calls made by the threads to be executed separately from the function calls of other threads. The outcome of using "thread stacks" will be discussed later on.

Loop parallelism is obtained by the parfor construct, which is a parallel version of the conventional for loop in C. The syntax for this construct is shown on the right side of Fig. 2.3. The body of the parfor, stmt, can be any legal statement in C, including a function call, a loop or a conditional statement. If *stmt* is a block (compound statement), it can declare its own private variables, which can not be

Fig. 2.3 The parfor construct

```
parfor ( index = e₁; index < e₂; index+ = e₃ )
{
      stmt
}
```

Fig. 2.4 Example of
`parfor`

```
int array[100];
parfor(int i=0; i< 100; i++){
      array[i] = 0;
}
```

Fig. 2.5 Increasing the work
done by each thread

```
int array[100000];
parfor(int i=0; i< 100000; i+=1000){
      int j;
      for(j=i; j<i+1000; j++) array[j] = 0;
}
```

referenced outside the scope of this parfor. In addition each iteration of the parfor
use a different set of local variables (including the parfor's index) which are thus
isolated from local variables of other iterations (unless passed by a reference through
a global variable). This point is discussed in greater detail in Sect. 2.3. The bodies
of the distinct iterates are executed in parallel. The meaning of the phrase "executed
in parallel" is discussed in Sect. 3.8.

For example, the code segment in Fig. 2.4 may be used to initialize an array of
100 cells. The `parfor` generates 100 threads, indexed by the integer variable `i`.
The index values ranges from 1 to 100 in increments of 1. Each thread comprises
a single statement, which sets one cell of the array to zero. In case of a larger array we can let each thread to zero more than one element as depicted in Fig. 2.5.
When using parallel constructs, one should keep in mind that spawning new threads
incurs a certain overhead. This overhead can be around few hundreds of assembler
instructions although for ParC threads it is usually smaller. Therefore, the threads
should be substantial enough so that the benefits of parallelization justify the overhead. Threads with a single instruction, as in the example of Fig. 2.4 are definitely
too small to be worthwhile hence code of the form depicted in Fig. 2.5 is preferable.
We remark that care must be given to the index expressions that are used in parallel
constructs. For example, the code in Fig. 2.5 is more efficient than the one depicted
in Fig. 2.6.

A distinct, local copy of the loop index is created for each iterate containing
the iteration-id similar to a regular sequential for-loop. The number of threads is

Fig. 2.6 A less efficient
version

```
int array[100000];
parfor(int i=0; i< 100; i++;){
    int j;
    for(j=0; j<1000; j++) array[i*1000+j] = 0;
}
```

Fig. 2.7 Using lparfor to
zero a large array

```
int array[100000];
parfor(int i=0; i< 100; i++){
    array[i] = 0;
}
```

$\lfloor \frac{e_2-e_1}{e_3} \rfloor + 1$ as in regular for-loops. The index variable in thread i is initialized to
$e_1 + (i - 1) \cdot e_3$. Note that this variable is only defined in the parfor and can not be
referenced directly outside of its scope.

Unlike the C's *for(int $i = e_1; i \leq e_2; i+ = e_3)stm$;*, the expressions e_1, e_2, and
e_3 are evaluated only once, before any threads are actually spawned. Thus, unlike
regular C, changing the index inside a parfor construct will not affect its evaluation:
This is done by using temporary variables to compute the loop's parameters before
the execution of the loop begins:

```
parfor(i=0;i<n;i+=x)
   {
      A[i]++;
      if(A[i] > 7)  i+=5;
      if(A[i] > 100) n+=5;
      if(A[i] > 5)  x+=i;
   }
if(i < n) x++;
from=0; to=n; by=x;
parfor(index=from ;index< to;index+=by)
   { int i;
     i=index;
     A[i]++;
     if(A[i] > 7)  i+=5;
     if(A[i] > 100) n+=5;
     if(A[i] > 5)  x+=i;
   }
if(i < n) x++;
```

Thus, changing the parfor's iteration-range during execution does not have the same
effect as changing these in regular for-loop nor is the loop's index affected in a
similar manner.

```
int array[100000];
int np=100000/P; parfor(int ii=0; ii< 100000; ii+=np){
    int i;
    for(i=ii; i<ii+np; i++) array[i] = 0;
}
```

Fig. 2.8 Equivalent parfor version of an lparfor

Unlike C, it is illegal to transfer control via a Goto-statement or via setjump/long-jump either into or out of a parallel construct. Note that transferring control via goto is legal in *C*, as illustrated in the following example:

```
#include <stdio.h>
main(){
int i,j=4,n=100;
for(i=0;i<n;i++){
   j=j+1;
   l:  if(i == 10) goto t;
   else j = j+10;
}
for(i=0;i<n;i++){
   j=j+1;
   t:  if(i == 10) goto l;
   else j = j+10;
}
printf("%d %d\n",i,j);
}
```

which has no meaning had we used parfor instead of for-loops since the second parfor has not been started when the first goto occurs.

It is often the case that the number of iterates in a parallel loop is much larger than the number of processors P. If such is the case, it would be better to create only P threads and have each of them execute $(\frac{e_2-e_1}{e_3} + 1)/P$ of the iterates in a serial loop. This procedure saves the overhead associated with spawning all the threads and increases the possibility of using fine-grain parallelism. ParC has a special construct that implements this optimization, called lparfor. Thus the use of lparfor in Fig. 2.7 is efficient and is equivalent to the parfor version of Fig. 2.8 where P is the number of processors.

Note, however, that the iterates must be independent for this procedure to work. lparfor explicitly implies that the iterations are independent. A correct program using parfor constructs may not be correct if lparfor is used instead. For example, the following parallel loop always halts, but not as an lparfor because the flag will never reset:

Fig. 2.9 The parblock construct

```
parblock
{
        stmt₁
:
.........
:
        stmtₖ
}
```

```
int x=1,z;
parfor(int i=0;i<n;i++)
   if(i == n-1){ z=f(); x=0;}
   else{
        while(x);
        A[i]=g(z);
   }
epar
```

Clearly one may always replace an lparfor with a parfor without affecting the correctness. The lparfor construct may be used to batch a number of small threads together in order to increase their granularity. However, such a procedure requires that these threads be independent.

The potential parallelism in recursion function calls and in a sequence of independent function calls $f(\ldots)$; $g(\ldots)$ is handled by the parblock construct whose syntax is given in Fig. 2.9. For example it can be used to parallelize the structure of divide and conquer algorithms.[1] Note that the three parallel constructs are redundant: a parblock and lparfor may be implemented using a parfor, for example, but such implementations would be bulky and degrade the code quality significantly.

Since parallel constricts can be freely nested then there is a need to determine what happens when a thread spawns another thread. For example in Fig. 2.10 we should determine if the for-loop $for(j = i; j < i + 1000; j + +)$ can continue execute its next iteration before all the threads spawned by the inner parfor (spawned in the current iteration of the $for(j = i; j < i + 1000; j + +))$ terminated. In ParC the rule is that the thread that executes a parallel construct is suspended until all the constituent threads have terminated. Thus, the for-loop in Fig. 2.10 is blocked until the threads spawned in its last iteration terminate (yielding no more than 100×1000 threads running at any time of the execution).

Upon execution, nesting of parallel constructs thus creates a tree of threads where only the leaves are executing while internal nodes wait for their descendants.

We now present a set of simple programs in order to demonstrate how to use parallel constructs to create parallel programs. As an example of parfor usage, consider a program that determines if all the elements of an array are equal, Fig. 2.11.

---

[1] In the sequel we will also use the short notation of $PF\ i = 1\ldots n\ [S_i]$ for the parfor construct and $PB\ [S_1, \ldots, S_k]$ for the parblock construct.

```
int array[100000][1000];
parfor(int i=0; i< 100000; i+=1000){
    int j;
    for(j=i; j<i+1000; j++)
        parfor(int k=0; k< 1000; k++) array[j][k] = 0;
}
```

Fig. 2.10   Nesting of parallel constructs

Fig. 2.11   Testing equality in parallel

```
int A[N];
int b=1;
parfor(int i=0; i<N; i++)
    if(A[i] != A[i+1]) b = 0;
```

Fig. 2.12   Testing equality in parallel using lparfor

```
int A[N];
int b=1;
lparfor(int i=0; i<N; i++)
    if(A[i] != A[i+1]) b = 0;
```

Fig. 2.13   Testing equality in parallel eliminating unnecessary comparisons

```
int A[N];
int b=1;
lparfor(int i=0; i<N; i++)
    if(A[i] != A[i+1] && b) b = 0;
```

The parallel program compares all elements in parallel. If one comparison fails, a flag (b) is set to zero. This program uses one parallel step instead of the N steps used by the sequential version. One can consider some issues of efficiency:

- Can we replace the parfor by a light lparfor? if so we improve the overhead for creating N threads (see Fig. 2.12).
- If we detected that two elements differ we need not complete the remaining iterations (see Fig. 2.13). Though (assuming that the b is tested first before $A[i]! = A[i + 1]$ is evaluated) we saved the comparison this version is still not efficient since it will execute N loop-iterations even if $b = 0$ is executed in an early stage (e.g., when $A[0] == A[1]$). Thus, the version in Fig. 2.14 is significantly better.

It is interesting to note that the effect of the version in Fig. 2.14 could have been obtained had we used break-statement as depicted in Fig. 2.15.

Fig. 2.14 Improving
efficiency by simulating
lparfor

```
int A[N];
int b=1, np=N/P;
parfor(int ii=0; ii<N; ii+=np){
    int i;
    for(i=ii; (i<ii+np) && b; i++)
        if(A[i] != A[i+1] && b) b = 0;
}
```

Fig. 2.15 Using
break-statement in a lparfor

```
int A[N];
int b=1;
lparfor(int i=0; i<N; i++){
    if(A[i] != A[i+1]) b = 0;
    if(b == 0) break;
}
```

Fig. 2.16 Recursive parallel
summing

```
int A[N];
int rsum(A,fr,to)
int A[],fr,to;
{
int a,b;
if(fr == to) return(A[fr]);
else
    parblock {
        a = rsum(A,fr,(to+fr)/2);
        :
        b = rsum(A,(to+fr)/2 +1,to);
    }
    return(a+b);
}
}
```

As an example of **parblock**, consider a recursive routine that computes the sum
of N elements of an array A, described in Fig. 2.16.

The parallel program computes the sums of each half of the array in parallel
and then adds them together. Hence, it needs $2 \log N$ parallel steps compared to the
$2N$ steps needed for the sequential version. The above program actually contains
a bug and may not work correctly. Assume that $(to + fr)/2$ rounds the result up to
$\lceil (to + fr)/2 \rceil$; then we have generated an infinite recursion, as depicted in Fig. 2.17.

Note that each call to *rsum*() is executed on a separate stack. Thus, when a thread
terminates, its stack can be re-used when generating new threads. Clearly, had we
used one stack to implement the calls of all the threads, we would suffer the following consequences:

Fig. 2.17 Infinite recursion and incorrect sums can be obtained

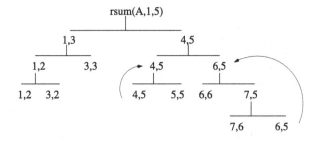

Fig. 2.18 Simple parallel programs for summing N numbers

```
int A[N];
int np=N/P,k,s=0,s_ar[P];
parfor(int l=0; l<P; l++)
{ int i;
    s_ar[l] = 0;
    for(i=l*np; i<(l+1)*np; i++)
        s_ar[l] += A[i];
}
for(k=0; k<P; k++) s += s_ar[k];
```

- The stack would have been a sequential "bottle-neck" because each call would require us to "lock" the stack pointer, preventing other threads from performing function calls in parallel.
- If the function calls of the threads are mixed in one stack, whenever a function returns, it will leave a "hole" in the stack that will be hard to use.

The sum of N elements (see Fig. 2.18) can be computed more efficiently by a divide and conquer algorithm designed for P processors. The program divides A into P segments, computes the sum of every segment in parallel and stores it in a global array $s\_ar[l]$. The local sums are summed sequentially in P steps. Hence, the program needs $\frac{N}{P} + P$ parallel steps, compared to N needed by the sequential program. This version of *sum* is more efficient than *rsum* because it spawns fewer threads $P \ll N$ than in *rsum*.

This summing program contain some faults as follows:

- If N is not divided by P then some elements at the last part of the array will not be included in the summing.
- It is multiplying by *np* every iteration.

Figure 2.19 shows how to correct these problems.

2.3 Scoping Rules

In general scoping rules associate between definitions of variables in different scopes. Scoping rules determine which assignments can update these variables and

```
int A[N];
int np=N/P,k,s=0,s_ar[P];
parfor(int l=0; l<N; l+=np)
{ int i,z;
    z = l/np;
    s_ar[z] = 0;
    for(i=l; i<l+np; i++)
        s_ar[z] += A[i];
}
for(k=l; k<n; k++) s += A[k]; /* remaining un-summed elements (at most N/P-1 steps) */
for(k=0; k<P; k++) s += s_ar[k];
```

Fig. 2.19 Correct version of summing N numbers, in $O(N/P)$ steps

which expressions can use these variables. In general each function call creates a new activation record that holds its set of variables. Thus the scope of a given call is all the activation records of other function calls whose variables can be updated or used directly through their names by the current function call. This is depicted in Fig. 2.20 showing that in the case of a single threaded code there is only one stack and the scope of each accesses to a variable is uniquely defined by searching the last occurrence of a function's activation record on the stack. However, in a multi-threaded code there is a multiple set of stacks and as depicted in Fig. 2.20 it is not clear what is the scope of $f4$.

Note that C has only two levels of nesting variables: local to a procedure and global. C, however, also has a form of hierarchical scoping for variables because each block of code may contain a data declaration section. Thus, within a single procedure, there is hierarchical scoping. As the following example illustrates, in C the scoping rules are not fully enforced.

```
int g1;
for(int i=0;i<n;i++){
int g2;
    g2 = i+g1;
    if (A[i] < g2)
    { int g3;
      g3 = g3 + g2*i;
    }
}
printf(" is g3 accumulative? %d\n",g3);
}
```

In ParC, this hierarchical scoping is used to provide various degrees of sharing of variables among threads. In parallel languages, scoping is often augmented with explicit declarations that variables are either private or shared. We find that explicit declarations are unnecessary, as the scoping naturally leads to a rich selection of sharing patterns. Since ParC allows parallel constructs to be freely nested inside other parallel constructions it naturally creates nested patterns of shared/private variables.

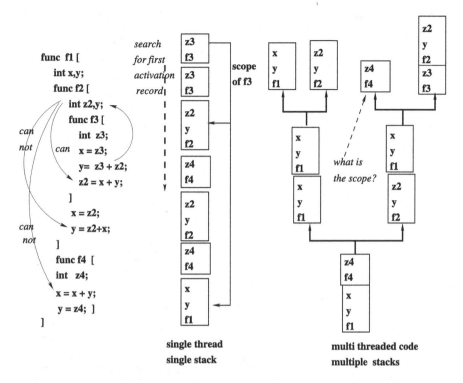

Fig. 2.20 Scoping rules in sequential environment versus scoping rules in multi-threaded code

As each iteration of a parfor/parblock creates a new thread we obtain multiple set of stacks for which the rule of:

```
Consider a reference to an ''external'' variable X made in f()
where X is defined in a different function F().
Search for the last occurrence of F() on the stack in order to
locate the right copy of X f() is referring to.
```

can not be applied.

ParC attempts to preserve the normal *C* language scoping rules. Thus, variables declared within a block (regardless of whether the block is parallel or sequential) can be accessed by any of its nested statements (parallel or sequential). This capability means that global variables are shared among all of the program threads; static variables and external variables are also considered global.

Local variables declared within a block are allocated to the thread's stack. The scoping rules, therefore, imply a logical "cactus stack" structure for nested parallel constructs, as each thread that is spawned adds a new stack that can be reused when the thread terminates. Note, however, that this is the case only for nested parallel constructs in the same procedure. Code in one procedure cannot access variables local to the procedure that called it unless they are passed as arguments. It cannot modify them unless they are passed by reference.

Fig. 2.21 Example to
illustrate scoping rules

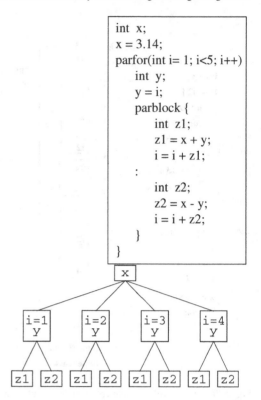

```
int  x;
x = 3.14;
parfor(int i= 1; i<5; i++)
      int  y;
      y = i;
      parblock {
            int  z1;
            z1 = x + y;
            i = i + z1;

        :

            int  z2;
            z2 = x - y;
            i = i + z2;
      }
}
```

The array in the example of Fig. 2.4 is shared by all of the threads, while the
index variable i is duplicated with a private copy in each thread. This is a special
case of the different sharing patterns that are possible in *ParC*.

The scoping rules of *ParC* are the same as those of *C*: variables may be declared
in any block, and their scope includes all blocks that are nested within the block in
which they are declared. If some of these nested blocks are executed in parallel, the
variable will be shared by all the decedent threads.

For example, consider the code segment in Fig. 2.21. The variable x is shared
by all the threads. The parfor construct creates four threads. Each has a private
copy of the index variable i that is initialized automatically by the system, and
another private variable y. When the parblock is executed, each of these threads
spawns two additional threads: one defines a private variable z1 and the other a
private variable z2. When one of these threads performs the instruction z1 = x
+ y, for example, it is adding the value of x, which is shared by everyone, to the
value of y, which it shares only with its brother, and stores the result in a private
variable that is inaccessible to other threads. The structure of the thread tree and the
copies of the various variables are also shown in Fig. 2.21. Note that the assignments
$i = i + z1, i = i + z2$ can affect each other only at the level of each parfor, but since
i is duplicated there can be no effect of these assignments between the threads of
the outer parfor.

The scoping rules described above are implemented by the ParC pre-compiler by changing the references to variables declared in surrounding blocks to indirect references through a pointer n(using $px = \&x$; $* px = y$ instead of $x = y$;). Thus, the run-time system does not have to:

- Chain stacks to each other explicitly to create a full-fledged cactus stack.
- Search along the set of stacks on the path from the current stack to the root stack to find the first occurrence of an activation record containing X for each external reference to X.
- Create special types of "shared addresses" to distinguish among the different copies of the local variables declared inside the parallel constructs. This is obtained through the use of indirect references via the $*px$ pointers.

Instead, direct pointers to the variables' location (typically on another thread's stack) are available. We call the resulting structure of stacks with mutual pointers into each other a *threaded stack*.

Figure 2.22 illustrates the implementation of the scoping rules with threaded stacks. The two threads in the parblock share the variables $i, x, A[\,]$ (but use only x, A) declared before the parblock in the external parfor. Each parfor iteration or parblock statement is transformed by the ParC compiler into a function ($f1, f2, f3()$ in the figure) that receives a pointer to i as its argument. The function names and the arguments are passed as parameters to the spawnPB, spawnPF functions. These spawn-functions are part of the thread system library. When it is called, it creates new threads on different processors/cores. As depicted in Fig. 2.22, each thread is complete with its own call stack. An activation record for the thread's function is constructed on the thread's stack, and the appropriate arguments are copied to it. The thread can then commence and behaves as if the function were called on a remote processor/core. Thus due to the execution of the program in Fig. 2.22 the *spawnPF* will generate four threads each with its own stack ($f3(0), f3(1), f3(2), f3(3)$ in the figure). Each of these four threads will spawn two new threads of the parblock yielding $1 + 4 + 8$ threads and stacks.

The issue of managing the cactus stack efficiently and the overhead involved with it is an important consideration when designing a multi-threaded system. The cactus stack is a direct consequence of the ability to nest parallel constructs and to mix them with recursive calls. These abilities form the main core of a free non-restricted parallel programming style. An alternative approach (for obtaining more efficient handling of stacks) is to sacrifice nesting + recursion and restrict the programmer to using a fixed set of P threads for the whole execution. This programming style is called Single Program Multiple Data (SPMD) and is equivalent to the following restrictions in ParC:

1. Use only *parfor* ($inti = 0; i < P; i + +)\{Seq - C - CODE\}$;.
2. Nesting of parallel constructs is not allowed.
3. *parfor* ()s can be used only in *main*().
4. The execution of parfor () should be unconditional.
5. Threads can communicate only through a global set of common shared variables.

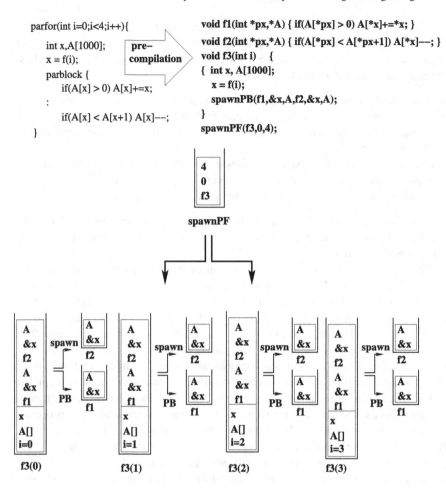

Fig. 2.22 Compilation of a ParC program and the resulting cactus stack generated by its execution

Thus, the recursive summing cannot be programmed in SPMD style. In SPMD style there is no need to support the cactus stack. Each iteration of the chain of parfor ()s composing the SPMD program is executed by one of the threads of the fixed *P* threads allocated at the beginning of the execution using its local stack. Figure 2.23 illustrates this fact showing that a set of three separate stacks can be used to implement a parallel program that agrees with the requirements of SPMD. In fact, as depicted in Fig. 2.23 we can execute an SPMD program using a fixed set of threads with only shared memory to hold global shared variables.

2.3.1 Using Static Variables

In *C*, static variables are declared inside functions but are shared or common to all invocations (calls) made to this function. The implementation is, therefore, to

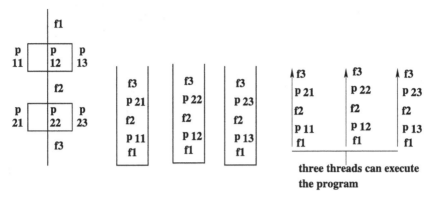

Fig. 2.23 SPMD allow to use separate flat set of stacks

```
parfor ( j; 0; N−1; 1 ) {
    parfor ( i; 0; N−1; 1 ) {
        static int s=0;         /* shared by all N threads * /
        int t;                  /* private to each thread * /

        s++;                    /* atomic incremental of 's' * /
        t++;                    /* private variables need not be protected * /
    }
}
printf("s will be N*N%d",s);
```

Fig. 2.24 A variable declared as static within the construct will actually be shared by all the threads of the construct!

allocate storage for such variables from the global heap space, rather than on the stack. In *ParC*, static variables declared in a parallel block become shared by all the threads that activate a function with that static variable (see Fig. 2.24).

2.3.2 Bypassing the Scoping Rules

The scoping rules of *ParC* make local variables declared in different threads separate entities. The goal is to let each thread use its own local copy safely without fear of being updated by another thread. However, due to the ability of C to pass the address of a variable through a global variable, it is possible to bypass the locality, allowing one thread to change the value of a local variable of another thread which is normally not visible to it. In regular C code one can use this ability to produce harmful effects such as accessing a local variable of a function after it has returned:

Fig. 2.25 Bypassing locality
using a shared variable

```
int *p;
    parfor( int i=1; i<4; i++)
    {
        int  Y;
        Y = i;
        P = &Y;
        *P = i;
        printf("<%d,%d>",i,Y);
    }
```

```
int *g,A[100];
int f(int z){
    int x,y;
    x= A[z];
    y= A[x];
    g = &y;
    return(x+y);
}

main(){
    *g = f(5);
}
```

In *ParC* this ability allows us to bypass the scoping rules, an ability that is potentially harmful, but can also be useful. Figure 2.25 demonstrates this ability by showing three threads that can potentially affect the local variables ($Y_{1,2,3}$) of one other. Let Y_i denote the local copy of the ith thread. One could expect that the program will print $\langle 1, 1 \rangle$, $\langle 2, 2 \rangle$, $\langle 3, 3 \rangle$ in different orders. However, other results are possible because one thread can change the value of Y of another thread if P has its address. For example $\langle 1, 1 \rangle \langle 2, 3 \rangle \langle 3, 3 \rangle$ will be printed by the sequence:

$$Y_1 = 1; \ Y_2 = 2; \ Y_3 = 3; \ P = \&Y_1; \ P = \&Y_3;$$

$$P = \&Y_2; \ Y_1 = *P = 1; \ Y_2 = *P = 2; \ Y_3 = *P = 3; \quad \langle 1, 1 \rangle \langle 2, 3 \rangle \langle 3, 3 \rangle$$

Or $\langle 2, 1 \rangle \langle 1, 3 \rangle \langle 3, 3 \rangle$ will be printed by the sequence:

$$Y_1 = 1; \ Y_2 = 2; \ Y_3 = 3; \ P = \&Y_3; \ Y_3 = *P = 3; \ P = \&Y_1; \ Y_1 = *P = 3;$$

$$P = \&Y_2; \ Y_2 = *P = 1; \quad \langle 2, 1 \rangle \qquad Y_2 = *P = 2; \quad \langle 1, 3 \rangle \langle 3, 3 \rangle$$

2.4 Effect of Execution Order and Atomicity

Another factor that should be considered is the fact that ParC assignments are not **atomic**. An operation is atomic if it is executed in one step by the hardware, and its result cannot be affected by the parallel execution of another operation. In ParC, the assignment $X = X + 1$ should be divided into atomic *load* and *stores* operations such that interleavings with other operations can take place. Hence, an instruction is atomic if it cannot be interleaved with any other operation. In order to compute all possible results of a ParC program, the user has to divide every expression and assignment into a sequence of load and stores, and then find all of the possible interleavings or execution orders.

The next program attempts to compute the sum of N elements in one step. If $X = X + 1$ had been atomic, in all execution orders X would have contained the sum of all of the elements in A. However, $X = X + 1$ is not atomic. Its atomic version is presented on the right side of the figure below. Clearly, there are execution orders where X will contain the value of the last store ($x = t$;). In other words, instead of $\sum A[I]$, X will contain the value of some $A[I]$.

| ```
int  A[N],X=0;
parfor( int i=1;i<N;i++){
    X = X + A[I];
}
``` | ```
int  X=0;
parfor( int i=1;i<N;i++){
    int t,*a,ai;
    t = X; /*load x*/
    a = A; /* load A[I] */
    a = a +I;
    ai = *a;
    t = t + ai;
    X = t; /*store */
}
``` |
|---|---|
| False summing program. | An atomic version demonstrating harmful execution orders. |

Clearly, interleaving instructions from different threads (execution order) may have an effect on program termination, in addition to the obvious effect on access to shared variables.

2.5 Parallel Algorithms for Finding the Minimum

In this section we study several basic parallel algorithms demonstrating some basic parallel programming techniques. These techniques are elementary but general enough so that they can be viewed as parallel programming techniques rather than specific algorithmic solutions to a single problem. Programming, testing and comparing different variants of the same problem may lead to a deeper understanding of the programming gap between algorithms and their implementation as parallel programs. The underlying algorithms solve the problem of finding the minimum of N elements stored in the array. Most of these algorithms are designed for a given

Fig. 2.26 Basic scheme of
divide and conquer using
$k = P$ parts

```
input A[N];
temporary partial_res[P];
parfor(int l=0; l<N; l+=t)
{ int i,z;
    z = (N/P);
    partial_res[l/z] = 0;
    for(i=l; i<l+z; i++)
        partial_res[l/z] op= solve(A[i]);
}
for(k=0; k<P; k++) combine(partial_res[k]);
```

number of processors. The algorithms vary in the number of processors needed. For example, when P (number of processors) is N^2, the minimum of N elements can be found in few parallel steps while for $P \leq N$ it takes about $\log N$ steps. When these algorithms are implemented in *ParC*, processors become threads. Hence, the number of processors used by the algorithm can affect the expected performance because of the overhead associated with the threads' creation.

2.5.1 Divide and Conquer Min

This solution is based on the summing algorithms described earlier (Fig. 2.16). A summing algorithm can be converted into an algorithm for finding the minimum by replacing the $+(x, y)$ operation with a $min(X, Y)$ operation. This procedure yields algorithms that use up to N threads and finds the minimum in $O(\log N)$ steps.

Basically, in this sort of solution the problem's input is split into $k > 1$ parts each is solved in parallel and independently of the rest of the parts. Finally a combine (conquer stage) finds the solution of the problem by processing all the results of k parts (sequentially or in parallel). Figure 2.26 illustrates the general scheme for divide and conquer when $k = P$.

2.5.2 Crash Min

The assumption used in this simple algorithm is that the number of available processors is N^2, where N is the problem size. In this case the power of common read and write to the same cell can be used to find the minimum in one step. The crush technique relies on the ability to use one shared memory cell to compute the boolean functions (e.g., AND) of n bits in one step as follows:

```
int b,A[N];

b = 1;
parfor(i=0;i<N;i++){
    if (A[i] == 0) b = 0;
}
printf(" the AND of A[1] to A[N] is %d",b);
```
Parallel AND of N bits

The crush method for finding the minimum of $A[N]$ can be described by picturing an $N \times N$ array $C[N][N]$ used to store the results of the comparisons between all elements of $A[N]$. For each i, j a TRUE is placed in $C[i][j]$ if $A[i] \leq A[j]$. If such is not the case, a FALSE is placed there instead. One or more FALSEs in the ith row of $C[][]$ indicates that the ith element is not the minimum. A parallel AND can be used to identify rows in $C[][]$ containing only TRUEs, a procedure that can be done in parallel by N^2 threads. The minimum is obtained by executing $min = A[i]$ for all rows in $C[][]$ with TRUE elements only. In fact, we need to check only the cells (in the imaginary array) that are above the main diagonal, so we need only $N \cdot (N-1)/2$ threads.

```
#define F 0
#define T 1
crush( ar, size )
int *ar,size;
{ int result[MAX],min;
    parfor(int i=0; i<size; i++)
        { result[i] = T; }
    parfor(int i=0; i<size-1; i++)
    {
        parfor(int j=0; j<size; j++)
        {
            if( ar[i] < ar[j] ) result[j] = F;
        }
    }
    parfor(int i=0; i<size; i++)
    {
        if ( result[i] == T ) min = ar[i];
    }
    return( min );
}
```
The crush method of finding the minimum in a constant number of steps

2.5.3 Random Min

The random algorithm uses N processors and advances in stages. In each stage there is a candidate for the minimum denoted by *min*. All threads whose element is greater than or equal to *min* are terminated because their value $A[i]$ is not the minimum. A set of $\sqrt{N}$ elements is chosen from the remaining candidates. Since there are N processors (or threads), the crash method can be used to find the minimum of this set. This minimum becomes the new candidate and the process repeats itself until all of the elements are greater than or equal to *min*. A simple probabilistic analysis shows that 6 steps are quite probably all that are needed.

```
#define F 0
#define T 1
random_min( ar , size )
int *ar,size;
{ int min,tag,sqr[ SQRMAX ];
   parfor(int i=0; i<SQRMAX; i++)
   { sqr[ i ] = BIGNUM; }
   for( min = BIG , tag == T; tag = T;)
   {
       tag = F;
       parfor(int i=0; i<size; i++)
       {
           if( ar[i] < min )
           {
               tag = T;
               sqr[ rand( SQRMAX ) ] = ar[ i ];
           }
       }
       min = crush( sqr , SQRMAX );
   }
}
```

Random method of finding the minimum in a constant number of steps

A simple calculation can be used to illustrate why this algorithm takes no more than a constant number of iterations.

- Let n be the size of $ar[]$.
- Since we are taking a random sample of $\sqrt{n}$ elements of the array, we may assume that the sample comes from a sorted array where the smallest element is $ar[0]$.

- The probability that an element chosen at random from $ar[]$ will not "fall" into the first segment of the smallest $\sqrt{n}$ elements is $1 - \frac{1}{\sqrt{n}}$. We use a sample of size $\sqrt{n}$. Thus, the probability that none of these elements will fall into the smallest $\sqrt{n}$ element is $(1 - \frac{1}{\sqrt{n}})^{\sqrt{n}} = \frac{1}{e}$.
- By repeating this process a constant number of times, we can reduce the above probability to any desired constant fraction, e.g., $\frac{1}{e^{100}}$.
- Clearly, once the sample contains an element in the smallest $\sqrt{n}$ elements, the number of remaining elements in $ar[]$ after the comparison with min is less than $\sqrt{n}$. Consequently, the next application of $crash()$ will find the correct minimum.

Note that we used a "trick" to select a random sampling of the remaining elements in $ar[]$. Hypothetically, we should have "packed" the remaining elements and generated a random permutation of them, which would have been a complex task. However, we used the fact that the results of parallel writes to $sqr[]$ are arbitrary to approximate a random sampling. In other words, when $k > \sqrt{n}$ elements are written in parallel to random locations in $sqr[]$, we assume that there is an equal probability that each of these k elements will not be "erased" by another write to the same location. This technique of using random mapping to "pack" $k \leq N$ elements from a larger array $A[N]$ into a smaller array $B[k]$ is based on the well known claim:

Claim 2.1 *Consider a process where L balls are thrown at random into k jars. If $L \geq k \cdot 2 \cdot \log k$, the probability that there will be an empty jar is less than $\frac{1}{k}$.*

The probability that a ball will hit a given jar is $(1 - 1/k)$. The probability that all $k \log k$ balls will miss that jar is $(1 - 1/k)^{k \log k}$. Given that $(1 - 1/k)^k = \frac{1}{e}$, this probability is less than or equal to $\frac{1}{e^{\log k}}$. Thus, for $L \geq k \cdot 2 \cdot \log k$, the above claim follows.

2.5.4 Divide and Crush

Assume that the number of processors P is $2 \cdot N$, and N is a power of 2. In each step, we divide the input into groups such there are enough processors for each group to execute the $crash()$. For the next step, we keep only the minimum elements of each group. In each step we have fewer minimum (candidates) and, therefore, more processors per group. Hence, the size of every group is the square size of the groups of the last step. Thus, the algorithm should terminate in $\log \log N$ steps. The last iteration takes place when the number of items left is smaller than $\sqrt{N}$. In Table 2.1 we show the relationship between group size, number of iterations and number of processors needed per group.

Table 2.1 Relationships between sizes in the divide and crush algorithm

Step	Items	Group size	# of groups	Processors per group
0	N	$2 = 2^{2^0}$	$N/2$	$2N/(N/2) = 4$
1	$N/2$	$4 = 2^{2^1}$	$N/(2 \times 4)$	$2N/(N/8) = 16$
2	$N/8$	$16 = 2^{2^2}$	$N/(8 \times 16)$	$2N/(N/(8 \times 16)) = 256$
3	$N/128$	$256 = 2^{2^3}$	$N/(128 \times 256)$	$2N/(N/(128 \times 256)) = 256 \times 256$
4	...			
5	...			

```
div_crush( ar , size )
int *ar,size;
{
    int b[ N/2 ];
    int gs; /* group size */
    int nbg; /* number of groups */
    int min; /* minimum value */
    gs = 2; nbg = size/2;
    while( size >= gs )
    {
        parfor(int i=0;i<nbg;i++)
        { /* find minimum of each group */
            b[i] = crash( &ar[ i * gs], gs);
        }
        parfor(int i=0;i<nbg;i++)
        { ar[i] = b[i]; }
        size = nbg;
        gs = gs * gs ;
        nbg = size/gs;
    }
    if( size == 1 ) return( ar[0] );
    min = crush( ar, size );
}
```

Divide and crush method for finding the minimum in $\log \log N$ steps

The following argument by Valiant's demonstrates that this result is optimal. Valiant considered a "stronger model" for algorithms that computes the minimum of n elements using P processors. In this model, at every stage the algorithm can perform only P comparisons and then, **based on the results of these comparisons alone**, remove those elements that are clearly not the minimum. This is a very re-

Fig. 2.27 A decision tree for finding the minimum of four elements with $P = 2$

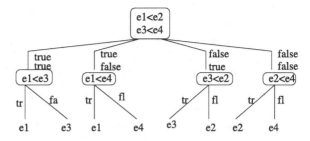

stricted model, a fact that becomes evident when we model it using a game between two players: the algorithm and the adversary. The algorithm player can ask the adversary only about comparisons between two elements. The adversary, on the other hand, does not even have to provide values for the n underlying elements. All he must do is give consistent answers. The only question is how long the adversary can delay the algorithm before the minimal element is located. The game's rules preclude the algorithm from using any other type of information (e.g., the value of some elements or their total sum). However, this is a natural restriction and a common way of obtaining lower bounds in computer science.

Another way of viewing such a restricted family of algorithms is as a decision tree wherein (see Fig. 2.27):

- Each node (except the leaves) represents a query of up to P comparisons involving up to $2P$ elements out of n initial elements.
- there are up to 2^P outgoing edges from every internal node marked by all possible outcomes of these comparisons.
- Each leaf is marked by a decision as to which element is the minimum.
- Such a decision tree is "legal" if one cannot find n elements $e_1, \ldots, e_n$ such that the decision in some leaf is "wrong."

We can obtain the lower bound by showing that the height of any decision tree is greater than $\log \log n$ for any decision tree that finds the minimum of n elements. Note that after each query the algorithm "knows" the transitive cluster of all the comparisons that were made up to this point. Thus, we can conclude that after each query the algorithm can filter out the elements that are clearly greater than some other elements. After each comparison, the algorithm can focus only on those elements that have not been compared to any other element or did not "lose" in any comparison.

Every comparison between two elements u, v can be represented by a "directed edge" $\langle u, v \rangle$ (the direction depends on the result of the comparison). Thus, at any stage of an algorithm A we can represent the computation by a comparison graph G_A. For example, applying $crash()$ on a group of elements yields a graph with an edge between every two elements ("clique") because each element is compared with all of the other elements. As explained before, after the edges have been added, we perform a transitive closure of the graph's end to remove all the elements that did

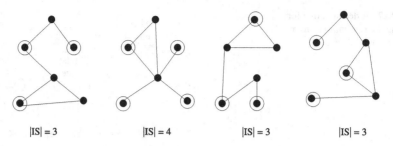

|IS| = 3 |IS| = 4 |IS| = 3 |IS| = 3

Fig. 2.28 Illustration of Toran's theorem

not win all of their comparisons (i.e., if $\langle u, v \rangle$ is an edge and $\langle v, w \rangle$ is an edge, then $\langle u, w \rangle$ is an edge). A given algorithm A can terminate when G_A does not contain two elements that have not been compared to each other (either directly or indirectly). This follows from the fact that if there are two uncompared elements (u, v) in G_A, then the minimum can be either u or v. Thus, we could have assigned values to the elements in such a way that the values would be consistent with all of the comparisons in G_A yet $u < v$ or alternatively chosen another set of values (equally consistent with G_A) with $v < u$.

Let an independent set *IS* in G_A be a set of nodes that are not connected to each other in G_A (after the transitive cluster, but before the filtering). An *IS* is maximal if we cannot add more nodes to it without violating the previous condition. It follows that for every algorithm, the size of the remaining elements (the remaining candidates for the minimum) is at least the size of the maximal *IS* in G_A. For example, the size of the maximal IS (MIS) of a directed chain with n nodes is 1 because after the transitive closure we have edges from the first node in the chain to all of the others.

The size of any maximal independent set in a directed graph G can be bounded from below by using a well known theorem by Toran:

Theorem 2.1 *The size of any maximal IS in a directed graph with n nodes and* $m \leq n$ *edges is greater than or equal to* $\frac{n^2}{2 \cdot m}$.

Consider, for example, the set of graphs in Fig. 2.28 showing that for $n = 6$ and $m = 6$ there is always an independent set with at least $\frac{6^2}{2 \cdot 6} = 3$ nodes.

Applying Toran's theorem to the minimum algorithm with $P = n$ processors implies that after the first query of up to P comparisons the size of the *IS* (remaining elements) in any G_A is greater than or equal to

$$a_0 = \frac{n^2}{2 \cdot P}$$

Thus, after the next query the size of the remaining elements is greater than or equal to

$$a_1 = \frac{a_0{}^2}{2 \cdot P} = \frac{n^4}{4 \cdot P^2 \cdot 2 \cdot P} = 2 \cdot P \left(\frac{n}{2 \cdot P} \right)^4$$

and in general

$$a_t = 2 \cdot P \left(\frac{n}{2 \cdot P} \right)^{2^t}$$

The algorithm cannot terminate before $a_t = 1$. Thus, for $P = n$

$$1 = 2 \cdot n \left(\frac{n}{2 \cdot n} \right)^{2^t}, \qquad \log 1 = \log^2 n + 2^t \cdot \log \frac{1}{2}, \quad 2^t = \log^2 n, \ t = \log \log n$$

2.5.5 Asynchronous Min

The underlying machine is an asynchronous one, so the scheduling in the execution of the previous algorithms can be different from the expected PRAM synchronous one. A simple method that is oblivious to the execution order is the *async_min*. In this method, a tentative minimum is held as a global variable. Each element $A[i]$ compares itself repeatedly to that global minimum. If it is bigger, then the thread terminates itself. Otherwise, it tries to update the tentative minimum to its own value. The algorithm terminates when there is no element bigger than the tentative minimum. A thread that has been suspended from the ready queue to the suspend queue (see Fig. 1.13) may benefit from the fact that a smaller element has updated the tentative minimum in that it may be spared some of its iterations. The algorithm is expected to terminate in $\log N$ steps because the probability that an element that has updated the tentative minimum is bigger than half of the remaining elements is high.

```
sync_min( ar , size )
int *ar,size;
{
int b=1,tent_min = MAX_VAL;
    while(b == 1) {
        parfor(int i=0;i<N;i++)
        {
            while ( A[i] < tent_min ) tent_min = A[i];
        }
        b = 0;
        parfor(int i=0;i<N;i++)
        {
            if ( A[i] < tent_min ) b = 1;
        }
    } }
```
Asynchronous minimum algorithm with expected time $\log N$.

As will be explained later on, if we join the two parallel-for statements, the program will not be correct and may compute the wrong result.

2.6 Recursion and Parallel Loops: The Parallel Prefix Example

The parfor and parblock constructs may be nested in arbitrary ways, creating a tree of threads where all the leaves are executing in parallel. This section illustrates how to directly compute $T_p(A(n))$ in a case where recursion and parallel for-loops are combined, where T_p is the number of parallel steps needed to solve a problem A with input size n by p processors. In this section T_p is a formula (probably recursive) that informally describes the number of synchronous parallel steps needed to compute the problem. Note that we cannot simply use the previous execution model and generate the set of all possible time diagrams of a ParC program, as this is simply not a "constructive" method to compute the time. The previous execution models should be regarded as proofs that execution time can be attributed to ParC programs. In this section we briefly consider the problem of obtaining an approximate formula to the execution time assuming that:

- There are no while-loops.
- The number of iterations each loop is executing is a known function of the input size.
- The number of threads that is spawned in every construct is also a known function of the input size.
- The input values do not affect the number of iterations in loops, thread generation and so forth.
- Synchronous execution of the program, step-by-step such that in each step the p processors are simulating a desired number of $P > p$ processors needed to execute all the instructions of the next step.

The program in Fig. 2.29 illustrates a combination of parfor and parblock inside parallel recursion. The program computes the partial sums of an array such that each cell is the sum of all cells that precede it (including itself). In other words, $A[i] = \sum_{j=0}^{j \leq i} A[j]$.

In order to estimate $T_p(prefix(n))$ one can use the following recursive equation:

$$T_p(n) = T_p\left(\frac{n}{2}\right) + \frac{n}{2p} + 1$$

where $T_p(\frac{n}{2})$ is the time needed to compute in parallel the partial sums of every half; $\frac{n}{2p}$ is the time needed to add the sum of all of the elements of the left half to all of the elements of the right half, using p processors; and $+1$ indicates the local computations such as $if(beg \geq end) \ldots$; and the computation of m. The solution for this equation is:

$$T_p(1) = 1 \qquad T_p(n) = \frac{n}{2p} + 1 + T_p\left(\frac{n}{2}\right) = \frac{n}{2p} + 1 + \frac{n}{4p} + 1 + \cdots = \frac{n}{p} + \log n$$

Fig. 2.29 Implementation of
parallel prefix computation
using divide and conquer

```
prefix( arr, beg, end )
int arr[], beg, end ;
{
        int m;
        if (beg ≥ end) return;
        m = beg + (end - beg + 1)/2 -1;
        parblock
                { prefix( arr, beg, m ); }
                ⋮
                { prefix( arr, m+1, end ); }

        parfor(int i= m+1;i <= end; i++)
        {
                arr[i] = arr[i] + arr[m];
        }

}
```

Note that this execution time is close to optimal in the sense that $\frac{n}{p}$ is a lower bound because each input must be read. The second term is also a lower bound because, as we proved in Sect. 1.6.3, using only summing operations, the value of the last element $A[n]$ cannot be computed in less than $\log n$ sequential sums. Thus, $T_p(n) = lowerbound_1 + lowerbound_2$, which is the optimal possible, as it is at most twice $max(lowerbound_1, lowerbound_2)$. We may even argue that an execution time which is the sum of lower bounds implies that we have a very efficient parallel program (even in a simplified model that does not take into account too many practical factors such as counting cache misses). Moreover, the additive factor $\log n$ is also an optimal factor because when n is increased or p is increased (but not both), $\frac{n}{p}$ dominates the $\log(n)$ factor.

Though a desirable estimation, the above computation of T_p is erroneous. This equation ignores the fact that the p processors should be divided between the recursive parallel computations used by the parallel prefix program. Assuming an equal division of the processors:

$$T_p(n) = \begin{cases} 1 + 2T_1(\frac{n}{2}) + \frac{n}{2} & p = 1 \\ 1 + T_{\frac{p}{2}}(\frac{n}{2}) + \frac{n}{2p} & p > 1 \end{cases}$$

This equation is solved by continuously expanding the second case $p > 1$ until after $\log p$ iterations, $p = 1$ and we are left with $T_1(\frac{n}{p})$:

$$T_1(n) \approx 2 \cdot T_1\left(\frac{n}{2}\right) + \frac{n}{2} = 4 \cdot T_1\left(\frac{n}{4}\right) + \frac{n}{2} + \frac{n}{2} = \cdots = \frac{n \log n}{2}$$

```
prefix( arr,beg, end )
int arr[n], beg,end ;
{
        int m,tmp[n];
        if (beg ≥ end) return;
        m = (end + 1)/2 -1;
        parfor(int i= 0; i<=end; i+=2)
        {
                tmp[i/2] = arr[i] + arr[i+1];
        }
        prefix( tmp, m );
        parfor(int i= 0; i<=end; i+=2)
        {
                arr[i] = tmp[i/2]; /* even locations are ready as is*/
                arr[i+1] = tmp[i/2] + arr[i+1]; /* odd locations must be updated*/
        }
}
```

Fig. 2.30 A better algorithm for computing prefix sums with an additive factor of $\log n$

$$T_p(n) = 1 + \frac{n}{2p} + 1 + \frac{\frac{n}{2}}{2\frac{p}{2}} + T_{\frac{p}{4}}\left(\frac{n}{4}\right)$$

$$= 1 + \frac{n}{2p} + 1 + \frac{n}{2p} + 1 + \frac{\frac{n}{4}}{2\frac{p}{4}} + T_{\frac{p}{8}}\left(\frac{n}{8}\right)$$

after neglecting minor factors such as using $\frac{n}{2p}$ instead of $(1 + \frac{n}{2p})$ (assuming $\frac{n}{2p} > 1$, we get

$$\log p\left(1 + \frac{n}{2p}\right) + T_1\left(\frac{n}{p}\right) = \log p\left(\frac{n}{2p}\right) + \frac{n}{p}(\log n - \log p) \approx \frac{n}{p}\log n$$

This last formula has a multiplicative factor of $\log n$ and thus is less desirable from a practical point of view than a formula with an additive factor of $\log n$. Such a formula can be obtained if we choose a different algorithm. The proposed "odd-even-prefix" algorithm (see Fig. 2.30) first sums each two consecutive elements (odd and even)in parallel. The result (half the size of the original array) is stored in a temporary array. Next, the algorithm recursively computes the prefix sums of the temporary array. Finally, the prefix sums of the original array can be computed in parallel by subtracting the original even element from the appropriate element of the temporary array.

Note that the parallel prefix can be computed in $T_p(n) = \frac{2n}{p} + p$ using the program in Fig. 2.31. The program divides the array into p chunks of $\frac{n}{p}$ elements and

Fig. 2.31 Efficient version of
the parallel prefix

```
int A[N];
int k,ar[P];
        parfor(int l=0; l<N-1; l+=N/P)
        { int i;
                ar[l] = 0;
                for(i=l; i<l+N/P-1; i++)
                        ar[l] += A[I];
        }
        for(k=1; k<P; k++) ar[k] += ar[k-1];
        parfor(int l=1; l<P; l++)
        { int i;
                A[l*(N/P)] += ar[l];
                for(i=l*(N/P)+1; i<(l+1)N/P-1; i++)
                        A[i] += A[i-1];
        }
```

computes the partial sums of every chunk in parallel. The parallel prefix of the partial sums is computed sequentially in $ar[i]$. These partial sums are added to the
elements of every chunk while computing the partial sums of every chunk.

The parallel prefix is a basic operation in many parallel computations. Consider,
for example, packing the non-zero elements of an array $A[N]$ into another array $C[]$.
Intuitively, the position of the element $A[i] > 0$ in the packed array $C[]$ is exactly
equal to the number of non-zero elements of $A[0, \ldots, i]$ or the prefix sum of $B[i]$
where $B[i] = 1$ if $A[i] > 0$, and zero otherwise (see Fig. 2.32). Many parallel programming languages such as OpenMP and MPI contain special constructs that implement prefix operations called reductions as primitive operations in the language.
Typically, the operation for reductions can be set by the user to any associative accu-
mulative operation such as multiplication or the max-operation. Note that we used
the associativity of the '+' operation when we performed parallel prefix operations
on different parts of $A[]$.

Clearly, the effect of a limited number of processors is significant, and one should
carefully divide the processors among the different parallel computations spawned
in a program. Note that such a direct computation of time can only be an approximation because the assignment of threads or computations to processors is not known
and is done dynamically by the underlying operating system. Hence, the execution
time of a program cannot be calculated, but some estimations can be computed, taking into account the effect of scheduling and other significant factors. For example,
consider the program in Fig. 2.33, where a depth-first scheduling will produce 1000
threads, while a breadth-first scheduling may produce 2^{1000} threads. Clearly, $T_p(f)$
is affected by the scheduling policy of the underlying operating system.

In spite of the dependency of T_p on the scheduling, one could define the T_p
of a program, assuming a "natural" breadth-first scheduling where processors are
divided equally among the different computations:

Fig. 2.32 Packing the
non-zero elements of an array

```
int A[N],B[N],C[N];
int k,ar[P];
    lparfor(int i=0; i<N; i++)
    { if(A[i] > 0) B[i]=1; else B[i]=0; }
    prefix(B,0,N-1);
    lparfor(int i=0; i<N; i++) {
        if(i==0&& B[0] > 0]) C[0]=A[0];
        else
            if(B[i] > B[i-1]) C[B[i]-1]=A[i];
    }
```

Fig. 2.33 The effect of
scheduling on the execution
time

```
int x=1;
f(x);

f(y)
int y;
{
    x = y;
    if (x<1000)
    parblock
    {
        f(y+1);
        :
        f(y+1);
    }
}
```

$$T_p(atomic - statement) = 1$$

$$T_p(LOOP\ i = 1 \ldots k\ S_i) = \sum_{i=1}^{k} T_p(S_i)$$

$$T_p(\{S_1, \ldots, S_k\}) = \sum_{i=1}^{k} T_p(S_i)$$

$$T_p\big(if(cond)S_1\ else\ S_2\big) = \max\,(T_p(S_1), T_p(S_2) + 1$$

$$T_p\big(PF\ i = 1 \ldots k[S_i]\big) = \begin{cases} \max_{i=1}^{k} T_{\frac{k}{p}}(S_i) & p \geq k \\ k \cdot \max_{i=1}^{k} T_{\frac{k}{p}}(S_i) & p < k \end{cases}$$

$$T_p\big(PB[S_1, \ldots, S_k]\big) = \begin{cases} \max_{i=1}^{k} T_{\frac{k}{p}}(S_i) & p \geq k \\ k \cdot \max_{i=1}^{k} T_{\frac{k}{p}}(S_i) & p < k \end{cases}$$

$$T_p(function - call) = T_p(body\ of\ the\ function + parameters) + 1$$

Note that this definition determines that processors are equally distributed among all the parallel computations of the parfor or parblock statements. This determination is made regardless of the **real** number of processors that a computation requires. Hence, if two computations are spawned where 4 processors are available, then each computation will receive 2 processors. However, it may be that one computation requires 3 processors and the other requires only 1. This possibility indicates that such a scheduling algorithm will prolong the execution time and should not be used by a real operating system. The notion of scheduling and how it is actually implemented will be discussed in the following sections.

2.7 Minimum Spanning Tree

In this section we consider a more complex problem and show how it's parallel solution is coded as a ParC program. For a given undirected graph G with distinct integer weights on its edges, the goal is to find a subset of the edges which is a minimum spanning tree (MST) of G. The algorithm is based on the fact that the minimum cost edge (v, u) of G (which is unique) is included in any MST of G. This is because for any MST T of G that does not include (u, v) we can add (u, v) back to T and by so creates at least one cycle. Now we can break these cycles by removing other edges with larger weights and obtain a new MST with a smaller weight than T. Many algorithms were developed for MST and here we show a simple generalization of the sequential algorithm that maintains a set of sub-MSTs organized where each sub-MST is organized as a star (all nodes of the sub-MST point to a common root). The algorithm merges stars by selecting a minimum cost edge that connects two stars.

For input connectivity matrix W, let $w(i, j)$ be the weight of the edge connecting between nodes i and j and $w(i, i) = infinity$ otherwise. The algorithm's description is as follows:

1. Let $W^0 = W$ be the initial connectivity matrix, $n_0 = n$ initial number of stars (each node a star of size 1) and $k = 0$ the step counter.
2. While $|n^k > 1$ do:
3. $k = k + 1$;
4. For each node $v \in W^{k-1}$ do
5. Find an edge (v, u) with minimal weight such that
6. $W^{k-1}(v, u) = \min_{(v,x)}\{W^{k-1}(v, x)\}$.
7. Add the edge (v, u) to the MST rooted at v.

8. Shrink each sub-tree to a star. This is done by performing "pointer-jumping"

$$while(p \longrightarrow next \neq star.root) \; v \longrightarrow next = v \longrightarrow next \longrightarrow next;$$

until all nodes in every sub-tree points to the root of that sub-tree.

9. Let n^k be the current number of stars.
10. Update the connectivity matrix $W^k = W^{k-1}$ restricted to all the roots of the current set of stars.

After each iteration we should have a set of stars that is smaller at least by half. The algorithm will terminate after at most $o(\log(n))$ iterations when only one star remains.

```
/* MINIMUM SPANNING TREE */
/* Parallel implementation of Sollin's algorithm */

/* INPUT :
      The graph is connected, undirected with  SIZE  vertices.
      W is a weight matrix of the edges. The highest value of
        an edge, SUP, and SIZE can be replaced by any other
        values.
   OUTPUT :
      An mst matrix where mst(i,j)=1 if the edge (i,j)
      belongs to the mst */

#include <stdio.h>

#define SIZE 11   /* number of vertices - size of problem */
#define SUP 100000  /* supremum value for weights */
#define TRUE 1
#define FALSE 0
#define MIN(a,b) ((a) < (b) ? (a) : (b))   /* returns
                                           MIN(a, b) */

typedef int mat[SIZE+1][SIZE+1];
mat w,   /* initial weighted matrix */
    w1,  /* iteration weighted matrix */
    w2,  /* auxiliary weighted matrix */
    mst;  /* MST matrix indication of the edges */
int c[SIZE+1],   /* vector of the minimum adjacent vertices */
    rs[SIZE],   /* the root vertices of the stars */
    n=SIZE;   /* number of vertices */

main()
{
   int nk,nk1,   /* number of rooted stars */
```

```
    i,j,
    isstar;   /* if all vertices are in rooted stars */
  parfor(int i=1;i<=n;i++)   /* initialize w with the top
                              value */
{
  parfor(int j=i;i<=n;j++)
    { w[i][j] = w[j][i] = SUP;  }
}
initialize();


parfor(int i=1;i<=n;i++)   /* initialize w1 and w2 to w */
{
  parfor(int j=i;i<=n;j++)
    { w1[i][j]=w1[j][i]=w2[i][j]=w2[j][i] = w[i][j];  }
}


nk=nk1 = n;
while (nk1 > 1) {  /* terminate when there is one star */
  /* creating the forest defined by c[] */
  parfor(int v=1;v<= nk;v++)
  {
    int x,u,a,b,i;
    x = w1[v][1];  u = 1;  /* x = 1st element in the v
                                  row */
    for (i=1; i<=nk; i++)  /* find minimum of the row */
     if (w1[v][i] < x) {
   u = i;
   x = w1[v][i];
   }
    c[v] = u;
    for (a=1; a<=n; a++)  /* restoring the original edges */
     for (b=a+1; b<=n; b++)
     if (w[a][b] == x) {  /* from the original matrix */
      mst[a][b] = mst[b][a] = 1;  /* add (v,c(v)) to the
                                          MST */
       a=b = n; }  /* exit loop */
  }


  /* shrink to rooted stars */
  parfor(int i=1;i<= nk;i++)  /* untie knots */
  {
    if (c[c[c[i]]] == c[i]) c[c[c[i]]] = c[c[i]];
  }
  do  {  /* perform pointer jumping */
    parfor(int i=1;i<= nk;i++)
     { c[i] = c[c[i]]; }
```

```
   isstar = star(nk);   }
while (!isstar);   /* until all vertices in rooted stars */


nk = nk1;
nk1 = numrs(nk);   /* computing nk */
/* assigning serial numbers to the rooted stars */
parfor(int i=1;i<= nk;i++)
{
  parfor(int j=1;i<= nk1;j++)
  {
if (c[i] == rs[j])   {
  c[i] = j;
  j=nk1;   }   /* break; */
  }
}


/* reinitialize w2 (with half of its previous dimension)
   to ensure that no previous values remain from
   the previous iteration in the smaller matrix. */
parfor(int i=1;i<=nk1;i++)
{
  parfor(int j=i;j<=nk1;j++)
{  w2[i][j] = w2[j][i] = SUP;   }
}
/* computing Wk */
/* determining the matrix elements,  find minimum
connecting edges */
/* between any two stars represented by elements
in the matrix of the */
/* previous iteration */
parfor(int i=1;i<=nk1;i++)
{
 int j,u,v,x;
 for (j=i+1; j<=nk1; j++)   {
x = SUP;
for (u=1; u<=nk; u++)
 for (v=u+1; v<=nk; v++)
  if (c[u]==i && c[v]==j || c[u]==j && c[v]==i)   /*stars
                                                    are
                                                    connect-
                                                    ed*/
     x = MIN(x, w1[u][v]);
w2[j][i] = w2[i][j] = x;
  }
}
```

```
    parfor(int i=1;i<=nk1;i++)   /* copy w2 to w1 */
    {
      parfor(int j=i;j<=nk1;j++)
      {   w1[i][j]=w1[j][i] = w2[i][j];   }
    }


  }   /* while */

    /* print result */
    /* the edge (i,j) belongs to the mst if and
    only if mst(i,j)=1 */
  printf("\n\n");
  for (i=1; i<=n; i++)   {
    printf("%2d  ",i);
    for (j=1; j<=n; j++)
      printf("%d ",mst[i][j]);
    printf("\n");
  }
}

/*************************************************************/
initialize()
{
}

/*************************************************************/
star(nk)
int nk;
{
  int i,
      s[SIZE+1],   /* vector of star indication to each
                      vertex */
      ret = TRUE;   /* boolean return value of the function */
  parfor(int i=1;i<=nk;i++)
    {   s[i] = TRUE;   }   /* initialize the s vector to TRUE */

  parfor(int i=1;i<=nk;i++)
  {
    if (c[i] != c[c[i]])   /* i does not point to root of
                              a star */
      s[i]=s[c[i]]=s[c[c[i]]]=FALSE;
  }


  parfor(int i=1;i<=nk;i++)
    {   s[i] = s[c[i]];   }

  parfor(int i=1;i<=nk;i++)
```

```
{   if (s[i] == 0)    /* return false if at least one vertex */
      ret = FALSE;     /* does not belong to a star */
}

   return(ret);
}


/****************************************************************/
/* computing the number of rooted stars.                      */
/* parameters : nk - the number of stars in the previous
iteration                                                     */
/* which is the current number of vertices.                   */
/****************************************************************/
numrs(nk)
int nk;
{
   int i,j,found,count;
   count=1;   /* current number of stars */
   rs[1]=c[1];
   for (i=2; i<=nk; i++)   {
     found = FALSE;
     for (j=1; j<=count; j++)
       if (c[i] == rs[j]) /* if i points to an existing root */
       { found = TRUE;  break; }   /* terminate search */
     if (found == FALSE)   { /* i points to a new root (c[i]) */
       count++;   /* increase number of current stars */
       rs[count] = c[i];   /* put new root in rs */
     }
   }
   return(count);
}
```

2.8 Exercises

1. Show how to transform lparfor, parblock using parfor. In other words, describe the transformations using the syntax of these constructs.
2. Can we use lparfor instead of the parfor in the code of Fig. 2.11?
3. Discuss the possibility of adding a "Light parblock" construct to *ParC*, and show how to implement it using lparfor.
4. What is the difference between the outputs of the following loops:

$$for(i = 0; i < n; i++) \ \{if(i\%2 == 0)i++; \ else \ printf(``\%d'', i); \}$$

$$\text{parfor } int \ i; 0; n - 1; 1 \ \{if(i\%2 == 0)i++; \ else \ printf(``\%d'', i); \}$$

5. Input and output statements can performed in parallel if they are supported by the operating system. Assume that a parallel machine allows the parallel execution of input and output statements as if they were atomic instructions.

(a) What does the output of the following nested loops program look like?
(b) What is the effect of transforming the inner loop into a parallel loop?
(c) What is the effect of transforming the outer loop into a parallel loop?
(d) What is the effect of transforming both loops into a parallel loop?

```
int i,j;

for(i=0; i<10; i++) {
    for(j=0; j<i; j++)
        putchar('*');
    putchar('/n');
}
```
nested loops.

6. The following drawing describes a chain of n links with $5n$ nodes. Each one stores a number and has several pointer fields. The middle node of every link points to a left son and a right son, and to the middle node of the next link. Finally, each son points to a grandson, which points to null. Clearly, the chain can be accessed only through the pointer p.

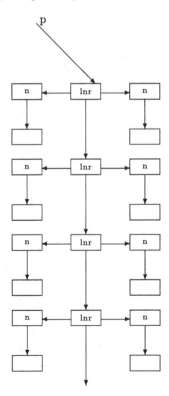

(a) Write a non recursive parallel program that computes the sum of all of the nodes in this chain.

(b) Write a recursive parallel program that computes the sum of all of the nodes in this chain.

(c) Compute the parallel time (in steps) in which each of the above programs traverses the chain. What is the minimal parallel time of any such program?

(d) Describe a data structure that would allow us to compute the sum in $\log 5n$ steps (without losing the chain structure).

(e) Write a program that computes the sum of all of the values in the chain in less than $2n$ steps.

(f) Compare the number of processors needed by each of the above programs, such that the maximal degree of parallelism is obtained.

2.8.1 Questions About Summing

Three summing algorithms were presented: one recursive (R-SUM), one with an external loop (LP-SUM), and the third with an internal sequential loop (PL-SUM). The following set of questions is based on these sum variants:

1. Show that R-SUM is correct, by proving that all possible running sequences satisfy a certain invariant.

2. Based on the previous question, show that without the sync, PL-SUM is incorrect. This can be done by giving two possible execution orders for computing the sum of 8 numbers, with different sum results.

3. Consider two alternative ways for implementing the parallel prefix problem described earlier. The odd-even parallel prefix uses different strategies to divide the input. In parallel, it sums its n inputs in pairs, yielding $\frac{n}{2}$ new inputs, and recursively computes their parallel prefix. These $\frac{n}{2}$ partial sums fit with the partial sums of the even places of the original n inputs. The partial sums of the odd places are computed in parallel by adding every odd input to the partial sum of its even predecessor. This procedure is depicted on the left hand side of the network diagram in Fig. 2.34. An alternative way to compute partial sums is to construct a tree of sub-sums like the one created in LP-SUM. The correct partial sums are computed by propagating the sums of sub-trees from the root to the leaves. The rule for this back propagation assigns the left son the value received by its father. The right son is given the sum of the left son and the value received by its father. This back propagation of sub-tree sums is depicted on the left hand side of the diagram in Fig. 2.34.

(a) Modify R-SUM such that it will implement the odd-even parallel prefix.

(b) Modify R-SUM such that it will implement the tree-like parallel prefix.

(c) Modify LP-sum such that it will implement the tree-like parallel prefix and use array cells to hold values stored at the tree nodes.

Fig. 2.34 Odd-even parallel
prefix network and a tree-like
parallel prefix network

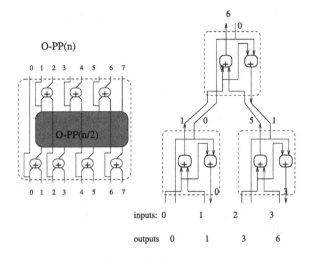

inputs: 0   1   2   3

outputs   0   1   3   6

(d) Compute the direct execution time for all three parallel prefix programs. Compare $N(R), T(R)$ and the memory usage of all parallel prefix versions (including the version presented here).

(e) Create a more efficient version for each of the previous parallel prefix programs by taking into account that the number of processors is fixed and relatively small. $P < N$, meaning it is similar to the final version of PL-SUM.

4. Modify the parallel prefix operation from summing to ranking every non-zero cell in the array.

5. Modify the parallel prefix operation from summing to packing such that all non-zero elements of the array will be packed from left to right, preserving the initial order.

6. Change the following program so that all possible atomic effects can be described by different execution orders. This should be done by changing every external access to a local one (as described earlier). Remove superfluous assignments from your program. Modify the underlying program such that there will be only 10 possible execution orders. Is such a transformation useful as a general parallel programming technique?

```
PF  i = 1 .. 10 [
     n = n -i;
     if((n+5) < (n*i)) n = n+5; else n = n-5;
]
```

7. Create a parallel version for $s2()$ in Sect. 7.8 where the first loop iterates until N, not $N/2$.

8. Show that the number of parallel steps performed by $p3()$ in Sect. 7.8 is optimal.

2.8.2 *Questions About Min Algorithms*

1. Program all five min algorithms described earlier, and test their correctness on the simulator.
2. For each of the five min programs, compute the expected execution time $T(R)$.
3. For each algorithm, determine the expected speedups $SP(R)$, $SP^o(R)$, $seq(R)$, $grain(R)$ and $glob_{bus}(R)$. Use the estimations given for the average number of iterations when needed (e.g., 6 in the case of random_min).
4. Test each algorithm on the simulator and compute all previous speedups for a specific N (large enough so that initialization at the beginning of the execution will not affect the results). Compare your calculations to the simulation results. Taking into account all of the factors, which algorithm is the best?
5. Justify the need for the second *pparfor* in *divide_crush*(). Explain why a direct substitution $ar[i] = crash(\ldots)$ is harmful.
6. Give an example showing that the *sync_min*() program can print an erroneous minimum if the external-while and the second *pparfor* are omitted.
7. Can the second *pparfor* in *sync_min*() be joined inside the first one?
8. Implement a version of *sync_min*() which uses *faa* instead of the external-while and the second *pparfor*.

2.8.3 *Questions About Snake Sorting*

Input: a two dimensional array A of size $N \times N$ of integers. The array in row order, if the rows are sorted in a snake-like order, will alternate in direction, with the first row going from left to right, the second row going from right to left and so forth. The last element in a row will be bigger than the first element of the next row. The sort algorithm that will be used throughout this test works as follows:

snake-sort(A)
LOOP Do $\log N$ times:
A Sort odd numbered rows to the right and even numbered rows to the left.
B Sort the columns (all of them downwards).
ELOOP

Assume that the sequential sort routines that the snake-sort uses to sort the rows and the columns are given, so you do not have to program them. Each one sorts a vector of K elements of A using $K \log K$ comparison steps:

l2r-row-sort($L, I, I + K$): Sort from left to right row L of A from I to $I + K$.
r2l-row-sort($L, I, I + K$): Sort from right to left row L of A from I to $I + K$.
col-sort($C, I, I + K$): Sort from bottom up column C of A from I to $I + K$.

All of these routines use a routine called "comp" that compares X and Y and sets the results as follows: NX to $max(X, Y)$ and NY to $min(X, Y)$.

```
comp(X,Y,NX,NY)
{
    if(X > Y) { NX = X; NY = Y;}
    else {NX = Y; NY = X}
}
```

Note that you should write your programs in ParC in free style, which means avoiding the "small" details of proper C programs. The program is acceptable as long as it does not ignore major complexities or aspects of the correct and full program. For example, in *comp(...)*, we skipped parameter definitions and address references.

1. Use the zero-one principle to show that after $\log N$ iterations, the array is sorted by rows (show that the algorithm sorts an array of zeros and ones).
2. Write a program in ParC style using no more than 15 lines that executes the snake-sort algorithm using the above routines. Compute the speedup of this program ($P < N$) in all three models: without overhead, a simple overhead model and a general overhead model. Each of the sequential sorts routines that you use takes $N \log N$ steps of *comp(...)*, so you have to consider those steps as well. In other words, count the steps of *comp(...)*. Note that you should count condition-expressions and function-calls as statements.

   For the simple overhead model: Determine the value of Z' (the length of the longest path in the program). Substitute the value of all parameters (S, N, Z') in the speedup bounds equation given in class. Are the above bounds close to the exact speedup you found in the first part?

   The snake-sort algorithm "assumes" that $P = N$. This assumption is reflected in the fact that at any given time there are always N processes. Use the chancing method for sorting algorithms (Budget and Stevenson) for the case where $P < N$. Recall that chancing for sorting means replacing every comparison with a sequential merge routine that merges to "big blocks" of $\frac{N}{P}$ numbers each. Modify the snake-sort program to spawn no more than P processes. Modify the *comp(...)* routine to "merge" "big blocks." The modification of *comp(...)* should be done by using a sequential version of the snake-sort algorithm. Before listing the modified program, indicate:

   - What is the division of A into blocks?
   - What is the merge step of two blocks?

3. Modify the snake-sort algorithm to support the case of $P = \sqrt{N}N$ efficiently. Hint: The extra processors should be used to parallel the sequential sort of rows and columns.

   - What is the time needed for this case?
   - Using the above modification, describe a new modification for the case of $P = N^2$. Give the time equation for this case (you do not have to solve it, in case it is not straight forward).

4. Assume that you can partition A between the local memories of the processors, and assume that you can map processes to processors. For the case $P = N$ and a

buss machine there is extra memory overhead for every access of a processes to a value which is not in his local memory.

- What is a reasonable memory overhead for a bus machine? (recall that only one processor can use the bus at a time).
- Describe a good partitioning of *A* to local memories and the processes mapping to processors (for the program of Q1).
- Compute the speedup using the simple overhead model and the extra overhead criteria you found before.

5. Modify your snake-sort program of Q1 such that it will spawn only *N* processes in the beginning (in a manner similar to the transformation from LP-SUM to PL-SUM). The program should be valid now only for a synchronized execution. Assume that you have a sync command, and that the *comp*(...) operation is atomic.

- If you iterate sync-snake-sort until *A* is in row order, will the program stop?
- Indicate what else is needed in order to make sync-snake-sort run asynchronously. Recall the example of an asynchronous algorithm for the transitive closure of a graph.

2.9 Bibliographic Notes

Details regarding the C programming language can be found in Merrow and Henson (1989). The simulator is described in Ben-Asher and Haber (1995). There are set of libraries for emulating various hardware features for the simulator as Shaibe (1989) and Zernik and Rudolph (1991).

Nesting of parallel constructs that allows the user to express the spawning of a large number of threads can be found in Vrsalovic et al. (1989). A "strong model" for algorithms that computes the minimum (also sorting and merging) of *n* elements using *p* processors, can be found in Valiant (1975). Other parallel programming languages include: Unified Parallel C (UPC), which is an extension of the C programming language designed for high-performance computing on large-scale parallel machines, including those with a common global address space (SMP and NUMA) and those with distributed memory, see El-Ghazawi and Carlson (2005). High Performance Fortran (HPF) (Koelbel 1994) which is an extension of Fortran 90 with constructs that support parallel computing. Building on the array syntax introduced in Fortran 90, HPF uses a data parallel model of computation to support spreading the work of a single array computation over multiple processors. This allows efficient implementation on both SIMD and MIMD style architectures. HPF features included new Fortran statements, such as FORALL and the ability to create PURE procedures, compiler directives for recommended distributions of array data and additional library routines including environmental inquiry, parallel prefix/suffix, data scattering, and sorting operations. Titanium (Yelick et al. 1998) is a high-performance Java dialect that includes parallel for each construct, multi-dimensional arrays that can be accessed in parallel, an explicitly parallel SPMD model a global address space through access to objects and objects fields. OpenMP (Dagum and Menon 2002) (Open Multi-Processing) is a common language to program shared memory machines (over C, C++ and Fortran). It include nesting of parallel for-loops and explicit control of scheduling policy. Unlike ParC its scoping rules allow only two modes of sharing: local variables and fully global variables. Finally, the CILK parallel programming language (Blumofe et al. 1995) is a parallel programing language that is based on spawn-thread construct rather than on the parfor construct. Spawning a thread is non-blocking and a special sync instructions is required to wait for spawned threads. Threads communicate through returned values that are collected by a sibling thread. Scheduling is done using Work-stealing paradigm where remote processors remove suspended threads from queues of other processors and execute them.

Scoping rules for nested parallel constructs as "cactus stack" implementation are presented in Hauck and Dent (1968), also described in Hummel and Schonberg (1991). More on scoping rules can be found in books dealing with programming languages as Scott (2009) and Sethi (1996). Scoping rules can be also dynamic as described in the books mentioned above, such that a global identifier refers to the identifier associated with the most recent environment (note that this cannot be done at compile time because the binding stack only exists at run-time). There are many works on obtaining atomic operations. Weihl (1990) supports atomic data-types by providing objects that provide serializability and recoverability of transactions on them. Eventually, guaranteeing atomicity yielded the transactional memory model wherein a sequence of instructions including load/store operations (code statements) in a parallel program is executed atomically. In transactional memory executing a code segment atomically does not imply exclusive lock over the full code but rather a weaker set of operations executed in a non-blocking way (Herlihy and Moss 1993; Marathe and Scott 2004).

Most of the algorithms on parallel sorting and maximum can be obtained from books on PRAM algorithms such as JáJá (1992) and Reif (1993). Some relevant and interesting lower bounds for problem discussed in this chapter can be obtained from Shiloach and Vishkin (1981). Alon and Spencer (1992) discuss Toran's theorem for Minimal Independence Set in graphs used to derive the lower-bound described at the end of this chapter. The parallel prefix is discussed in Snir (1986), Ladner and Fischer (1980) and in Hillis and Steele (1986).

Sollin's algorithm for Minimum Spanning Trees (MST) is presented in Sollin (1965). The first algorithm for finding a MST was developed by Boruvka in 1926 (see Nesetril et al. 2001). Commonly used algorithms that run in polynomial time Prim's and Kruskal's described in Cormen (2001). The fastest randomized algorithm for MST is Karger et al. (1995) and is based on Boruvka's algorithm and a reverse version of Kruskal's algorithm. While Chazelle's (2000) is the fastest deterministic algorithm and is close to linear time in the number of edges. Parallel algorithms for finding MST that are based on the Boruvka, Prim and Kruskal, do not scale well to additional processors. Chong et al. (2001) developed a parallel algorithm for an EREW PRAM with linear number of processors, in optimal logarithmic time (a better randomized algorithm can be found in Pettie and Ramachandran 2004). Bader and Cong (2006) present a practical version for parallel MST with good speedup. Distributed algorithms for finding the MST were studied extensively (see Gallager et al. 1983; Awerbuch 1987; Garay et al. 2002). A lower bound of $\Omega(\frac{\sqrt{V}}{\log V})$ where v is the number of nodes was shown by Peleg and Rubinovich (2002).

References

Alon, N., Spencer, J.H.: The Probabilistic Method. Wiley, New York (1992)

Awerbuch, B.: Optimal distributed algorithms for minimum weight spanning tree, counting, leader election, and related problems. In: Proceedings of the Nineteenth Annual ACM Symposium on Theory of Computing, pp. 230–240. ACM, New York (1987)

Bader, D.A., Cong, G.: Fast shared-memory algorithms for computing the minimum spanning forest of sparse graphs. J. Parallel Distrib. Comput. **66**(11), 1366–1378 (2006)

Ben-Asher, Y., Haber, G.: On the usage of simulators to detect inefficiency of parallel programs caused by bad schedulings: the simparc approach. In: HiPC (High Performance Computing), New Delhi, India (1995)

Blumofe, R.D., Joerg, C.F., Kuszmaul, B.C., Leiserson, C.E., Randall, K.H., Zhou, Y.: Cilk: An efficient multithreaded runtime system. In: Proceedings of the Fifth ACM SIGPLAN Symposium on Principles and Practice of Parallel Programming, pp. 207–216. ACM, New York (1995)

Chazelle, B.: A minimum spanning tree algorithm with inverse-Ackermann type complexity. J. ACM **47**(6), 1028–1047 (2000)

Chong, K.W., Han, Y., Lam, T.W.: Concurrent threads and optimal parallel minimum spanning trees algorithm. J. ACM **48**(2), 297–323 (2001)

Cormen, T.H.: Introduction to Algorithms. The MIT Press, Cambridge (2001)

Dagum, L., Menon, R.: OpenMP: an industry standard API for shared-memory programming. IEEE Comput. Sci. Eng. **5**(1), 46–55 (2002)

El-Ghazawi, T., Carlson, W.: UPC: Distributed Shared Memory Programming. Wiley-Interscience, New York (2005)

Gallager, R.G., Humblet, P.A., Spira, P.M.: A distributed algorithm for minimum-weight spanning trees. ACM Trans. Program. Lang. Syst. **5**(1), 66–77 (1983)

Garay, J.A., Kutten, S., Peleg, D.: A sub-linear time distributed algorithm for minimum-weight spanning trees. In: Proceedings of 34th Annual Symposium on Foundations of Computer Science, 1993, pp. 659–668. IEEE, New York (2002)

Hauck, E.A., Dent, B.A.: Burroughs' B6500/B7500 stack mechanism. In: AFIPS Spring Joint Comput. Conf., vol. 32, pp. 245–251 (1968)

Herlihy, M., Moss, J.E.B.: Transactional memory: architectural support for lock-free data structures. In: Proceedings of the 20th Annual International Symposium on Computer Architecture, p. 300. ACM, New York (1993)

Hillis, W.D., Steele, G.L. Jr.: Data parallel algorithms. Commun. ACM **29**(12), 1170–1183 (1986)

Hummel, S.F., Schonberg, E.: Low-overhead scheduling of nested parallelism. IBM J. Res. Dev. **35**(5/6), 743–765 (1991)

JáJá, J.: An Introduction to Parallel Algorithms. Addison Wesley Longman, Redwood City (1992)

Karger, D.R., Klein, P.N., Tarjan, R.E.: A randomized linear-time algorithm to find minimum spanning trees. J. ACM **42**(2), 321–328 (1995)

Koelbel, C.H.: The High Performance Fortran Handbook. The MIT Press, Cambridge (1994)

Ladner, R.E., Fischer, M.J.: Parallel prefix computation. J. ACM **27**(4), 831–838 (1980)

Marathe, V.J., Scott, M.L.: A qualitative survey of modern software transactional memory systems. Tech. Rep., University of Rochester Computer Science Dept. (2004)

Merrow, T., Henson, N.: System design for parallel computing. High Perform. Syst. **10**(1), 36–44 (1989)

Nesetril, J., Milková, E., Nesetrilová, H.: Otakar Boruvka on Minimum Spanning Tree Problem: Translation of Both the 1926 Papers, Comments. History. DMATH: Discrete Mathematics, vol. 233 (2001)

Peleg, D., Rubinovich, V.: A near-tight lower bound on the time complexity of distributed MST construction. In: 40th Annual Symposium on foundations of Computer Science, 1999, pp. 253–261. IEEE, New York (2002)

Pettie, S., Ramachandran, V.: A randomized time-work optimal parallel algorithm for finding a minimum spanning forest. In: Randomization, Approximation, and Combinatorial Optimization. Algorithms and Techniques, pp. 233–244 (2004)

Reif, J.H.: Synthesis of Parallel Algorithms. Morgan Kaufmann, San Francisco (1993)

Scott, M.L.: Programming Language Pragmatics, 3rd edn. Morgan Kaufmann, San Mateo (2009)

Sethi, R.: Programming Languages: Concepts & Constructs, 2nd edn. Pearson Education India, New Delhi (1996)

Shaibe, B.: Performance of cache memory in shared-bus multiprocessor architectures: an experimental study of conventional and multi-level designs. Master's thesis, Institute of Computer Science, The Hebrew University, Jerusalem (1989)

Shiloach, Y., Vishkin, U.: Finding the maximum, merging and sorting in a parallel computational model. J. Algorithms **2**(1), 88–102 (1981)

Snir, M.: Depth-size trade-offs for parallel prefix computation. J. Algorithms **7**(2), 185–201 (1986)

Sollin, M.: Le trace de canalisation. In: Programming, Games, and Transportation Networks (1965)

Valiant, L.G.: Parallelism in comparison problems. SIAM J. Comput. **4**(3), 348–355 (1975)

Vrsalovic, D., Segall, Z., Siewiorek, D., Gregoretti, F., Caplan, E., Fineman, C., Kravitz, S., Lehr, T., Russinovich, M.: MPC—multiprocessor C language for consistent abstract shared data type paradigms. In: Ann. Hawaii Intl. Conf. System Sciences, vol. I, pp. 171–180 (1989)

Weihl, W.E.: Linguistic support for atomic data types. ACM Trans. Program. Lang. Syst. **12**(2), 178–202 (1990)

Yelick, K., Semenzato, L., Pike, G., Miyamoto, C., Liblit, B., Krishnamurthy, A., Hilfinger, P., Graham, S., Gay, D., Colella, P., et al.: Titanium: A high-performance Java dialect. Concurrency **10**(11–13), 825–836 (1998)

Zernik, D., Rudolph, L.: Animating work and time for debugging parallel programs—foundation and experience. In: ACM ONR Workshop on Parallel and Distributed Debugging, pp. 46–56 (1991)

Chapter 3
Locality and Synchronization

The discussion so far has assumed a shared memory address space with uniform access cost to every address. This assumption is not practical and in particular for multicore machines where some of the memory references made by a parallel program can be significantly longer than other memory references. In this chapter we consider a simplified model of parallel machines that demonstrates this claim and is used as a "formal" model to study ParC's memory references. Though this model is not simulating a multicore machine it can be regarded as an intermediate stage between a uniform cost of shared memory references and the complexity of real multicore machines.

We first consider a general argument showing why inherently shared memory machines will always expose non-uniform cost to memory references:

- We consider a parallel program that access N different memory cells in $O(N/P)$ steps where P is the number of cores or processors. Moreover during execution each core may, in an unpredictable way, access any of these N addresses.
- Any shared memory machine with P processors/cores must be divided into P memory modules $M_1 \ldots M_P$ to basically allow parallel access. If the program accessed N memory addresses in $T < O(N/P)$ steps then each of these memory modules should have served at least $\frac{N}{P \cdot c}$ cells of the original N cells accessed by the program (c is a suitable constant).
- A communication network must connect any processor to all the memory modules since each processor/core can potentially access any address that passes through a memory module.
- Memory modules have two ports allowing to serve two concurrent memory reference simultaneously.
- One of the two ports of each port must be connected to the communication network while the other port can be connected directly to some P_i.
- Thus there are two possible types of shared memory references:
  - A "fast" reference made by a processor to the memory module it is directly connected to.
  - A "slower" reference made by a processor through the communication network to the rest of the memory modules.

Y. Ben-Asher, *Multicore Programming Using the ParC Language*,
Undergraduate Topics in Computer Science,
DOI 10.1007/978-1-4471-2164-0_3, © Springer-Verlag London 2012

Fig. 3.1 A Shared memory
machine model with
non-uniform access cost

SHARED   MEMORY   MACHINE

Note that each processor can access $1/P$ of the shared memory address space attached to it using fast memory references while the remaining $\frac{P-1}{P}$ memory cells must be remotely accessed. We argue that a real shared memory machine is usually built such that each processor has part of the shared memory space directly attached to it, while all the remaining parts of the shared memory space are accessed indirectly via some communication network. This construction results in a non-uniform memory access machine, where some of the memory references executed by the processor are faster than others.

A possible schematic structure of such a shared memory machine that captures this non-uniform memory access scheme (NUMA) is described in Fig. 3.1. Here a switch is used to implement fast "local" access to some part of the shared memory and slower accesses to the rest of the address space through a communication network. Temporarily, we will use this simplified description of a shared memory machine to model the complex behavior of multicore machines that are the target architecture of ParC.

In architectures with non-uniform memory access, it is very important that a large part of the memory references made by a program will be made locally. Clearly, the code of the program and local variables of threads should be accessed via local memory references. Therefore, the programmer must have some way to coordinate the mapping of threads to processors and the mapping of data structures to memory modules. In ParC, this mapping is done through the scoping rules and through a new "mapped" version of the parfor construct.

3.1 Locality of Memory Operations via the Scoping Rules

Variables and data structures (V_i) that are declared within a thread (T_i) are unknown to other threads, except for descendants of the declaring thread T_i. It is therefore reasonable to require that such variables reside in a memory module close to the processor that runs T_i. Thus, all accesses to V_i made by this processor are in fact local memory references. Given that the local variables of threads (V_i) are allocated on the thread's stack, making access local implies that T_i's stack should be allocated in the memory module adjacent to the processor that runs T_i. If run-time threads migration is used, it is not possible that all the accesses to V_i made by T_i will be local. Thus, ParC requires that:

1. No thread migration should be used, if a thread T_i is started to be executed by a processor P_i then it should always be executed by P_i. Note that this does not imply that P_i can not execute other threads nor does it imply that the execution of T_i can not be suspended.
2. The stack of a thread T_i will be at the local memory module attached to the processor that executes T_i.

Note that we distinguish between:

Local/Shared variables which are determined by the scoping rules of *ParC* and

Local/Global memory references which is access made by a processor to variables that are allocated in its local memory module.

The semantics of *ParC* require that all memory references made to local variables must be made as local memory operations. This requirement, however, does not imply that all access to shared variables are necessarily made by global memory operations because shared variables accessed by a processor can reside in its local memory module.

For example, consider the program in Fig. 2.21. $Y = I$ is composed of local accesses, while in $Z = X + Y$ only the accesses to Z are local. Figure 3.2 contains the code of two threads that computes in parallel if there are two values $i < N/2$ and $j \geq N/2$ for which $f(i) == f(j)$. Thread-a has two arrays: *parta*[] where all the values of $f(i) < N/2 \&\& i < N/2$ are marked (by thread-a), and *nexta*[] where all the values of $f(i) < N/2 \&\& i \geq N/2$ are marked by the other thread, thread-b. Similarly, thread-a has two arrays: *partb*[] where all the values of $f(i) \geq N/2 \&\& i \geq N/2$ are stored, and *nexta*[] where all the values of $f(i) < N/2 \&\& i \geq N/2$ are stored by thread-a. Clearly, if the same index is marked in *parta*[], *nexta*[] or in *partb*[], *nextb*[], then there are two values $i < N/2, i \geq N/2$ for which $f(i) == f(j)$. Note that half of the memory references are local. Had we used two global arrays to mark the values, all of the references would have been global. Note that we assumed that all arrays are initialized to 0.

This solution should be compared against the naive solution of using a global shared array $A[N]$ and execute the code:

$$if\big(A[f(i)]++>1\big) \qquad fc = 1;$$

Even if we assume that $A[f(i)]++$ is executed atomically, this program although shorter performs @ $\cdot N$ global memory references while the program in Fig. 3.2 is likely to perform only $N/2$ global memory references out of the $2N$ references made tp *parta*, *nexta*, *partb*, *nextb*. By this we assumed that for each thread of the program in Fig. 3.2 half of the $f(i)$'s values it evaluates will be in the range $0 \ldots N/2$ and vice versa for the other thread.

```
int  *a,*b,fa=0,fb=0,fc=0;

    parblock
    { int i,parta[N/2],nexta[N/2];
        *a= nexta;
        fa= 1;
        while(fb==0);
        for(i=0;i<N/2;i++){
            int v;
            v = f(i);
            if(v < N/2) parta[v]=1;
            else *b[v]=1;
        fa= 0;
        while(fb==1);
        for(i=0;i<N/2;i++)
            if(parta[i]==1 && nexta[i] == 1)fc=1;
        }
        :
    { int j,partb[N/2],nextb[N/2];
        *b= nextb;
        fb= 1;
        while(fa==0);
        for(j=N/2;j<N;j++)
            if(f(j) >= N/2) partb[f(j)-N/2]=1;
            else *a[f(j)-N/2]=1;
        fb= 0;
        while(fa==1);
        for(j=0;j<N/2;i++)
            if(partb[j] == 1 && nextb[j] == 1)fc=1;
    } }
```

Fig. 3.2 Sharing of local arrays via a global pointer

3.2 Locality of Memory Operations Through Partitioned Arrays

So far we have used only two forms of variables: shared and locals, however many applications and algorithms requires a third type of variables which is called "partitioned". These are large shared data structures, which are partitioned between several threads. In such partitioning each thread has one part of the partitioned variable which acts as:

- A local variable for all the memory references made by this thread,
- Shared (non-local) variable for all the memory references made to this part by other threads.

Thus if most of the memory references a thread executes are made to its local-part, then they will be counted as local references even though the all partitioned parts are shared. When a thread access other parts of the partitioned data-structure, these accesses may incur full overhead of an access to a shared variable. Typically, large variables like 2D-pictures or matrices are best processed in parallel as partitioned data-structure. In this case each thread will mainly compute and update its local part, but also will access neighboring parts to get updated. In general the assumption that for parallel machines it is always possible to partition shared data such that the memory references made by one thread to its part will always cost as local references is only approximation. In reality, using partitioned structures only increase the probability that memory references made by one thread to its part will always cost as local references.

Another property of partitioned variables is that unlike local variables which disappear when their thread terminates, partitioned variables linger on and can be referenced by other newer threads. This happens even though the threads that have created the parts terminated. In this respect partitioned variables act as static variables of functions. Partitioned variables thus serve as persistent patterns allowing a new set of threads to re-access the local parts of a partitioned structure made by another set of threads that by now have terminated.

In ParC partitioned variables are handled by combining two statements: the mapped lparfor construct and the malloc instruction. The *malloc*() instruction allocates space on the heap as with regular-C, but in ParC, the space allocated by *malloc*() is always local to the thread that executes it. As explained earlier, the lparfor construct creates $P = number\ of\ processors/cores$ threads each executing a "chunk" (equal part) of the lparfor iterations in a sequential loop. The mapped version, which is distinguished by adding the letter 'm' to the parallel constructs, guarantees that these chunks are mapped to processors/cores on a one-to-one basis according to the processor IDs. This is based on the assumption that processors/cores have consecutive ID numbers that can be used to allocate chunks to processors/cores in a persistent manner. Thus, corresponding chunks or mlparfor-threads in distinct constructs will be mapped to the same processor. Note there is no need to use processors-ids in the code just to use consecutive mparfor-construct in order to allocate their threads to processors in a consistent way. If the user wants to create exactly one iteration of the mparfor on each processor, she must use the number of available processors/cores as follows:

$$mparfor(int\ i = 0; i < proc\_no; i + +)\{itteration\_code;\}$$

where *proc_no* is predefined global variable.

A persistent shared array that is partitioned across P threads, one per processor, may be created as shown in Fig. 3.3. The resulting memory layout of the partitioned array is depicted in Fig. 3.4. First, a global array of pointers is declared. Then, a set of threads is spawned by a mapped lparfor. Each thread allocates persistent local memory using the *mallocc*(). The implementation of ParC guarantees that *malloc*()'s space is allocated on a local heap of the processor that executed this *malloc*(). The addresses of the local memory blocks are assigned to the global array.

```
#define  SIZE      1000
#define  NUM       proc_no
#define  PART      (SIZE/NUM)

#define  arr(i)    arr_p[(i)/PART][(i)%PART]

int  *arr_p[NUM];

mlparfor(int k= 0; k < NUM; k++ )
{
    arr_p[k] = (int*)malloc( PART );
}
mlparfor(int k= 0; k < NUM; k++ ) {
    /* use with the arr macro */
    arr(i)=0;
}
```

Fig. 3.3 Implementation of a persistent shared array that is partitioned among threads

Fig. 3.4 Memory layout of a
2D partitioned array

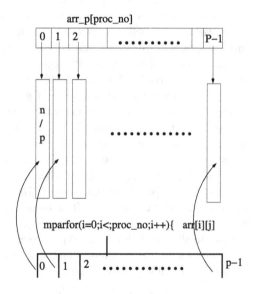

The use of two consecutive *mlparfor* guarantees that no thread tries to use a pointer
that has not been assigned yet.

Note that every access to an element of the partitioned array in Fig. 3.3 is not
efficient since it involves a non-local access $arr\_p[k][j]$ through the global pointer
array. This can be fixed by copying $arr\_p[k]$ to local memory as described in the example of Fig. 3.5. In the example of Fig. 3.5 a number of arrays may be manipulated
in parallel (Fig. 3.5). When we want to sum one of the arrays, as in the calculation
of an inner product of two vectors, P threads are spawned and each sums the local

```
#define MAPPED -1

int   *A[P], *B[P], *C[P];
int   res=0;

mlparfor (int i=0; i< P; i++ ) {

    A[i] = (int*) malloc(N/P);
    B[i] = (int*) malloc(N/P);
    C[i] = (int*) malloc(N/P);
}

/* initialize and use A and B, and multiply into C */

mlparfor (int i=0; i< P; i++ ) {

    int   k, *a=A[i], *b=B[i], *c=C[i];

    for (k=0 ; k<N/P ; k++)
        c[k] = a[k]*b[k];
}

/* inner product is sum of C */

mlparfor (int i=0; i< P; i++ ) {

    int   k, sum=0, *c=C[i];

    for (k=0 ; k<N/P ; k++)
        sum += c[k];
    atomicADD( &res, sum );
}
```

Fig. 3.5 Inner product of partitioned arrays

part of the array c[] holding the multiplications. Then these partial sums are added together but through local pointers so that most of the array references are efficient.

Figure 3.6 contains an example of a 2D array a[][] where each element is updated to be the sum of its four neighbors. Since a[][] is allocated through the use of *mparfor(...)* it is in fact partitioned between the processors. The elements in Fig. 3.6 are referenced as any two dimensional array and fit in well with the C notion of a vector of pointers to vectors. The mapped version of lparfor ensures that the indexed threads will always be mapped to the same physical processor. Note that in Fig. 3.6 the second *mlparfor* starts from 1 to $N-2$ because the elements of column 0 and column $N-1$ do not have the four neighbors needed for the summing operation. Note that we assume that the *ParCl* system maps thread i created in *mparfor($i = 0; \ldots$)* to processor with $ID = i \bmod proc\_no$ in order for this code to work well for the first and last columns of a[][]. Thus, it is better to let the index of *mparfor* be used with *steps* $= 1$ because otherwise the mapping of threads to processors can be hard to track. In this example the access to $a[k][i]$ involved a global

```
/* partitioned array; efficient */
int  *a[N];

mlparfor ( int k=0; k<N; k++)
{
    a[k] = (int *) malloc( N*sizeof(int) );
    initialize(a[k]);
}

mlparfor ( int k=1; k<N-1; k++)
{
    int  i;
    for (i=1; i<N-1; i++) {
        a[k][i] = a[k-1][i] + a[k][i-1]+
            a[k+1][i]+ a[k][i+1]; } }
}
```

Fig. 3.6 Using the partitioned 2D array

```
/* partitioned array; efficient */
int  *a[N];

mlparfor ( int k=0; k<N; k++)
{
    a[k] = (int *) malloc( N*sizeof(int) );
    initialize(a[k]);
}

mlparfor ( int k=1; k<N-1; k++)
{
    int  i,*ak=a[k],*akp1=a[k+1],*akm1=a[k-1];
    for (i=1; i<N-1; i++) {
        ak[i] = akm1[i] + ak[i-1]+
            akp1[i]+ ak[i+1]; } }
}
```

Fig. 3.7 Using the partitioned 2D array with full locality

memory reference through $a[k]$. However, a good compiler will usually put $a[k]$ in a register and thus save this extra global memory reference, as depicted in Fig. 3.7.

Figure 3.8 illustrates an incorrect declaration of a shared 2D array that does not yield a partitioned structure.

Finally we show how these methods of partitioned arrays and local memory references through local variables are combined to create an efficient version of matrix multiplication. Figure 3.9 obtains an efficient matrix multiplication as follows:

- The matrix A is partitioned and every one of the p threads will multiply N/p rows of A with every column of B. Since A and C are partitioned this can be done locally from the perspective of A and C.

```
/* whole array declared; inefficient */
int   a[N][N];

mlparfor ( int k=0; k<N; k++)
{
    initialize(a[k]);
}

mlparfor ( int k=1; k<N-1; k++)
{
    int   i;
    for (i=1; i<N-1; i++) {
        a[k][i] = a[k-1][i] + a[k][i-1]+
            a[k+1][i] + a[k][i+1]; } }
```

Fig. 3.8 Incorrect use of mapped construct

```
mlparfor ( int from=0; from < N; from+=N/p)
{
    int   j, k, t, sum, *a, *b, *b_arr, *c;
    int   to=from+N/p;

    b = (int *) malloc(N);

    for (k=from; k!=(to-1)%N; k=(k+1)%N) {
        b_arr = B[k];
        for (j=0; j < N; j++)
            b[j] = b_arr[j];

        for (j=from; j < to; j++) {
            a = A[j];
            c = C[j];
            sum = 0;
            for (t=0; t < N; t++)
                sum += a[t] * b[t];
            c[k] = sum;
        }
    }
}
```

Fig. 3.9 Improved version of matrix multiplication

- Since the computation of each $C[i][j]$ is not dependent on the computation of other elements we can et the order such that for each j we compute $C[0][j], \ldots, C[N][j]$ (as partitioned between the threads). In this way, for each thread we copy the next column of B to a local copy $b[]$ and multiply this column with all the rows A that are local to the current thread. Thus, the cost of copying the column of B to a local array b is amortized by the fact that it is being re-used N/p times.

- Finally, since each thread copies all the columns of B to a local copy we would like them to access different *remote* columns of B at any given time. This reflects the assumption that multiple concurrent accesses to the same elements by different threads may slowdown the execution (we later justify this assumption). Thus by letting each thread to use a different order ($k = bot$; $k! = (bot - 1)\%N$; $k = (k + 1)\%N$) of copying the columns of B we minimize possible conflicts between the treads.

3.3 Synchronization ·

Synchronization is the ability to create some correlation in absolute time between a group of threads that are to be executed in parallel. The correlation itself can take many forms ranging from "exact" correlations like the one requiring that **all the threads execute this statement at the same time** to weaker notations like the one stating that **no two threads execute this statement at the same time**. For instance, the fact that the next statement after parfor or parblock cannot be executed unless all the threads spawned by the parfor or parblock have terminated is, in fact, a form of weak synchronization. Thus, synchronization is a mechanism allowing us to impose some partial order between the statements of different threads that are being executed in parallel, where a parallel execution indicates that no such order had existed prior to the synchronization.

Synchronization in a parallel programming language can be expressed by imposing semantic restrictions on the parallel execution as follows:

- Restricting or imposing a condition on mutual or simultaneous access to common variables and data structures.
- Using special primitive instructions whose execution yields the desired condition.
- Adding parallel constructs whose execution imposes the desired order.

We distinguish between the following types of synchronizations:

- Synchronization via accesses or locks on shared variables and shared data structures.
- Synchronization through execution of control structure, e.g., through parfor statement.
- Synchronization through the execution of statements such as calling a special function.

The approach adopted for ParC is to have few synchronization mechanisms from each type.

Fig. 3.10 Synchronization
via parallel constructs

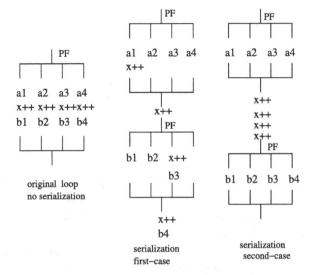

original loop
no serialization

serialization
first–case

serialization
second–case

3.4 Synchronization Through Shared Variables

The first way to impose synchronization is to use ParC's nesting of parallel constructs. Consider two consecutive parallel-for constructs. Clearly, the threads spawned by the second parallel-for cannot start before all the threads of the first parallel-for have terminated. Thus, the ability to nest parallel constructs can be used to impose some sort of synchronization. Figure 3.10 (left) depicts a parallel-for that invokes four threads, each executing some initial code a_i, an increment $x + +$ and a terminating code b_i. Since $x + +$ is not atomic (equivalent to $t_i = x$; $t_i = t_i + 1$; $x = t_i$), we may want to impose serial execution on all four $x + +$s. Figure 3.10 (right) depicts two ways of imposing serial execution of $x + +$s using two consecutive parallel-for loops. Note that in both approaches we had to impose more serialization than what is required by the condition that **no two $x + +$ will be executed in parallel**. The first approach prevents an execution where $b1$ is executed after $a4$, and the second approach prevents any overlapping between a_i and b_j. Thus, it is natural to consider other ways of imposing synchronization between the threads.

Another way of imposing synchronization between the threads is to use shared variables as flags and use busy-waiting loops in other threads. Figure 3.11 illustrates how some synchronization can be imposed by active-waiting for a change in a shared flag (a procedure known as "busy-waiting"). In the case depicted on the right hand side of Fig. 3.11, the busy-waiting of the threads guarantees that $b1$ and $b3$ will be executed after $F = 0$ of thread-2.

The conditions imposing serialization of a code segment are known as **critical sections** (CS). A code segment that is enclosed by a critical section indicates that it should not be executed in parallel with other code segments that are enclosed in a critical section. A thread can start executing a critical section only if no other thread is currently executing a critical section. It is possible to implement (CS) using

Fig. 3.11 Synchronization
via shared variables

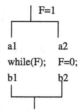

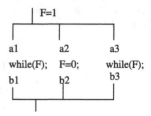

only shared variables and busy-waiting provided that all read/write operations to the
shared memory are atomic. The following example illustrates Peterson's algorithm
for CS for the case of two threads. However, the example can be easily extended to
the case of P threads.

Peterson's algorithm for two threads uses three shared variables: $F[0] == 1$
when thread $T0$ would like to enter its CS, $F[1] == 1$ when thread $T1$ would like
to enter its CS and $turn = 1/0$, indicating that priority should be given to thread
$T0/T1$. Intuitively, setting $turn = 0$ thread $T0$ grants $T1$ the possibility of entering
the CS first and vice-versa for $T1$.

<pre>int   F[2]={0,0},turn=0;
 	
parblock {
/* enterCS thread-T0*/
F[0]= 1;
turn = 0;
while(F[1] && turn == 0);
thread-0: critical code
/* exitCS thread-0*/
F[0]= 0;
}
:</pre>
	<pre>{
	/* enterCS thread-T1*/
	F[1]= 1;
	turn = 1;
	while(F[0] && turn == 1);
	thread-1: critical code
	/* exitCS thread-1*/
	F[1]= 0;
	}</pre>

Critical section thread-0.	Critical section thread-1

Correctness Assume in negation that both threads are executing instructions from
their CS-codes in parallel. In this case $F[0] = 1$ and $F[1] = 1$ because both threads
have executed $F[0] = 1$ and $F[1] = 1$ before entering their CS-codes. Consequently, in order for both threads to exit the $while()$-loop it must follow that
$turn = 0$ and $turn = 1$, which is impossible because:

- before entering $while(F[1]\&\&turn == 0)$; $T0$ executes $turn = 0$; Hence, the
  only hope for $T0$ to find $turn == 1$ is for $T1$ to execute $turn = 1$;.

- before entering $while(F[0]\&\&turn == 1)$; T1 executes $turn = 1$; Hence, the only hope for T1 to find $turn == 0$ is for $T0$ to execute $turn = 0$;.

Thus, both threads cannot enter the CS simultaneously.

Starvation   One of the threads $T0$ is constantly blocked in its $while(F[1]\&\&turn == 0)$ while $T1$ enters its critical section repeatedly. This situation can not happen because $T1$ will execute $turn = 1$; every time it attempts to enter its CS. Since $T0$ is executing $while(F[1]\&\&turn == 0)$;, executing $turn = 1$; will let $T0$ enter its CS **before** $T1$. Since $T1$ is in $while(F[0]\&\&turn == 1)$;, $F[0] == 1$. Hence, $T1$ will be blocked in its while-loop, allowing $T0$ to enter. Thus, starvation is not possible. In addition, the above scheme is clearly "fair" because if both $T0$ and $T1$ attempt to enter their CSs constantly, the accesses will be equally partitioned between the two threads.

Mutual blocking   Both threads are waiting in their while-loops, preventing one another from entering the CS. As an example of such a situation, consider the parallel execution of

```
parblock {
    while(x >= 10) x--;
} : {
}
    while(x <= 10) x++;
```

Mutual blocking can occur at the point $x = 10$ where one thread increments x to 11 and the other resets it to 10. In the case of CS, mutual blocking is clearly not possible because $turn$ must have some value that will allow only one of the threads to enter its CS.

Self blocking   Assume that $T0$ exits its CS and does not attempt to access its CS. Clearly, in this case $T1$ can use its CS because it will not be blocked in $while(F[0]\&\&turn == 1)$;. As before, the exiting $T0$ executed $F[0] = 0$;.

3.5 Fetch and Add Synchronization

Fetch-and-add, denoted faa(var, value), is an atomic operation that modifies *var* by *value*. $X = $ faa$(\&V, exp)$ returns the old value of V to X, and adds exp to V. In other words, $X = V$; $V = V + exp$;. Since faa is executed atomically (no interleavings inside faa), the effect of executing several faa in parallel is the same as executing them in some sequential order. The following program will print ten numbers from 0 to 9, while the final value of g will be 10.

```
int   g;
g = 0;
parfor (int I=0;  I<10;I++)
{
    int   t;
    t = faa(&g,1);
    printf("<%d,%d>",i,t);
}
```

```
10 faa performed in parallel:
<1,9><2,7><3,8><4,5><5,1><6,4><7,3><8,6><9,2><10,0>.
```

Fetch-and-add has been shown to be useful in a large number of algorithms. An important feature of faa is that it can be used to implement "wait-free" interactions, where wait-free implies that the completion of faa in a given thread does not depend on the actions of other threads. Thus, although all operations have been executed in parallel the outcome is as if they were executed atomically. The use of busy-waiting is always blocking as it depends on another thread to reset a shared flag. For instance, these features of faa can be used to compute the sum of N elements in one step, which is erroneous otherwise.

`int   A[N],X=0;` `parfor (int I=0;  I<N;I++) {` `    X = X + A[I];` `}`	`int   X=0;` `parfor (int I=0;  I<N;I++) {` `    faa(&X,A[I]);` `}`
False summing program.	Correct summing with faa.

The different values returned by parallel calls to faa can be used to synchronize threads when accessing a common resource. For example, a LIFO parallel queue structure can be implemented using faa. Consider an array $A[N]$ used as a queue with the following operations:

$+(x)$ add x to $A[]$.
$-()$ remove item from $A[]$.

Semantics For every time unit t (after the queue has been initialized) there is a pointer P on $A[]$, such that if i additions and j removes took place in those t time units, then P points to the $i - j$ element of $A[]$ and all the $i - j - 1$ left elements of A are non empty (i.e. $A[i] \neq \emptyset$).

This semantic has several weaknesses:

- It does not differentiate between sequential and parallel accesses to the queue. Therefore, $[+(a)|| - ()|| + b()]$ and $\{+(a); -(); +b()\}$ may yield that the queue contains one item 'a', yet it is obvious that for $\{+(a); -(); +b()\}$ the queue must contain 'b'.

Table 3.1 Execution order
for parallel additions and
deletions to $A[]$

	+(a)	+(b)	−()	−()	+(c)
a:	1	2	4	3	5
b:	8	9	6	10	7

- It does not differentiate between a parallel queue and a parallel stack. The same definition will hold if we replace $+(x)$ by $push(x)$ and $-()$ by $pop()$.

`int  A[N],P=0;`
 	
`+(x){`
`int F;`
`a:   F = faa(&P,1);`
`b:   A[F] = x;`
`}`
	`-(){`
	`int F;`
	`a:   F = faa(&P,-1);`
	`b:   A[F-1] = Ø;`
	`}`

`Adding an element to the queue.`	`Deleting an element from the queue.`

Consider a program which adds three elements and removes two elements from $A[]$:

$$PB\big[+(a); : +(b); : -(); : -(); : +(c);\big]$$

A specific execution order for this program is described in Table 3.1. One possible way of describing the execution of the faa algorithm is to use "a pointer table" in which the position of every pointer (i.e., variables affected by faa) is denoted. In our case only P and the local F_x should be traced, where F_x is the local variable of the $x()$ operation. Table 3.2 follows the execution order of Table 3.1. The execution returns $A[0] = a$ and $P = 1$, indicating that $A[]$ contains one element, which is the correct result for 3 additions and 2 deletions. Note that another execution order might yield $A[0] = a$, $A[1] = b$, $A[2] = c$, however, P will always be 1.

The validity of this algorithm stems from two simple claims, which are valid after the execution of any sequence of accesses:

- There is no $i < P$ such that $A[i] = \emptyset$. Otherwise there could have been a step $F_x = faa(\&P, 1)$ (where $F_x = i$) without any writing of $A[F_x] = x$, which contradicts the definition of $+(x)$.
- Let i be the number of additions and j the number of deletions; then $P = i - j + 1$. This claim follows from the faa definition.

One problem with this algorithm and the above "proof" is that P might exceed the boundaries of A. Observe that, if the final value of P should be less than zero, no additions or deletions to negative places $F < 0$ should take place because A is empty anyway. If the final value of P is positive, then any addition to negative places is also redundant because it must have been matched or overwritten by some

		A[0]	A[1]	A[2]
Table 3.2 Pointer table for parallel queue accesses	initial	$P\uparrow$		
	1	$F_a\uparrow$	$P\uparrow$	
	2		$F_b\uparrow$	$P\uparrow$
	3		$P\uparrow$	$F_-\uparrow$
	4	$P\uparrow$	$F_-\uparrow$	
	5	$F_c\uparrow$	$P\uparrow$	
	6	$A[0]=\emptyset$		
	7	$A[0]=c$		
	8	$A[0]=a$		
	9		$A[1]=b$	
	10		$A[1]=\emptyset$	

deletion (i.e., the one that moved P to this place). In other words, if the final value of P is positive, then the number of additions and deletions to negative indexes is equal, and there is no need to actually execute them. A similar argument holds for additions and deletions that exceed the value of N. In other words, additions and deletions to indexes greater than N can be skipped. This observation can be used in the following version:

```
int  A[N],P=0;                   -(){
                                 int F;
+(x){                            a:F = faa(&P,-1);
int F;                           b:if((F-1 >= 0)&&(F-1 < N))
a:F = faa(&P,1);                 b:    A[F-1] = Ø;
b:if((F >= 0)&&(F < N))          }
c:   A[F] = x;
}
```

Skipping additions and deletions	when overfull or underfull situations occur.

There is a more substantial problem with the above naive implementation of the queue–it is erroneous. The error is due to the ability of delete operations $A[k]=\emptyset$ to override correct values in $A[k]$ for $k < i - j$ (i.e., $A[k]$ should contain some inserted element). For example, in the execution order described in Table 3.2 it is sufficient to change the execution order, letting $A[0]=\emptyset$ be the last instruction updating $A[0]$ so that $A[0]$ will be empty. A correct version of the queue can be obtained if we attach a counter to each cell $A[k]$ indicating if there were more insertions than deletions to $A[k]$. Thus, if this counter is positive, then clearly the value of $A[k]$ should not be equal to $\emptyset$. The modified version of the queue algorithm uses such an array of counters $C[]$ and the update of $A[]$'s elements is done based on the counter in $C[k]$. Note that the counter is updated in a non-blocking mode using *faa*(). The update of the counters *faa*($\&(C[F])$, $1/-1$) must be performed before $A[]$'s elements are updated. In this way any update $A[F] = x$ or $A[F-1] = \emptyset$ is counted before it is executed.

int A[N],C[N]={0},P=0;	-(){
```+ (x) { int F; a: F = faa(&P,1); c: faa(&(C[F]),1); b: A[F] = x; }```	```int F; a: F = faa(&P,-1); c: faa(C[F-1],-1); b:if(C[F-1] <= 0)) b: A[F-1] = Ø; }```
Adding an element to the queue.	Deleting an element from the queue.

A more complicated example of faa's usefulness appears in the quicksort program. Here faa is used to allocate distinct cells in the array ARRAYtmp to the different threads so that all the parallel increments of l, r yield distinct and consecutive values. The atomic wait-free property of this faa can remove the need for mutual exclusion or unnecessary blocking serialization.

A sequential version that implements the quicksort algorithm is presented in Fig. 3.12. Two arrays are used alternately to copy elements that are smaller or larger than the first element in the segment. The first element is copied to the output array at a location that is between the set of smaller values and the set of larger values. The recursion ends when the segment is empty or includes a single element. If there is a single element, it is copied to the output array.

The parallel version in ParC is presented in Fig. 3.13. An lparfor is used to compare the elements against a splitting value in parallel, dividing them into those that are larger and those that are smaller. As this procedure implies parallel access to the indices 1 and r, the atomic fetch-and-add (faa) instruction is used to increment and decrement them. Then a parblock is used to perform the two recursive calls in parallel. The initial steps of quicksort are demonstrated in Fig. 3.14. The leader 5 is compared in parallel to all of the elements. This comparison divides the array into two parts, $0 \longrightarrow 3$ and $5 \longrightarrow 8$, which can be sorted in parallel.

ParC also contains Semaphores providing an interface through which a thread can suspend itself while waiting for a shared variable to change its value. Variables of type **semaphore** may be declared, and the **P** and **V** operations may be applied to them with the usual semantics.

```
int   final[n];

void quick_sort(int *ARRAY, *ARRAYtmp, FROM , TO )
{
     int   l=FROM, r=TO;

     if ( FROM == TO )
         final[FROM] = ARRAY[FROM];
     if ( FROM >= TO ) return;

     for ( i=FROM+1; i<=TO; i++ )
     {
         if ( ARRAY[i] < ARRAY[FROM] )
             ARRAYtmp[ l++ ] = ARRAY[i];
         else
             ARRAYtmp[ r- ] = ARRAY[i];
     }

     final[l] = ARRAY[FROM];

     quick_sort( ARRAYtmp, ARRAY, FROM, l-1 );
     quick_sort( ARRAYtmp, ARRAY, r+1, TO );
}
```

Fig. 3.12 A *C* program implementing the quicksort algorithm. The first element, ARRAY[FROM], is used to split the array

3.6 The Sync Instruction

This instruction blocks any thread generated by a parallel construct until all the threads spawned by that construct reach this barrier. Thus, a thread that executes a sync is suspended until all its siblings also execute a sync. It is sufficient that one thread out of the set of threads spawned by a parallel construct will not perform the sync (through conditional execution or through an infinite loop) to deadlock the remaining threads in an infinite loop. Note that if a subset of these threads terminates before a synch is executed then only the remaining threads have to perform this sync. In particular, if, at a given moment, all the threads that did not started to execute a sync terminate, the threads waiting at the sync can continue across the sync.

Intuitively, the effect of a sync can be described as a door that is locked with several locks (see Fig. 3.15). Each thread in a parallel construct has a key to one of the locks. Whenever the thread executes a sync, it releases its lock and waits. When the last lock has been removed, the door is opened and threads can enter. When the last thread has entered through the door, the door is locked again using all the locks so that it can be used for the next sync of the current parallel construct.

The use of sync may seam redundant since two consecutive parallel constructs also creates a barrier. This is because the threads of the second parallel construct can not be executed until all the threads of the first construct terminates. Figure 3.16

```
int    final[n];

void quick_sort(int *ARRAY, *ARRAYtmp, FROM , TO )
{
     int   l=FROM, r=TO;

     if ( FROM == TO )
          final[FROM] = ARRAY[FROM];
     if ( FROM >= TO ) return;

     lparfor (int i= FROM+1; i<= TO; i++ )
     {
          if ( ARRAY[i] < ARRAY[FROM] )
               ARRAYtmp[ faa(&l,1) ] = ARRAY[i];
          else
               ARRAYtmp[ faa(&r,-1) ] = ARRAY[i];
     }

     final[l] = ARRAY[FROM];

     parblock
     {
          quick_sort( ARRAYtmp, ARRAY, FROM, l-1 );
          :
          quick_sort( ARRAYtmp, ARRAY, r+1, TO );
     }
}
```

Fig. 3.13 A parallel version of the quicksort program

Fig. 3.14 First steps in
quicksort of 9 numbers

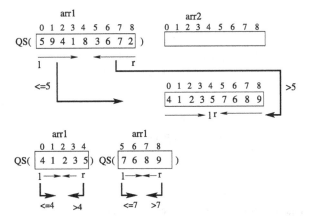

contains two alternatives codes one that uses sync and one that use two consecutive
lparfor to compute the same outcome. In this example, each element of an array $a[i]$

Fig. 3.15 The sync door,
blocking all threads from
entering until all locks have
been removed

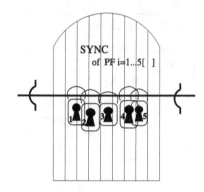

```
int   a[N];

parfor (int i= 0; i<N; i++)
{
    int  k;

    while(f(...)) {
        k=i;
        while(a[k] > a[i] && k < n) k++;
        sync;
        a[i] += k;
        sync;
    }
}
```

```
int   a[N], tmp[N];

    int  k;

while(f(...)) {
    lparfor (int i= 0; i<N; i++){
        k=i;
        while(a[k] > a[i] && k < n)k++;
        tmp[i] = k;
    }  lparfor (int i= 0; i<N; i++){
        a[i] += tmp[i];
    }
}
```

Fig. 3.16 Sync versus parallel constructs allowing the use of temporary variables

seeks in parallel the index of the first element above i $k > i$ such that $a[k] < a[i]$.

```
int   *P;

      parfor (int I= 0;  i<10;  i++)
      {
            int L;
            L = I;
            P = &L;
            printf("<%d,%d> ",L,I);
            sync;
            *P = L;
            sync;
            printf("(%d,%d) ",L,I);
      }epar

      printf("-%d-",*P);
```

Fig. 3.17   The effect of sync on the use of shared variables

Once, found k is added to $a[i]$ and the whole process is iterated in a while-loop until some global condition $f(...)$ becomes false.

- The search for k must be separated from the update $a[i]+=k$ since we can not modify $a[i]$ while other elements are seeking to find their k.
- Though the two alternatives obtain the same result, the first alternative (the one that uses sync) does have the advantage of passing k directly after the sync while the second alternative need a shared array $tmp[]$ to pass k to the second parfor.
- However, the second alternative can use lparfor while the first alternative must spawn N threads since otherwise sync will not work.

Thus, there is some tradeoff between using Sync and using consecutive parallel constructs for synchronization.

The sync instruction is mainly used to coordinate different (possibly parallel) references to shared variables. Consider the effects of *sync* in the program in Fig. 3.17. The program prints any possible permutation of $\langle 1, 1 \rangle \ldots \langle 10, 10 \rangle$. Let L_i denote the local variable of the ith thread of the *pparfor*. P is a global pointer that points to some L_i, depending which of the $P = \&L_i$ has "won" or performed last. After the first *sync* all 10 threads write their local L_i to the L_i pointed to by P. The next sequence of printing depends on which pair of statements $P = \&L_i$ and $*p = L_i$ has won. Assume that $P = \&L_8$ has won and $*P = L_5$ has won. In this case the program prints any possible permutation of $(1, 1) \ldots (5, 8) \ldots (10, 10)$, indicating that thread 5 wrote its value to L_8 of the 8'th thread. The last printing of $*P$ will print 5.

The printing sequence is not changed by omitting the second sync because only one $*P = L_i$ can win before the printing of L_8 takes place (in case $P = \&L_8$ won). However, the last value of $*P$ can be different from L_8 because another $*p = L_i$ can win after $*p = L_8$ has been executed.

Without the first sync, the first sequence of printing can be affected and many values can be changed, for example:

$$P = \&L_4 \quad \langle 5, 5 \rangle \quad *P = L_5 \quad \langle 5, 4 \rangle$$
$$P = \&L_8 \quad \langle 9, 9 \rangle \quad *P = L_9 \quad \langle 9, 8 \rangle$$
$$P = \&L_3 \quad \langle 6, 6 \rangle \quad *P = L_6 \quad \langle 6, 3 \rangle$$

The second sequence of printing can also be affected because the local values of some of the L_i do not match i; e.g., $(5, 4)$, $(9, 8)$, $(6, 3)$ are expected.

3.7 Controlling the Execution by Using the Yield and Switch Instructions

Another aspect of synchronization is formed by letting the programmer control the way threads are scheduled by ParC's virtual machine. As described earlier at any time there is a set of ready-to-run threads that are waiting in the ready-queue and a set of suspended threads waiting in the suspend-queue to be moved to the ready queue. When the current thread is preempted (context-switch) or terminated the processor/core selects another thread from the ready-queue and starts to execute it. In here we consider two direct mechanism through which the programmer can affect this scheduling process and use it for maintaining a desired pattern of synchronization:

switch_on, switch_off are two flags that when activated allow the user to create non-preemptable/re-preemptable threads. Non-preemptable thread are more efficient since it saves the overhead of executing a context-switch. Non-preemptable threads actually occupy the processor until their termination. A non-preemptable thread may be preempted if it is forced to wait a for a spawn, sync instruction or any other suspending operation it initiates. Note that this instruction cannot be used to guarantee mutual exclusion because it has no effect on threads running on other processors.

yield is an instruction that preempts its current thread and put it at the end of the ready-queue. It is useful to wait for an event while yielding the current processor to executes another thread.

Switch_on is useful to create a *clock − thread* that constantly increments a time counter. Other threads running in parallel can use this time counter to sample the current time and thus determine time-order (before/after) between events. This clock saves the overhead of calling the system clock and is more accurate (useful for program monitoring and debugging). The clock thread can be terminated by reseting a suitable flag.

Threads often communicate through shared variables. In these cases some threads may need to wait until a certain value has been computed. A trivial solution is to use a loop to wait until a common variable has been set to a desired value. The obvious drawback of the "busy-waiting" through a while-loop is that it consumes unnecessary processor time. A possible solution is to let the waiting thread "give-up" its processor for a while. This is done by the "yield_proc" command, which throws the current thread back into the queue. The property of the yield_proc instruction is that the yielding thread will resume only after all the other threads already in the queue have a chance to run (the queue is a FIFO one). Thus, yielding increases the running time of the thread for which it is waiting. By putting itself at the end of the queue, the waiting thread makes sure that it will be rerun only after the thread it is waiting for runs for a while. The use of yield_proc is, then, as follows:

| ```
int x=1;
parblock {
    x = f();
    :
    while(x == 1);
    g(x);
}epar
``` | ```
int x=1;
parblock {
    x = f();
    :
    while(x == 1) yield_proc;
    g(x);
}epar
``` |
|---|---|
| Busy-wait | Waiting by yielding. |

However, constantly "yielding" ignores the overhead associated with the yield_proc (moving the processes back and forth from the queue). A better solution is for the process to execute "busy-waiting" for some period of time and then, if its condition has not been met, execute yield_proc. The goal is to do busy-waiting until the thread has wasted as much as it would have cost it to use yield_proc. Thus, it invests equal overhead in both strategies because the thread cannot waste more than half of the time on the overhead needed to yield. All that is left is for the above thread to determine the exact global time it needs to spend on busy-waiting.

Note that the thread can be swapped to the queue by a context-switch interrupt. In that case the thread need not yield and can continue its busy-waiting by dedicating one thread and processor to be used as a global clock.[1] In order for a thread to be used as a clock, it should always run and never be swapped to the queue. The switch_off command prevents the clock process from being suspended. The final code is as follows:

```
#define yield_overhead 300

int x=1;
int cl=0; stop = 1;

parblock{
    /* clock processes */
    switch_off;
    while(stop == 1) cl++;
    :
    parblock {
```

---

[1] Not all systems allow the reading of a hardware clock with sufficient granularity.

```
        x = f();
        :
        {
        int t,i;
        while(x == 1){ /* loop until the condition is met */
            i = 0; t = cl;
            /*busy-wait*/
            while( (i < yield_overhead) && (x == 1)) i++;
            /* if the counter'i' differs from the clock then
            there was a context switch, otherwise yield */
            if((x == 1) && (i > (cl -t -20)) ) yield_proc;
        }
        g(x);
        stop = 0;
        }
    }epar
}epar
```
Mixing busy-waiting with yielding, using a clock thread.

The clock processes can be also used for monitoring the program's execution. For example, the following program computes the maximal synchronization time of ten processes:

```
int cl=0; stop = 1;
int tm,k,max_t[10];

parblock{
    /* clock processes */
    switch_off;
    while(stop == 1) cl++;
    :
    parfor(int i=0; i< 10;i++)
    {
    int j,t1,t2;

        for(j=0;j<10000;j++);
        t1 = cl;;
        sync;
        t2 = cl;;
        max_t[i] = t2 - t1;
    }
    tm = 0;
    for(k=0;k<10;k++) if(tm < max_t[i]) tm = max_t[i];
    printf(" It took %d to synchronize 10 processes",tm);
    stop = 0;
}epar
```
Monitoring the program using a clock thread.

3.8 Fairness Related Issues

In this section we consider the problem of "fair" execution order. Intuitively, we can partition the possible set of all possible execution orders into fair and unfair orders. An unfair order is an order that allows some threads to continue while "starving" other threads by not assigning a physical processor that will execute them. More formally, fairness can be defined in several ways:

Weak sense At any stage of the computation, there is a finite time duration wherein each thread is advanced at least once, implying that eventually each thread will terminate if it does not enter an infinite loop.

Strong sense For a given correct program R, there is a fixed a priori time duration d_R such that at any stage of the computation, after d_R time units each thread that is ready is advanced at least once. Intuitively, this is a weak synchronous execution, wherein every d_R time units each thread is advanced (full synchronous execution is obtained when $d_R = 1$).

Clearly, if the program generates threads at an exponential rate, fairness in the strong sense is not possible because at a certain stage there will be more threads than any finite d_R. Thus, fairness in the strong sense is possible only for programs that span a fixed number of threads during the whole execution of the program (e.g., the number of spawned threads does not depend on the input). Given that there is a limit to the number of activities any parallel machine can hold, any program which, at a given stage, spawns more threads than this limit will automatically crash or terminate. Thus, practically we can assume that the number of threads that are "alive" at any stage is fixed for any program that completes its execution.

The fairness of the execution results from the way in which the scheduler of the underlying parallel machine works. There are three possibilities:

- Executes a context-switch every fixed amount of time using the system clock. When a thread is preempted it is inserted at the end of the ready-queue. Thus, there is no possibility to starvation and strong fairness is obtained where

$$d_r = contextswitch\_delay \times max\#threads$$

- Execute a context-switch only in while-loops that may access shared variables. This creates weak-fairness, since if a thread is starved and the amount of threads that is generated is bounded, then there must be another thread that is executing a while-loop waiting for a shared variable to be changed. Thus by executing a context-switch in every while-loop that may access shared variables we prevent such a starvation. This option has been selected for ParC due to its ability to reduce the overhead of the context-switch operation.
- Do not execute any context-switch let threads run to completion. The user must explicitly control the scheduling by inserting yield instructions in the code.

Fairness through preemption is useful to handle cases of busy-waiting and synchronization through shared variables as depicted in Fig. 3.18. Here, assume that we have only three processors each executing a *while*(*flag* == 0); thread. Hence, only by preempting one of the current threads, the forth thread will be executed setting the flag to one freeing all the other three threads.

Fig. 3.18 Code solved
preemption even for a
machine with three
processors

```
int   flag=0;
parblock
{
        while  (flag  ==  0);
    :
        while  (flag  ==  0);
    :
        while  (flag  ==  0);
    :
        flag = 1;
}
```

3.9 Scheduling Policy

Another related issue that affects the execution of code is the order in which threads
are pulled from the ready-queue by the processors. The ready-queue can be managed
as a FIFO-queue or as a LIFO-queue or at a random order of selection. Note that, at
any given time the ready queue is accessed in parallel by a set of processors whose
threads have been terminated or suspended. Thus, the ready-queue is managed as a
parallel queue similar to the parallel-queue described in the previous chapter where
parallel insertions $+(X)$ or deletes $-()$ operations are supported.

The implications of the scheduling order on the resulting execution time and fairness can be subtle. Consider the parallel program $f()$ whose execution is described
in Fig. 3.19. In this example there is a recursive function $f()$ that spawns ten threads
$t0, \ldots, t9$ such that:

- $t0$ sets $x = 10$,
- $t1, \ldots, t8$ waits for x to be greater than 9,
- $t9$ checks the value of x and if it is smaller than 10 it increment x and calls $f()$
  again.

If the scheduling order is LIFO (last-in-first-out) then $t9$ of every invocation of $f()$
will be executed first (assuming one or two processors). Thus $f()$ will be called
10 times leading to the generation of 100 threads. However, if the scheduling order
was FIFO and $t0$ is executed first then $f()$ will be invoked only once since $x = 10$
will be executed first. Clearly this example can be reversed such that LIFO will be
preferable over FIFO. In ParC, the default scheduling is FIFO, however, via simple
hacking the user can change this to any desired order.

3.10 Forced Termination

In regular C loops iterations are controlled by three instructions:

continue that skips the remaining of the current iteration and moves to the next
iteration of the loop.

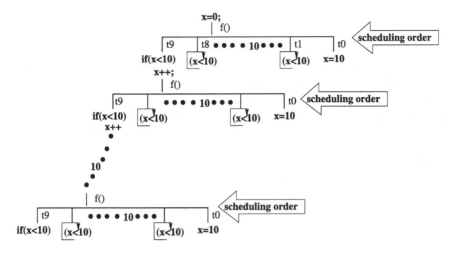

Fig. 3.19 Scheduling order that leads to superfluous generation of threads

break terminates the loop and continue the execution after the last iteration of the loop. Note that break can be used to exit from case-structures, however, since in ParC the switch-statement was not extended to parallel construct this use of break is not considered.

return terminates the current function-call terminating all level of nested loops and resume the execution after the last call.

Due the fact that in ParC parfor iterations spawns threads then the direct use of *break, continue, return* in parallel constructs must be to terminate these threads as follows:

pcontinue is the analogue of continue and when executed in the body of a parfor it kills the iteration/thread that executes it. Thus pcontinue skips the current iteration. Pcontinue has no effect on its siblings threads, and similarly due to the nesting-rules of parallel constructs in ParC it has no effect on threads that have been spawned by it before it executed pcontinue. If the last thread executes pcontinue the whole parfor terminates with it. Finally, a thread that executes pcontinue before a sync is counted as if it has executed this sync.

pbreak terminates all the remaining threads of the current parfor. Clearly all the threads spawned by the current thread and its siblings threads must be terminated as well. It thus kills the current sub-tree of threads including those that are currently running by a processor, those residing in the ready-queue and all those threads that have been suspended. The execution resumes after the current parfor.

preturn acts similar to return by terminating all the threads that were spawned by the current functions including those that are currently running and those that are suspended or those that are in the ready-queue.

go-to operation are not allowed between parallel constructs and their iterations as well. The use of **setjmp** and **longjmp** in the scope of a parallel construct is not allowed.

```
int count=0;
parfor(int i=0;i<10;i++)
{
    if(i % 2 == 0) pcontinue;
    if(i > 4)    pbreak;
    if(i==3) f(i);
    printf("I=%d\n",i);
}
printf("count=%d\n",count);

int f(int m)
{
    parfor(int j=0;j<m;++){
        if(j == 2) preturn;
        printf('j=%d\n",j);
        while(1) count++;
    }
}
```

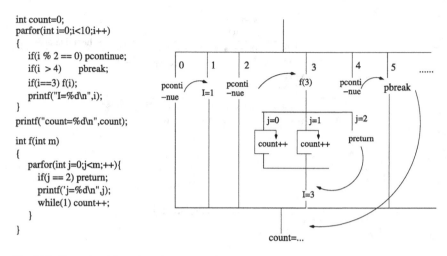

Fig. 3.20 Example of Pcontinue, Pbreak and Preturn

continue, break can be used only in the scope of sequential loops not in parallel constructs and so it the return-statement.

An example that clarifies the differences between these instructions is provided in Fig. 3.20. Here, *pcontinue* skips over iterations $i = 0, i = 2, i = 4$ so that iteration $I = 1$ prints its value and iteration $I = 3$ calls $f(m)$. $f(3)$ spawns three threads out of which two increments *count* using an infinite loop. The last thread spawned in $f(3)$ ($J = 2$) executes preturn which terminates the tree of threads spawned by $f(3)$ printing $I = 3$. Thread $I = 5$ executes pbreak thus terminating threads $I = 6, \ldots, I = 9$.

As to the mechanism that kills all the threads in a sub-tree, it follows that all threads (suspended, running, and those in the ready-queue) must be killed before new threads are generated. This is because new threads can be generated by threads of the sub-tree in a faster rate than the rate in which they are killed. The thread killing-mechanism must be implemented as a global operation that halts the scheduler and the generation of any new thread spawned from the sub-tree that is being killed. This can be done by using thread-ids that are formed by adding their iteration-id as a suffix to the id of the thread that generated them (e.g., $root.son_i.son_j$). In this way it is possible to identify and block the generation of new threads by a sub-tree of threads that is currently being killed.

Figure 3.21 includes a search procedure for an element x in a binary tree. Since the search is recursive and parallel then preturn is used to kill all the threads generated by the recursive parblock construct once the value has been found. The value is returned through a global pointer *found*. Note that only the first call to *search()* initiates a thread that waits by executing a busy-wait for x to be found.

The use of preturn,pcontinue and preturn might be simulated through shared memory synchronization, for example, stopping a search by using a common flag, see Fig. 3.22. The advantages of using *pbreak, pcontinue, preturn* are mainly in their

```
node *found=NULL;
search(node *root, int x, int level)
{ if(level == 0)
    parblock {
    {
        if(root->val == x){
            found = root;
        } else parblock {
            if(root->left != NULL) search(root->left,x,level+1);
            :
            if(root->right != NULL) search(root->right,x,level +1);
        }
    } : {
        while(found == NULL); /* busy-wait */
        preturn();
    } }
else {
    if(root->val == x){
        found = root;
    } else parblock {
        if(root->left != NULL) search(root->left,x,level+1);
        :
        if(root->right != NULL) search(root->right,x,level +1);
    }
}
}
}
```

Fig. 3.21 Use of preturn to stop a recursive search

```
search( arr, n, x )
int  arr[], n, x;
{
    int  flag=1;
    parfor (int i= 0; i<p-1; i++ )
    { int  j;
        for(j=i*n/P;j< (i+1)*n/p;j++) {
            if (arr[j] == x) flag=0;
            if (flag == 0) break;
        }
    }epar
    return(flag);
}
```

Fig. 3.22 Terminating a parallel search using a common flag

readability and the fact that a local search might contain other heavy calculations
that are stopped by *pbreak* or *preturn*, but not necessarily by a flag. Moreover, the

operating system may perform a termination on waiting threads while a *flag* control mechanism should wait until all of the threads have been selected and started to run.

3.11 Exercises

3.11.1 Replacing Sync with f&a()

The following program is executed by a parallel machine M which uses the following rules:

1. M has three processors.
2. m performs a context switch every three instructions.
3. No thread migration and processors cannot be idle as long as the queue is not empty.
4. Local variables are mapped to local memory on the processor board.
5. One of the sons' activities is mapped to the same processor which has executed the spawning thread (the father thread).

```
int g=0;

f(n)
int n;
{ int x;
    parblock {
        int i;
        sync;
        for(i=0;i<n;i++){ g = g+1; x=g+i; }
    } : {
        if(n > 1) f(n/2);
        sync;
        *x = y + 2;
    } : {
        int i;
        for(i=0;i<y;i++) { g = g+1; x=g+i; }
        sync;
    }
}
f(8);
```
A sync in three activities in a recursive program.

1. Draw the execution graph G such that:
   (a) Add declarations of variables and parameters, with different thread ids, to every variable.

(b) Loops should contain only inner instructions.

(c) G should be drawn such that all syncs whose execution depend on one another can be connected by a straight dashed line.

2. Using the M definition, assign a processor/time index to every instruction in G. Explain the effect of *sync* on the execution time.

3. Choose a mapping of all variables to the three processors of M and describe how the M definition improves the ratio between local and global memory references.

4. For an arbitrary call $f(n)$;:

(a) Explain why the final value of g is not necessarily zero.

(b) What are the minimal and the maximal final values of g?

(c) Describe in words three execution sequences, one for the maximal value of g, one for the minimal value and one for the value $g = 0$.

(d) What is the effect on the possible values of g of (a) changing $g = g + 1$ to *faa*$(\&g, 1)$;, (b) changing $g = g - 1$ to *faa*$(\&g, -11)$;, (c) changing both $g = g - 1$ and $g = g + 1$ to *faa*$(\&g, +/ - 1)$;?

3.11.2 Draw Program

Consider the following sequential program.

```
#define N 256
int n,A[N][N],B[N][N],T[N][N];
line(x,y,l,dx,dy)
int x,y,l,dx,dy;
{ int i;
   B[x][y] = 1;
   for (i=0;i<l;i++){
      x=x+dx; y=y+dy;
      B[x][y] = 1; } }
drow(d,l)
int d,l; {
   int i,j,k;
   for (i=0;i<n;i++)
      for (j=0;j<n;j++)
         if(A[i][j] == 1){
            k=0;
            if(A[i][j+1] == 0) k = k+1;
            if(A[i][j-1] == 0) k = k+1;
            if(A[i+1][j] == 0) k = k+1;
            if(A[i-1][j] == 0) k = k+1;
            if( (k >= 3) && (d == 1)){
               line(i,j,1,0,1); line(i,j,1,0,-1); }
            if( (k >= 3) && (d == 0)){
               line(i,j,1,1,0); line(i,j,1,-1,0); }
         }
}
```

```
    if (d == 1) d = 0; else d=1;
    for (i=0;i<n;i++)
       for (j=0;j<n;j++)
          if((A[i][j] == 1) || (B[i][j] == 1)) A[i][j] = 1;
    if(l > 2) drow(d,l/2);
 }
 main()
 {
    int i,j;
    scanf("%d",&n);
    for (i=0;i<n;i++)
       for (j=0;j<n;j++) B[i][j]=A[i][j]=0;
    A[n/2][n/2] = 1;
    drow(1,n/4);
    for (i=0;i<n;i++){
       for (j=0;j<n;j++) printf("%1d",A[i][j]);
    }
 }
```
draw program

1. What is the operation of *draw* on A[][]?
2. Write the code obtained from *draw* by a direct parallelization.
3. For the execution of *draw* with p processors and array size n, compute the following:

   Tp the direct execution time defined in Sect. 2.6.
   $T(R)$ the estimated time. This includes the computation of: N, D, W, S_s, S_l, S_g, F_{bus}. Execute *parfpaint* on the simulator and compare the time statistics to the previous times.

4. Create a simple, fully recursive version of *draw* (without 'IF') and transform it into a parallel program. Compute the direct execution time and the estimation time for this program. Discuss the advantage of the recursive version compared to the non recursive one. Execute the new program on the simulator and compare the results to those of the previous version.

3.12 Bibliographic Notes

There are many levels and types of NUMA architectures (Larowe and Schlatter Ellis 1991) for shared memory machines. Given a hierarchy of memory devices $d_0, d_1, d_2, \ldots$ (e.g., $d_0 = registers$, $d_1 = L1\_cache$, $d_2 = DRAM\_memory$) a NUMA machine is formed by using an interconnection network (bus, crossbar, ...) to connect separate d_is of different CPUs while sharing by using a single memory device of all the remaining levels $d_{i+1}, d_{i+2}, \ldots$. Once this is done we have two options regarding the shared level d_i:

- Either each d_i of a CPU contains a different part of the memory space and the communication network allows all the other CPUs to access a given d_i remotely.
- or there are duplications of memory cells among the different d_is and the communication network is used to impose coherency between the d_is.

NUMA architecture implies that some of the memory references made by the underlying cores/CPUs will be to their local d_i and will be thus fast, while other memory references will be slow due to the need to maintain consistency.

Though there are many alternatives to create NUMA architectures, the following can be regarded as the basic set of levels used by NUMA machines:

- Register level NUMA. This is the basic level of NUMA wherein register usage forms the fastest level and next level (cache or memory) is clearly slower. Basically compilers optimize the use of this level by efficiently allocating variables to specific registers (Muchnick 1997).
- Vector level NUMA. Vector operations are used to speedup parallel operations on arrays. They are supported by vector registers that allows operations like vector addition and vector load/store as separate assembler instructions. Vector operations are generated automatically by compilers using several compilation schemes. Reader is referred to Karrenberg (2010) for a comprehensive vector compilation technique including the use of predicated/masked vector operations for vectorizing if-then-else statements.
- Cache coherent NUMA (ccNUMA). Caches at each core form the third level of memory hierarchy. Since the cache is partitioned to three levels $L1, L2, L3$ (where $L1$ is the faster and smallest in size) we have different NUMA levels as well. Typically, multicore (Blake et al. 2009) machines are generated by sharing $L2$ between several cores and impose cache coherency between the $L1$ caches of each core. Thus we obtain a NUMA machine with several costs of memory references depending if its $L1 - hit, L2 - hit$ and so forth.
- Last level of sharing is formed over a cluster of computes where d_i is the different memories at each machine. In order to form shared memory complete pages are moved between the different machines. In distributed shared memory (DSM) systems (Keleher et al. 1993; Nitzberg and Lo 2002) the range of shared memory addresses is partitioned between the different machines, implemented by validating/invalidating page-table entries of pages that do/do-not belong to the partition currently allocated to this machine. This form of shared memory creates sequential consistency as no memory cell is duplicated in more than one machine however it may result in too frequent expensive page migrations. Consequently several DSM systems tried to relax the consistency model that is maintained by the underline DSM system, e.g., Keleher et al. (1992) or Ben-Asher and Podvolny (2001).

Constructs for explicit array partition have been used in particular in High Performance Fortran (HPF) (Loveman 1993). HPF contains directives for data distribution among multiple processors, and for alignment of different data structures and in particular multi-dimension arrays. André et al. (1990) describe Pandora, a language annotation that allows the user to express data partitioning and mappings between data and threads. Explicit techniques to partition data structures where also proposed in Amza et al. (2002) proposing special form of parfor-loops where arrays can be partition using arbitrary distribution functions. Explicit Data Placement (XDP: Bala et al. 1993) is another technique for explicit data-partition for SPMD programs with explicit operations to move data between the processors after the partition is made.

Many works address the issue of automating data partition, and in particular array partition to improve locality of parallel shared memory programs. Balasundaram et al. (1991) described a performance estimator to guide data partitioning decisions based on the measured performance of a set of kernel routines. Gupta and Banerjee (1992) collect and combine constraints on data partition of arrays across multiple loops such that the communication of array cells is minimized. Agarwal et al. (2002) show an automatic technique for tiling of loop nests such that cache reuse (locality) is optimized (for Fortran programs). Lim et al. (2001) use an affine loop transformation to improve data locality combining two loop transformations and loop-fusion to replace intermediate array references by scalars and blocking (loop-tiling). Chatterjee et al. (1993) consider automatic array alignment for Fortran-90 programs, where data alignment is an important aspect in improving data locality of caches. Khanna et al. (1997) study the theoretical problem of partitioning an array to p intervals such that the maximal weight of each interval is minimized. Approximated solutions to this problem can be useful in data partition problems.

References

Agarwal, A., Kranz, D., Natarajan, V.: Automatic partitioning of parallel loops and data arrays for distributed shared-memory multiprocessors. IEEE Trans. Parallel Distrib. Syst. **6**(9), 943–962 (2002)

Amza, C., Cox, A.L., Dwarkadas, S., Keleher, P., Lu, H., Rajamony, R., Yu, W., Zwaenepoel, W.: Treadmarks: Shared memory computing on networks of workstations. Computer **29**(2), 18–28 (2002)

André, F., Pazat, J.-L., Thomas, H.: Pandore: A system to manage data distribution. In: Intl. Conf. Supercomputing, pp. 380–388 (1990)

Bala, V., Ferrante, J., Carter, L.: Explicit data placement (XDP): A methodology for explicit compile-time representation and optimization of data movement. In: Symp. Principles & Practice of Parallel Programming, pp. 139–148 (1993)

Balasundaram, V., Fox, G., Kennedy, K., Kremer, U.: A static performance estimator to guide data partitioning decisions. In: Symp. Principles & Practice of Parallel Programming, pp. 213–223 (1991)

Ben-Asher, Y., Podvolny, D.: Y-Invalidate: A new protocol for implementing weak consistency in DSM systems. Int. J. Parallel Program. **29**(6), 583–606 (2001)

Blake, G., Dreslinski, R., Mudge, T.: A survey of multicore processors. IEEE Signal Process. Mag. **26**(6), 26–37 (2009)

Chatterjee, S., Gilbert, J.R., Schreiber, R., Teng, S.H.: Automatic array alignment in data-parallel programs. In: Proceedings of the 20th ACM SIGPLAN-SIGACT Symposium on Principles of Programming Languages, pp. 16–28. ACM, New York (1993) ISBN 0897915607

Gupta, M., Banerjee, P.: Demonstration of automatic data partitioning techniques for parallelizing compilers on multicomputers. IEEE Trans. Parallel Distrib. Syst. **3**(2), 179–193 (1992)

Karrenberg, R.: Automatic packetization. Technical report, Saarland University, Informatics (2010)

Keleher, P., Cox, A.L., Zwaenepoel, W.: Lazy release consistency for software distributed shared memory. Comput. Archit. News **20**(2), 13–21 (1992)

Keleher, P., Cox, A.L., Dwarkadas, S., Zwaenepoel, W.: Treadmarks: Distributed shared memory on standard workstations and operating systems. Rice University, Dept. of Computer Science (1993)

Khanna, S., Muthukrishnan, S., Skiena, S.: Efficient array partitioning. In: Automata, Languages and Programming, pp. 616–626 (1997)

Larowe Jr., R.P., Schlatter Ellis, C.: Experimental comparison of memory management policies for NUMA multiprocessors. ACM Trans. Comput. Syst. **9**(4), 319–363 (1991)

Lim, A.W., Liao, S.W., Lam, M.S.: Blocking and array contraction across arbitrarily nested loops using affine partitioning. ACM SIGPLAN Not. **36**(7), 103–112 (2001)

Loveman, D.B.: High performance Fortran. IEEE Parallel Distrib. Technol. **1**(1), 25–42 (1993)

Muchnick, S.S.: Advanced Compiler Design and Implementation. Morgan Kaufmann, San Mateo (1997). ISBN 1558603204

Nitzberg, B., Lo, V.: Distributed shared memory: A survey of issues and algorithms. Computer **24**(8), 52–60 (2002)

Chapter 4
Multicore Machines

Multicore machines are an extension of the single core personal computer that include several processors (cores) and a shared memory. As such, they are suitable for running parallel programs, including ParC, that use shared memory. Multicore machines replace single processor personal computers and are thus widely used. In this work we will use the term "core" instead of processor or CPU to indicate that several cores are packed in a single chip or actually in one die, functioning as a multi-processor machine. Basically, the parallelism available in multicore machines is used by the operating system to execute several unrelated processes in parallel (e.g., running two compilations and a web search on different cores). We will demonstrate that multicore machines can be used to execute parallel programs efficiently, programs that spawn many threads all communicating through shared memory. However, as an extension of a single core machine designed for personal computers, the mechanism using the shared memory is not as effective as it would have been had it been designed from scratch as a parallel machine. In fact, the shared memory of multicore machines is basically a simulation of shared memory over the single port memory module of the single core personal computer. Thus, it is important to understand how the shared memory of multicore machines works in order to determine how ParC can be implemented and used by multicore machines.

As indicated earlier, shared memory is memory that holds a set of shared variables common to several threads that are executed in parallel by a set of cores. Thus, if one core executes a write operation $x = 1$; and immediately afterwards another core reads this value by executing $if(x == 1)\ldots$, it should observe that the value of x is now 1. Any implementation of shared memory should support the following properties:

- A memory module is usually a sequential device allowing only one access at a time. However, shared memory must support multiple parallel accesses of all cores. Consequently, shared memory must be assembled by a set of P separate memory modules $M_1, \ldots, M_P$ so that the P cores can at least have the ability to access it in parallel.
- A communication mechanism allowing each core to update every M_i must be implemented. Otherwise, information from one core can not be accessed by another.

Y. Ben-Asher, *Multicore Programming Using the ParC Language*,
Undergraduate Topics in Computer Science,
DOI 10.1007/978-1-4471-2164-0_4, © Springer-Verlag London 2012

- Regular memory modules used in personal computers are typically 100 slower than the cores used for processing. Thus, any memory system must use local caches between the cores and the slower memory module to overcome the large memory latencies of regular memories. When a core is trying to read/write a shared variable x, it will first attempt to fetch/modify x from a copy stored in the cache of this core. The use of caches is a must in modern machines because it is the only way to speed up memory access times. Thus, any shared memory machine should assume that cores first read/write from/to their local caches. A problem occurs if a local cache copy of x is not updated to the most recent value amongst all of the recent updates of x made by all of the other cores. Thus, a coherence protocol must be used to guarantee that the value of x read by one core is consistent with the most recent update of x.

Shared memory in a multicore machine relies on the operation of the local caches that each core is using. These local caches act as the P memory modules that can be accessed in parallel by the P cores. Hence, the first step in understanding multicore machines is to understand how a single cache works.

4.1 Caches

A cache is basically a 2D table of cells with k rows and w columns. The cache's cells hold copies of the recently used variables. Unlike memory modules, the cache can hold a non-consecutive set of memory addresses. Therefore, the cache acts as a search device capable of answering queries such as: "Is the memory address 6025 currently stored in the cache or not?" The cache of a core is significantly faster than memory modules. However, at any given time, it can hold only a small fraction of the memory cells used by the program executed by its core. Basically, the cache stores the last k memory addresses used by the current program.

Thus, we assume that the next variable that a program will access is likely to be one of the recent variables it accessed in the past, e.g., re-accessing the index of a loop is likely to occur frequently when the loop is being executed. Another mechanism used by caches to increase the probability that the next memory reference a program makes will already be in the cache is to fetch a set of consecutive memory cells every time an address is fetched from memory to the cache. For example, we would likely assume that if a program accesses $A[i]$, its next sequence of memory references will be to $A[i + 1], A[i + 2], \ldots, A[i + k]$. In general, caches are complicated devices that can use several mechanisms to increase the probability that the next memory reference will be a cache "hit," allowing faster access to variables compared to the longer access times it would have taken to fetch these variables from the memory. In this section we consider a very simplified model of caches sufficient to understand their use in multicore machines. Recall that the cache is smaller than the main memory, and thus, only a small fraction of the variables can be stored in the cache at any given time. Hence, the cache is managed dynamically: a row can be evicted (flushed) from the cache to the main memory to make room for new variables. The cache is managed as follows:

- Each row holds w consecutive addresses from the memory, where typically there are $w = 4, 8, 16$ memory cells.
- The mapping of a variable to a cache line is done based on its address in the main memory. The least significant $\log w$ bits of the address will determine the position of a variable in a row, while the previous $\log k$ bits (before the $\log w$ bits) are used to determine the row.
- Read/write operations are first directed to the cache if the desired variable is not stored in the cache and a "cache miss" occurs. A cache miss is handled by fetching the suitable w words from the memory and bringing it to the correct line in the cache. The core is blocked until the cache is updated from the main memory.
- The remaining $n - \log k - \log w$ bits forming the prefix of the addresses of the w cells that are in a cache line are used to tag this cache line. In this way, it is possible to tell if a given address is currently in the cache. Another tag, "valid-bit," indicates if the values found in a cache line are valid or not. In other words, are they the most updated value of this address? Note that in this form of direct mapping each memory address can be mapped to only one cache line. If there are n memory cells, then each cache line is shared by $\frac{n}{k \cdot w}$ variables.
- In order to increase the utilization of the cache lines, caches are made to be "l-way associative," allowing the use of l different cache lines to store any given address. Figure 4.1 illustrates the difference between a direct mapping cache and a 2-way set associative cache.
- When the cache is full and a new variable must be stored, one of the l-way-associative lines is "flushed" to the main memory and the new variable is stored in this line. The cache line that is evicted from the cache is the Least Recently Used (LRU) row. On a practical level, LRU works well. However, poor patterns of memory references can cause large numbers of misses. Consider, for example, a loop that repeatedly accesses $w_1 \longrightarrow w_2 \longrightarrow \cdots \longrightarrow w_{l+1}$ all mapped to lines $0, 1, \ldots, l-1, 1$ in the same l-way associative set. After the first rows $0, 1, \ldots, l-1$ have been filled, the last address w_{l+1} will cause a miss. The LRU will evict line 0, which is accessed next. Thus, w_1 will be a cache miss as well causing w_2 to be evicted from the cache. In general, each w_i that is accessed will evict the next address that is accessed. In this case, had we kept $w_1, \ldots, w_l$ constantly in the cache, we would have had a miss only for w_{l+1}.
- It is common that a cache miss will prefetch more lines than the needed addresses, assuming that the next set of addresses that will be needed is consecutive or has a fixed offset. Note that prefetching will not solve this "bad" example because the "distance" between w_i, w_{i+1} is likely to be greater than the prefetching range.
- Usually, a memory cache transaction can involve more than one line, flushing and fetching a block of lines.

There are two possible variants of memory updating in caches:

Write through (WT) The information is written to both the line in the cache and to the line in the main memory.

Write back(WB) The information is written only to the line in the cache. The modified cache line is written to the main memory only when it is replaced.

Fig. 4.1 2-way set
associative versus a direct
map cache

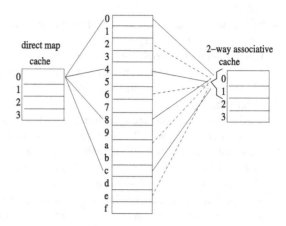

Pros and cons of each variant:

- WT: Read misses can not result in writes to the memory. In other words, if a cache line is evicted from the cache, there is no need to update the memory with its content.
- WB: No repeated writes to the same location.

We remark that WT always combines with write buffers so that the core is not blocked until the write to the main memory is completed.

4.2 Basic Mode of Operation of Multicore Machines

Multicore machines are parallel machines that simulate shared memory using caches, so that the set of memory modules that constitute the shared memory is the local cache of each core. As claimed earlier, for speed and efficiency each core of a multicore system keeps a cache that is periodically updated from a common shared memory module called the main memory. The set of P caches and the main memory are connected by a bus that acts as a communication network. Each core can read/write values from the shared memory through its local cache. Figure 4.2 illustrates the structure of a multicore machine and some basic operations that are used to access the shared memory:

- Every core is connected to a common bus.
- A read/write operation of a shared variable can be directed to the local cache if one of the cache's rows contain this variable. Otherwise, a cache miss occurs. Note that local read/write operations are faster than all other operations (about 5 ns in Intel and AMD machines) and can be made in parallel by all of the cores.
- Caches snoop on that bus to detect update operations made by some other core to the memory.
- Processors can update their caches based on the values snooped on the bus.

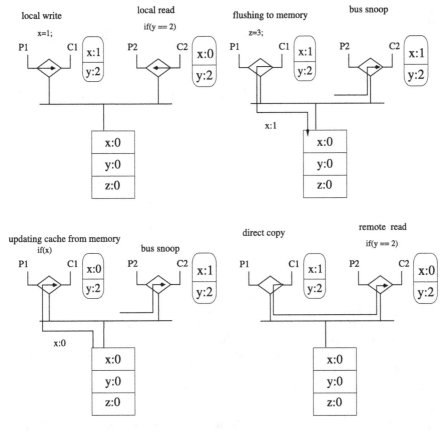

Fig. 4.2 Basic operations in a multicore machine

- Remote memory operations between a cache and the main memory can occur when

  1. a cache miss occurs and a cache line is brought from the memory or
  2. a cache line is evicted from the cache and "flushed" to the main memory.

  These types of transactions are significantly slower (150 ns in Intel and AMD multicore machines). Note that only one transaction with the main memory can occur at a given time. A memory transaction made by one core can be executed in parallel with local read/write/snoop operations in other cores.

  It follows that the general architecture of multicores can permit memory inconsistency. Consider the dual core machine in Fig. 4.3 executing the following steps:

  1. Initially, $x, y, z = 0$ are stored in the main memory and the two caches are empty.
  2. P1 is the set $x = 1$, which resides in its local cache. At the same "time," P2 executes $z = x$ and obtains $x = 0$ from the main memory.
  3. P1 executes $y = 2$; residing in its local cache.

Fig. 4.3 Memory coherence
violated on a multicore
machine

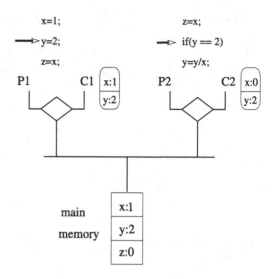

4. P1 executes $z = x$ but this time its cache is full and $y : 2$ is flushed to the main memory while z, x resides in its local cache.
5. P2 executes $if(y == 2)$. Given that y is not in its local cache, $y : 2$ is brought from the main memory to its local cache.
6. P2 executes y/x. Given that x is stored in its local cache, the value $x : 0$ is brought from the cache.
7. The operation y/x in P2 is a division by zero and the program crashes.

The memory inconsistency is reflected by the fact that in spite of the fact that $y = 2$ was executed after $x = 1$, P2 "sees" the updated value of y but not the updated value of x. Hence, the shared memory of a multicore machine needs a management scheme that ensures that all cores keep an updated version of all data values stored in the shared memory. This is called memory coherence. Thus, a protocol must be devised to ensure memory coherence in multicore machines.

4.3 The MESI Protocol for Memory Coherence in Multicore Machines

Memory consistency is the heart of the multicore machine, allowing us to view it as a single shared memory machine and not as a set of sequential machines connected by a communication network. There are many protocols for memory consistency that have been proposed and studied. However, we focus mainly on the Modify-Exclusive-Shared-Invalidate (MESI) protocol that is widely used by commercial vendors. In the data cache, MESI maintains consistency with the caches of other cores and with an external memory module.

Intuitively, the MESI protocol uses the following ideas. MESI is based on a data ownership model where:

- at any given time, either all copies of a variable in all of the caches are updated,
- or, at most one core can have a "dirty" copy that is not consistent with the main memory.

A copy of a variable in a cache is "dirty" if it has a different value than the most updated value (last write) of this variable. Writes are typically not broadcasted to all of the cores, but cache lines containing a requested address are transferred to the cache of the core that needs it. Writes of invalid data will cause data invalidation in other caches.

In the MESI protocol, a two bit tag is used to designate the status of each address of the shared memory in the caches. The MESI protocol is specified by a transition diagram including the following states and actions (as described in Fig. 4.4):

Modified(Dirty) state When the status of a cache line is modified, the data value in the cache has been altered but is not currently held in the cache of any other core. This status indicates that the address must be written back to the shared memory before it is overwritten by another word. Thus, in this state, a modified cache line resides exclusively in this cache and its content is modified relative to its state in the main memory.

Exclusive state When the status is exclusive, the data value in this cache line is held only by the current core and has not been modified. When it is time to overwrite this value in the cache, it does not need to be written back to the shared memory. Thus, in this state a cache line in an exclusive state resides exclusively in this cache and the content is the same as that of the memory.

Shared state The shared status means that copies of this value may be stored in the caches of other cores. Thus, in this state, a line that resides in this cache may be shared with other caches as well, but all of the values of this line in all of the caches are the same. The content of the memory is for a line in a shared state that is updated as well.

Invalid state The invalid status indicates that this cache line is not valid. In order to validate its data, the cache line must be updated from the main memory.

Apart from the states, MESI is defined using a set of actions that each core performs in order to

- Detect that a change has occurred in the status of a local cache line due to some action issued by other cores or by the current core. Here an action serves as an event that can be detected by any core.
- In order to complete a change in the state of a cache line, the current core may need to issue an action.

Thus, MESI is defined as an automaton where a change in the current state of a cache line is triggered by an action and results in another action. The actions are performed using a bus broadcast mechanism (including the snoops). Hence, all of the actions are (a) atomic and (b) serialized. The set of actions used by MESI include the following:

PrRd/PrWr Processor read/write, a core read/write of a value to/from the memory.

BusRd/BusRdX/BusWB Are the bus actions where:

BusRd Asks for a copy with no intention of modifying it. Data could come from memory or another cache.

BusRdX Asks for a copy with the intention of modifying it. This operation should invalidate all other copies residing in other cores.

BusRd(S) Refers to a shared line asserted on a BusRd transaction, and *BusRd(S')* indicates that the line is not shared. The shared signal that is asserted is a value returned by another core as a result of a *BusRd* operation. Thus, if $core_i$ issued a *BusRd* operation of the variable, the shared signal S/S' is asserted depending on whether or not another $core_j$ has the value of the variable in its cache. The shared signal is thus part of the events that trigger a new state even though it is obtained as a result of an action performed due to a change in state. This may cause some confusion because the way automata are written is *new_state : event* $\longrightarrow$ *action*. Thus, even though the S/S' are written in the action section, they are actually part of the event that triggers a new state. Hence, MESI requires a shared signal to detect if other caches have a copy of a given cache line. State changes in MESI due to shared signals include: *Invalid* $\longrightarrow$ *Shared* if a shared signal is asserted by any other cache and *Invalid* $\longrightarrow$ *Exclusive* otherwise.

Flush Updates memory; the cache controller puts the content on the bus and the memory is updated. If there is cache-to-cache sharing, only one cache flushes the data.

A diagram of the states of the MESI protocol is presented in Fig. 4.4 and the following table, where each entry is of the form *event/action*:

$fr \rightarrow$	M	E	S	I
M	PrRd, PrWr/−	−	BusRd/Flush	BusRdX/Flush
E	PrWr/−	PrRd/−	BusRd/Flush	BusRdX/Flush
S	PrWr/BusRdX	−	PrRd/−, BusRd/Flush	BusRdX/Flush
I	PrWr/BusRdX	PrRd/BusRd(S')	PrRd/BusRd(S)	−

The MESI protocol implies the following conclusions regarding the state of the cache lines in every core:

in state modified(M) the cache line is valid for use, the memory copy is updated, other caches do not contain copies of this line, and an update to this line does not cause a bus transaction. We may draw this conclusion due the fact that $S/I \longrightarrow M$ transitions yield *BusRdX* actions, which lead to state-I for all other cores (considering the column that leads to state-I in the MESI table). In the case of $M/E \longrightarrow M$ transitions, we already assume that no other core contains a copy of this cache line. Hence, there is no need for any operations. The fact that the cache line is valid follows from the fact that in order to be in state-M in a core, a cache line must be updated by a PrWr by this core. The fact that the memory is not updated results from the fact that a change to state-M does not involve a flush.

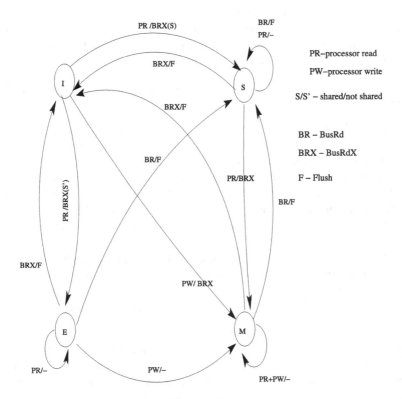

Fig. 4.4 Diagram of the states of the MESI protocol

in state Exclusive(E) the cache line is valid, the memory copy is updated, other caches do not contain copies of this line, and an update to this line does not cause a bus transaction. The argument for the previous case of state-M is also valid here. The claim that in this case, the memory is also updated is due to the fact that:

1. The only way to reach state-E (except already from state-E) is from state-I (see the column of state-E in the MESI table of states).
2. In this transition $I \longrightarrow E$, so we know that the cache line is not shared. Thus, it is held by one core at most.
3. All of the other transitions to I involved a flush operation (see the column for state-I). Hence, the memory is updated.

in state Shared(S) the cache line is valid, the memory copy is updated, other caches may contain copies of this line. An update to this line will cause a bus transaction, and by snooping, will update other caches containing this line. The fact that in this case the memory is updated is due to the fact that:

1. All transitions to state-S involve a flush operation (based on the state-S column) except the $I \longrightarrow S$ transition.
2. All of the transitions to state-I involve a flush to the memory.

All other claims can be proved similarly.

in state Invalid(I) the cache line is not valid, the memory copy is probably not updated, and other caches may contain updated copies of this line. An update to this line will cause a bus transaction, which will follow immediately.

From the perspective of the core, the MESI transition table can be interpreted as follows:

Read-hit line is in state M, E or S Data is provided to the core by the cache and no bus cycle is initialized. The next state remains the same as before.

Read-miss line is in state I Data item does not exist in the cache; a read bus cycle will be generated by the core. An intent to read request is broadcasted on the bus to all of the other cores' caches. If the line is obtained from another core's cache, the next state will be S because this line is clearly shared. If the line is obtained from the memory, the next state will be E because the line is now exclusively in this cache.

Write-hit line in states M, E, S The local cache is updated with the change and the next state will be M. If the current state is S or I (a cache miss), then a write-through cycle is generated on the bus to update the memory and/or invalidate the contents of other caches. The state transition occurs after the write-through cycle completes on the bus.

Note that memory writes are buffered before they are issued to the memory such that another memory update issued, even by the same core, can reach the memory before a current update. Thus, there is no guarantee of synchronization between completion of the memory writes on the bus and the execution instructions after the current write. A serializing instruction needs to be executed to synchronize writes with the next instruction if necessary.

4.4 Counting MESI's Transitions and Overhead

In this section we follow a detailed example of how MESI executes several instructions in parallel. Figure 4.5 illustrates the first stages of MESI when three cores execute:

step	P1	P2	P3
0:	int reg1;	int reg1;	int reg1;
1:	reg1 = x;		reg1 = z;
2:	x = 1;	z = 2;	
3:		x = 2;	reg1 = x;
4:	reg1 = z;		x = 3;
5:		reg1 = y;	reg1 = y;

Fig. 4.5 Steps 1, 2, 3

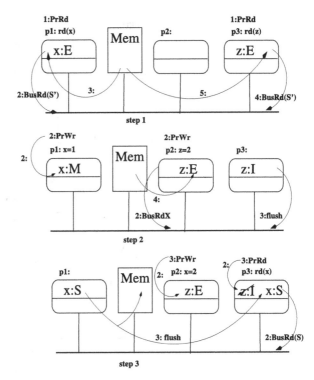

Step 1 In both loads, a cache miss happens so each cache puts a BusRd onto the bus for the information. The main memory owns the data and will provide the up-to-date data. P1's cache loads x in the E state. P3's cache loads z in the E state as well.

Step 2 P1 has x in the exclusive state, so on the cache hit, it does not need to have a bus transaction. z is not in P2's cache, so the cache places a BusRdX to gain exclusive access. The main memory provides the data because it is not stale even though P3's cache has the data. z is loaded in M state and P3's cache invalidates its copy of z.

Step 3 P2 executes another store to z. It already has exclusive access to z and the store results in a cache hit. No bus transaction is issued by P2's cache. P3 wants to load x. This results in a cache miss and the cache issues a BusRd transaction. P1's cache asserts the S signal because it has a dirty x and provides the up-to-date data through a flush. P1 changes its state to S. P3's cache loads x in the S state.

Step 4 (described in Fig. 4.6) P3 executes a store to x. Both P1 and P3 have an up-to-date, unmodified x. Since x is in state-S, P3 issues a BusRdX transaction that invalidates x in P1's cache. P1 wants to load z and flush x out. However, since x is in state-I, no flush is needed. P1's cache does not have z, so it issues a BusRd transaction. P2's cache turns on the S signal, so P1's cache knows to load z in the S state. P2's cache provides z for P1 and cancels access to the main memory through a flush.

Fig. 4.6 Steps 4, 5

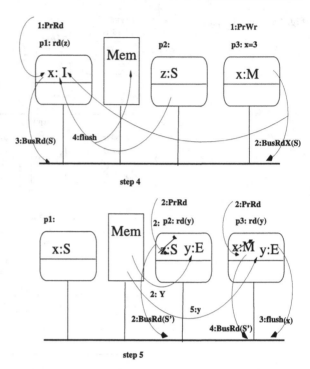

Step 5   (described in Fig. 4.6) P2 wants to load y. This generates a cache miss. P2's cache issues a BusRd transaction. The S signal is not asserted, so it knows that it has exclusive access to y. The main memory provides the data for y. Should the state of z be changed in P1 because it is the only cache that has a copy of z?

As can be seen, we have executed 10 instructions in 5 steps using 6 BusRd operations and 4 memory-flush operations. Clearly, since all BusRD/flush operations are made sequentially over the bus, and the overhead of each operation is relatively high, the execution time of this code will be longer than a sequential execution of this code using one core.

4.5 The MESI Protocol Preserves Sequential Consistency

Sequential Consistency (SC) can be defined as follows: "For any core the sequence of values that are read is consistent with a single serialization of the writes made by all cores." In this respect each read operation can be regarded as if it is between two writes in this sequential order of the writes. All of the cores should see assignments to two variables in the same order. In general, MESI is sufficient to guarantee serialization as follows:

- Writes and reads that are not cache hits are serialized due to the use of the BusRd action.

- Write atomicity: If a read returns the value of a write, that write has already become visible to all of the other caches. This is evident by looking at all of the *PrRd* actions in the MESI states table that are either cache hits in M or S states or involve *BusRd(S/S')* actions. Clearly, a *BusRd* action that returns a value must obtain it after the BusRdX operation that modified it has completed its action (due to the bus serialization). In the first case, any cache hit implies that all of the other cores have already invalidated their copies or the value being read is in a shared state. This implies that all previous writes have been completed.

Formally, the SC validity of the MESI protocol can be argued as follows:

1. All writes that do not involve BusRd or BusRdX are made in modified or exclusive states. Hence, only one core can perform a sequence of such writes to the same address. Thus, any consecutive sequence of such writes made by $core_i$ to the same address can be replaced by the last write Wl_i whose value will be read or moved to another core in the future.
2. All other writes made in other states involve a bus operation and thus can be sequentially ordered in one global total order (denoted by OW) following the order in which they occurred on the bus.
3. Similarly, all of the read operations that involve bus operations can be ordered in a global total order OR.
4. Given that both OW and OR used the bus, there is one global total order GWR, which is a merge of OW and OR.
5. Given that each Wl_i was read using a bus transaction, the Wl_is can be imbedded in GWR such that each Wl_i is inserted before the remote read operation that obtained its value. Let $GWRl$ denote the resulting order.
6. It follows that at every time of the execution each core's cache contains an ordered sub-sequence of read-write operations from $GWRl$. Consequently, any two ordered reads performed by a core $W_i = R_t(); \ldots; W_j = R_{t+k}()$ must satisfy that $i \leq j$ in the $GWRl$ order.
7. It thus follows that all of the values returned by read operations (either due to bus transactions or local hits) are consistent with $GWRl$.

Figure 4.7 illustrates the effect of the sequential ordering of BusRdX (BRX) and BusRd (BR) on imposing memory coherence. Here, two cores modify a shared variable x to be either 1 or -1 and write after executing $y = 2$ and $z = 3$. Two other cores $P2$, $P3$ read y and z, obtaining $y + z == 5$. As the order of the writes is the same for all of the cores, it must follow that if both $P2$ and $P3$ obtained $y = z == 5$ then for both, either $x == 1$ or $x == -1$. Thus, it should follow that regardless of how we order the reads of x in $P2$ and in $P3$, we will get that $x(P3) == x(P2)$. As depicted in Fig. 4.7, there is no possibility that $P3$ will obtain $x == 1$, because it can initiate the $read(x)$ only after $read(y) + read(z)$, which can happen only after the conflict between $x = 1$; and $x = -1$ has been resolved. We assumed that initially all of the variables were in state 'S' with a value of 0.

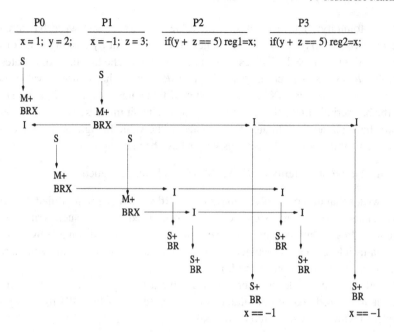

Fig. 4.7 Writes of shared variables appear in the same order for all cores

4.6 The MOESI Extension

The MOESI protocol is an extension of the MESI protocol that adds a new status called **owned**. A core can write to a cache line it owns even if other cores are holding copies. The owner state indicates that this cache holds the most recent copy of the data. When a core modifies data it owns, it is responsible for updating the copies being held by other cores. The MOESI protocol is used in multicore CPUs in which core-to-core communication is much faster than access to the main memory.

A comparison between MESI and MOESI yields the following:

```
MESI                              MOESI
* read-exclusive bus transaction: * One cache can hold a block of
    1- Write to a shared or            data in the owner state while
       invalid block.                  the others are in a shared
    2- Invalidate other copies         state.
       of the block.
                                  * The owner of a cache block
* Modified block has to be          updates other caches reading
  written back to memory            the block.
  when another cache reads
  the invalid block                * The copy in the main memory
                                     can be stale.

                                  * Writing the modified cache
                                     back to memory can be avoided.
```

MOESI (see Fig. 4.8) contains one additional state, "owned," on top of the MESI protocol. The O state is implemented to facilitate cache-to-cache transfer when the

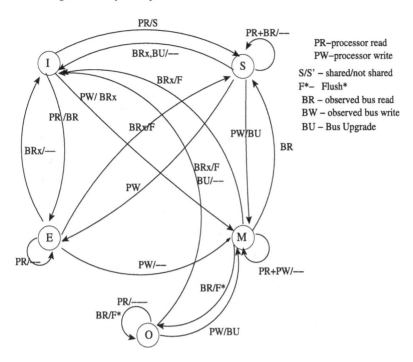

Fig. 4.8 Diagram of the MOESI protocol

cache line is modified by a processor P (in M state) and can be supplied directly by P. Similar to the S state, a cache line in the O state in one processor will be present in at least one other processor's cache. Note that the memory will have a stale version of this line. In the MOESI state diagram below, we also introduce a new transaction called BusUpgr (Bus upgrade) to substitute for BusRdX in some transitions where we can simply invalidate the cache lines of others without incurring an actual data exclusive read. In this simulation, cache-to-cache transfers take place only during the action of flush in which the requested cache line is sent directly to the requester by the processor having the same line in E, M or O state without updating the memory. Note that all the other "flush" transactions will update the memory and a request will receive the line from the memory.

Figures 4.9, 4.10 and 4.11 follow the execution of three instructions by three cores, comparing the different actions and states that result from using MESI as opposed to MOESI.

4.7 Preserving the Locality Principle of ParC

Parallel systems often allow thread migration where a thread that was executed in one processor is suspended and its execution is then resumed by another processor.

➜ P1: Load A   ; P2: Load B ; P3: Load B
P1: Write A=7; P2: -   ; P3: Write B=5
P1: Read B   ; P2: Read A ; P3: -

	MESI			MOESI		
	P1	*P2*	*P3*	*P1*	*P2*	*P3*
Processor Op	RD	RD	RD	RD	RD	RD
Status	Miss	Miss	Miss	Miss	Miss	Miss
Bus Transaction	RD(!s)	RD(!s)	RD(s)	RD	RD	RD
Cache	A [E]	B [E] -- -Flush to memory B [S]	*provided from memory B [S]	A [E]	B [E] -- snoop B [S]	*provided from P2 cache B [O]

Fig. 4.9 MESI vs. MOESI after executing the first instruction of each core

P1: Load A   ; P2: Load B ; P3: Load B
➜ P1: Write A=7; P2: -   ; P3: Write B=5
P1: Read B   ; P2: Read A ; P3: -

	MESI			MOESI		
	P1	*P2*	*P3*	*P1*	*P2*	*P3*
Processor Op	WR	--	WR	WR	--	WR
Status	Hit	--	Hit	Hit	--	Hit
Bus Transaction	--	--	Upgr	--	--	Upgr
Cache	A [E] A=7 [M]	B [E] B [S] -snoop B [I]	B [S] B=5 [M]	A [E] A=7 [M]	B [S] -snoop B [I]	B [O] B = 5 [O]

Fig. 4.10 MESI vs. MOESI after executing the second instruction of each core

The locality principle of *ParC* forbids this and requires that although threads may be suspended, they must be resumed in the same processor where their stack resides. As explained earlier, this requirement preserves the *ParC* locality principle where

P1: Load A   ; P2: Load B ; P3: Load B
P1: Write A=7; P2: -   ; P3: Write B=5
➔ P1: Read B   ; P2: Read A ; P3: -

	MESI			*MOESI*		
	P1	*P2*	*P3*	*P1*	*P2*	*P3*
Processor Op	RD	RD	-	RD	RD	-
Status	Miss	Miss	-	Miss	Miss	-
Bus Transaction	WB A RD(S)	RD(!S)	Flush	WB A RD	RD	Upgr
Cache	~~A [E]~~ ~~A=7 [M]~~ B [S]	~~B [E]~~ ~~B [S]~~ ~~B [I]~~ A [E]	~~B [S]~~ B=5 [M] B [S]	~~A [E]~~ A=7 [M] B [O] *P3 is the provider	~~B [E]~~ ~~B [S]~~ ~~B [I]~~ A [E]	~~B [O]~~ ~~B=5 [O]~~ B [S]

Fig. 4.11   MESI vs. MOESI after executing the third instruction of each core

memory references to local variables of a thread T that are made by T must be executed as fast as local memory references. This rule of implementation is true for the abstract machine model where each processor/core has a separate, fixed part of the shared memory address space. Multicore machines deviate from this model. As illustrated the memory range of addresses stored in each cache changes dynamically. Consequently, memory references to local variables in multicore machines are not guaranteed to be fast operations. Moreover, even if all of the variables reside in the cache, the use of MESI can lead to violation of the locality principle of *ParC*. In a multicore machine (even without thread migrations) a local variable v of a thread T residing in core p_i can be updated by a descendent thread of T residing in another core p_j. In this case, v_i will be in an exclusive state in p_j's cache. Hence, the next time that T references v will be a cache miss violating the locality principle of *ParC*.

In order to preserve the locality principle of *ParC* in multicore machines, its implementation must satisfy the following conditions:

- All local memory references must be cache hits.
- All reads of local variables must be to shared or exclusive cache lines.
- Updating local variables should be in exclusive state.
- Non-local memory references may result in a cache miss or BusRd.

The fact that threads do not migrate is clearly necessary but not sufficient to guarantee these conditions.

Clearly, extending the no-migration rule to the requirement that all descendent threads that can access a local variable of T must be executed by the same core where T resides is not practical. Such a requirement may lead to fully sequential execution where all threads are executed by the same core. We can, however, relax this requirement so that it will allow the scheduler more freedom:

- Let a thread T_j be a descendent of thread T_i at run time.
- We say that T_j may conflict with T_i if T_j can reference a local variable of T_i statically. By the term "statically" we mean a direct reference of T_j, at source code, to a local variable of T_i. This excludes indirect references of T_j through pointers to local variables of T_i. Note that T_j cannot reference local variables of T_i through function calls because the scoping rules of C do not allow this.
- If T_i is alive at the creation of T_j, then T_j must be scheduled in the same core that is currently executing T_i.

While the above practice will preserve the locality principle of *ParC*, it may affect load balancing. Consider the following code segment. Due to access to x, all threads of the external parfor statement must be executed in the same core. Similarly, the threads spawned by the inner parfor must be executed in the same core because they access y, a local variable of each thread spawned by the external parfor. It is clearly better to distribute the threads of the outer parfor between the cores and pay the MESI overhead for the few non-local accesses to x than eventually execute all threads sequentially. Thus, in practice, we may relax the above locality rules requiring that: two threads T_i, T_j should reside in the same core if some constant fraction of the number of memory references that T_j executes are to local variables of T_i.

```
#define N 10
int x,A[n];
parfor int   i;1;N;1{
int i,y,B[n]=0;
    y = x+A[x];
    B[0] = y;
    for(i=1;i<n;i++) B[i] = y+ B[i-1];
    parfor int   j;1;N;1{
    int i,z,C[n]=0;
        z = y+1;
        C[0] = z;
        for(i=1;i<n;i++) C[i] = z+ C[i-1];
        y = C[n-1];
    } epar
        x = y+B[n-1];
} epar
```

The locality principle requires that all threads must be executed in the same core

In conclusion, although this is a simplified model compared to the complexity of the MESI protocol, its rules of locality promote some locality on multicore machines:

- A local variable v of a thread T, may be invalidated if it is accessed by a descending thread of T that is executed by a core other than the one executing T. Note that in this case, we should prefer to schedule a descendent thread on the same processor as the spawning thread.
- A local variable can be evicted from the cache due other variables that are mapped to the same cache line. However, the chances of this problem occurring are not high if the caches are sufficiently large.
- Given that threads do not migrate, their local variables have a strong probability of remaining in the cache until their execution is resumed.

4.8 False Sharing of Cache Lines

In this section we discuss several types of optimizations that can be applied to reduce the number of MESI cache misses and the overhead involved with the resulting BusRD and flush operations. Although the approach assumes that the user will implement these optimizations manually by modifying the source code, we believe that they can also be applied automatically by a suitable compiler.

This is a situation in which two or more variables $x_1, x_2, \ldots, x_k$ reside in the same cache line but are updated separately by different cores. Had these variables been mapped to different cache lines, all of the updates would have been executed by local cache operations because each cache line would be in state E. However, as $x_1, x_2, \ldots, x_k$ are mapped to the same cache line L, each update of x_i by core p_i will invalidate the copies of L in all of the other caches. Consequently, each access to x_i will result in $BusRdX/BusRd$ transactions wherein L ping-pongs between the different caches in vain. Consider, for example, the two threads

| ```
int  B[N],A[N],x,y,w,z;
pparblock {
    int i;
    for(i=0;i<N;i++){
        if(x > 100)
            x = x + A[i];
        else y = y - w+z;
    }
} : {
``` | ```
int i,w,z;
for(i=0;i<N;i++){
    if(w > 100)
        w = w + B[i];
    else z = z - x+y;
} } epar
``` |
|---|---|
| False sharing of variables x and y. | |

Assuming that the else-parts are executed much less often than the then-parts, the first thread will usually access x, while the right thread will usually access w. If

x, y, z, w are mapped to the same cache line, there will be $O(N)$ BusRdX transactions due to the race conditions on x and w between the two threads. The solution in this case is to separate the set of variables into two cache lines. At the source level, this separation can be accomplished as follows:

| ```
int  A[N],x,y,B[N],w,z;
pparblock {
    int i;
    for(i=0;i<N;i++){
        if(x > 100)
            x = x + A[i];
        else y = y - w+z;
    }
} : {
``` | ```
int i;
for(i=0;i<N;i++){
    if(w > 100)
        w = w + B[i];
    else z = z - x+y;
} } epar
``` |
|---|---|
| eliminating false sharing | by separation. |

Here, $B[N]$ separates x, y from w, z, significantly reducing the chance that x, y and w, z will be mapped to the same cache line. Obviously, the compiler can prevent such cases by explicitly assigning suitable addresses to x, y and w, z.

This code can be further optimized using the following observation. MESI race conditions between local variables of different threads are not likely to occur because each thread has a distinct stack area. Hence, cache lines containing variables from different stacks will likely reside in different cache lines. Thus, by using local variables instead of shared global variables (if possible), we can reduce the number of cache misses caused by race conditions. In the following example x, y and w, z have been made to be local variables. The updates between the threads have been made through two variables $s1, s2$ that are being updated in the less frequent else-part.

| ```
int  A[N],s1,B[N],s2;
pparblock {
    int i,x,y;
    for(i=0;i<N;i++){
        s1 = x;
        if(x > 100)
            x = x + A[i];
        else { s1=x+y;
        y = y - s2; }
} } : {
``` | ```
int i,w,z;
for(i=0;i<N;i++){
    if(w > 100)
        w = w + B[i];
    else { z = z - s2;
    s2= w+z;  }
}
} epar
``` |
|---|---|
| Avoiding false sharing through | the use of local variables. |

4.9 Controlling Cache Line Sharing at Different Times

In this section we consider cases where grouping a set of shared variables such that they sit in one cache line can reduce the total number of bus transactions made by the MESI protocol. This is the opposite case of false sharing where we group variables' decelerations so that they will use the same cache line. In the following example, the variables x, y, z are constantly updated by the N threads. Due to the separation in the declaration of x, y, z by $A[n]$ and $B[n]$, it is likely that x, y, z will be mapped to different cache lines. Assuming that each thread is executed by another core implies that the three cache lines containing x, y, z will travel back and forth on the bus, slowing the execution considerably.

```
#define N 10
int x,A[n],y,B[n],z;
parfor int   i;1;N-2;1{
int j,s=0;
    x = y+ (A[i-1]+A[i+1])/2;
    y = z+ (B[i-1]+A[i+1])/2;
    z = x+ (B[i-1]+A[i+1])/2;
    for(j=0;j<n;j++) s+=A[j];
} epar

x,y,z are likely to be mapped to different cache lines.
```

The proposed solution is to group x, y, z on one cache line but to separate the access to this line in time by the different threads. In the following code the local for-loop has been divided into two parts, one executed before the segment wherein x, y, z are updated and the other after this segment. In each thread, the first part of the for-loop lasts for a different number of iterations. Consequently, the probability that the execution of two x, y, z-segments will overlap in time is low. In this case, only one BusRdX operation will be needed to move the cache line containing x, y, z from the cache where it is now valid to the cache of the core that begins to execute this segment.

```
#define N 10
int x,y,z,A[n],B[n];
parfor int   i;1;N-2;1{
int j,s=0;
    for(j=0;j<(n/N)*i;j++) s+=A[j];
    x = y+ (A[i-1]+A[i+1])/2;
```

```
    y = z+ (B[i-1]+A[i+1])/2;
    z = x+ (B[i-1]+A[i+1])/2;
    for(j=j;j<n;j++) s+=A[j];
} epar
```

x,y,z are likely to be mapped to different cache lines

Another similar case involves reordering the iterations of loops that are executed in parallel and accessing the same arrays. The assumption behind this approach is that each loop will execute its iterations in a different order so that the probability that two loops will reference the same part of the array simultaneously is reduced. Typically, this can happen when the same code is executed in parallel by different cores, particularly if the threads of a parfor statement contain heavy loops that are not dependent on the parfor index. This is the case with the following code (left-side) that counts all of the occurrences of an array's elements in a matrix. In this case, since the iterations of the inner loop are independent, it is possible to reorder them such that each core will begin the execution from a different place chosen at random (see the right-side of the example).

```
int M[n][n],B[n],C[n];
parfor int i;0,n-1;1; {
    int j,k;
    for(j=0;j<n;j++)
      for(k=0;k<n;k++)
        if(M[i][k] == B[j])C[j]++;
} epar
```
Searching all of the occurrences
```
int M[n][n],B[n],C[n];
parfor int i;0,n-1;1; {
    int j,k,x=rand()%n;
    for(j=x;j != x-1;(j++)%n)
      for(k=0;k<n;k++)
        if(M[i][k] == B[j]) C[j]++;
} epar
```
rearranging the iteration order

In the modified version, each loop begins from a random iteration. Thus, if the arrays B[] and C[] are partitioned between the different cores, then (most likely) simultaneous access to the same parts of B[] and C[] will not occur.

Another issue we need to consider is the use of Volatile Registers (VR) in multicore machines. Compilers usually eliminate loads/operations in loops and hold temporary values of variables in registers. Thus, if a variable x is shared between several threads and the compiler replaces all references to x with references to a register in a loop, x will no longer be visible to the MESI protocol. In such a case, updates made to x during a loop would not be visible to other threads. Volatile variables in C can be used to force the compiler not to use registers to update x, in case this is important. In the case of ParC, the compilation method of ParC makes all accesses to shared variables through a pointer pass as parameters. In this case, the compiler cannot eliminate the load/store operation by the use of a register.

4.10 Prefetching Data

A known compilation technique for overcoming cache misses is to prefetch variables that will be needed later on. In dealing with the prefetching of a variable for the MESI protocol in a multicore machine, we should bear in mind the following points:

- Caches contain automatic prefetching mechanisms in the hardware. We focus on software prefetching that is accomplished by inserting explicit prefetch instructions into the source code.
- It is better to prefetch arrays because the memory access pattern of arrays is usually regular and it is possible to predict the set of addresses that will be used next.
- It is better to apply prefetching in loop iterations where a prefetch at the i th iteration can be used to fetch the values that will be used in the next iteration.
- Prefetching should not block the execution of the code and should be overlapped with a useful computation. This goal can be achieved in two ways:
  - The prefetch instruction is implemented in the hardware such that it does not block the core. In addition, while the prefetching is executed, the core should execute instructions that do not collide with the prefetching (i.e., the current code should not generate load/store operations that would be a cache miss).
  - A special, dedicated thread, executed by the current core, is prefetching values for the current thread.
- Prefetching incurs a similar overhead as that of a memory reference. Thus, it is important to overlap its execution with a sufficient number of arithmetic operations of local memory references (shored cache hits) that will hide the latency of the prefetching operation.
- Attention must be paid to the fact that prefetching will not invalidate copies of prefetched variables in other caches. Thus, prefetching data to the cache of one core may help one thread but destroy useful content in other caches.

The simplest form of prefetching is in loops, prefetching the array elements that will be needed for the next iteration. Note that there are enough arithmetic operations in every iteration of the for-loop to cover the latency of the prefetch instruction.

In this case, there is little overlap between the N/Z threads of two array elements. Only $(A[i-1], A[i-2]$ are accessed by both thread i and thread $i-1$. Thus, the expected number of MESI BusRDx transactions is only $O(N/Z)$.

| ```
#define N 100000
#define Z 1000
int x,A[n],y,B[n],z;
parfor int   i;1;N;Z{
int j,t,s=0;
   for(j=i;j<i+Z;j++){
      t= (A[j-1]+A[j-2])/2;
      s += t *t;
      A[j]= s*t;
} epar
``` | ```
#define N 100000
#define Z 1000
int x,A[n],y,B[n],z;
parfor int   i;1;N;Z{
int j,t,s=0;
   for(j=i;j<i+Z;j++){
      prefetch(&A[j+1]);
      t= (A[j-1]+A[j-2])/2;
      s += t *t;
      A[j]= s*t;
} epar
``` |
|---|---|
| Initial code | with prefetching |

This can be further improved if we prefetch every $k > 1$ iterations (k items), thus reducing the total number of prefetching operations:

```
#define N 100000
#define Z 1000
int x,A[n],y,B[n],z;
parfor int   i;1;N;Z{
int j,t,s=0;
   for(j=i;j<i+Z;j++){
      if(j % k == 0)
         prefetch(&A[j+1],k);
      t= (A[j-1]+A[j-2])/2;
      s += t *t;
      A[j]= s*t;
} epar
```

with improved prefetching

A different form of prefetching is to insert special code before every heavy loop. The goal of this code is to sample the set of addresses that the loop will reference and prefetch the pages that will be used by the loop to the current cache. In general, the sampling of a given loop is done by generating a pseudo-loop that realizes a subset of the memory references of the original loop. Local copies of shared arrays and variables (denoted by $x, a[], b[], c[]$ in the following example) are used instead of the original ones, so that the sampling loop will not affect the correctness of the execution. The loop itself is executed in jumps of PSIZE (LSIZE is used for while-loops) so that the overhead involved with the sampling code will be negligible. Clearly, there is no need to sample consecutive array references because most of the addresses will be to the same cache lines. Finally, the following example demonstrates how safe sampling can be done. Note that we assume that the function-call to $f()$ has no side effects, i.e., there are no updates of memory references.

```
int i,X,A[n],B[n],C[n];
lparfor(i=0;i<n;i++){
  A[i]=B[i+5];
  if(A[i] != B[i]) C[i]=B[i];
  else C[i] = B[i-1];
  for(j=i;j<n;j++)
    A[A[i+j]]=f(B[i-1]);
  while(X > 0){
    A[X]=X; X-;}
}
```
Initial code

```
int i,X,A[n],B[n],C[n];
int i,x,a[n],b[n],c[n];
x = X;
mapped lparfor(i=0;i<n;i+=PSIZE){
  a[i]=B[i+5];
  if(a[i] != B[i]) c[i]=B[i];
  else c[i] = B[i-1];
  for(j=i;j<n;j+=PSIZE)
    a[a[i+j]]=f(B[i-1]);
  i=0;
  while(X > 0 && i++ < LSIZE){
    a[x]=x; x-;}
  prefetch(&A[i],&B[i],&C[i],&A[x]);
} mapped lparfor(i=0;i<n;i++){
  A[i]=B[i+5];
  if(A[i] != B[i]) C[i]=B[i];
  else C[i] = B[i-1];
  for(j=i;j<n;j++)
    A[A[i+j]]=f(B[i-1]);
  while(X > 0){
    A[X]=X; X-;}
```
with a sampling loop

Note that we concentrate on computations that are dependent on the loops' indices. In the case of a conditional statement, we use the union of the **then** and the **else** parts while the loops are executed as long as their condition does not become *undef*.

It is also possible to perform the prefetching in the form of a helping thread that, concurrent with the main thread, prefetches the data items before the main thread needs them: We use the mapped version to make sure that the ith helper thread and the ith main thread will run on the same core. In this way, the data items that are prefetched by a helper thread will reside in the same cache that is used by the appropriate main thread.

```
int i,X,A[n],B[n],C[n];
int i,x,a[n],b[n],c[n];
x = X;
mapped parblock {
  mapped lparfor(i=0;i<n;i+=PSIZE){
    a[i]=B[i+5];
    if(a[i] != B[i]) c[i]=B[i];
    else c[i] = B[i-1];
    for(j=i;j<n;j+=PSIZE)
      a[a[i+j]]=f(B[i-1]);
    i=0;
    while(X > 0 && i++ < LSIZE){
      a[x]=x; x-;}
    prefetch(&A[i],&B[i],&C[i],&A[x]);
  } } : {
  mapped lparfor(i=0;i<n;i++){
    A[i]=B[i+5];
    if(A[i] != B[i]) C[i]=B[i];
    else C[i] = B[i-1];
    for(j=i;j<n;j++)
      A[A[i+j]]=f(B[i-1]);
    while(X > 0){
      A[X]=X; X-;}
}
```
Using a sampling thread

4.11 Exercises

1. Consider the following trace of a parallel code executed over MESI.

   - Is the following sequence possible for the MESI protocol?
   - If not, specify all of the violations of the MESI protocol.
   - Is the following sequence possible for the MOESI protocol?
   - If not, specify all of the violations of the MOESI protocol

```
 1  CPU0 reads a0 from memory [not shared] - state E
 2  CPU0 reads a0 from cache - state E
 3  CPU0 updates a0 in cache ONLY - state M
 4  CPU0 updates a0 in cache ONLY - state M
 5  CPU1 reads a0, CPU0 cache intervenes and
    supplies
 -  data to cache and memory - state S
 6  CPU1 updates a0 in cache & memory and
    invalidates
 -  all other caches with address a0 - state E
 7  CPU1 updates a0 in cache ONLY - state M
 8  CPU0 write a0
 -  CPU0 reads a0, CPU1 cache intervenes
        and supplies data to cache and memory (S),
 -  CPU0 then writes to a0 in cache & memory
    invalidating all
 -  other caches with address a0 - state E
 9  CPU0 reads a2 from memory (E) and then writes
    to a2-state M
10  CPU0 flushes a2 to memory, reads a2 from
    memory (E)
 -  and then writes to a0 - state M
```

2. Consider the following code executed by two threads:

$$int \quad x = 0, y = 0; \qquad Thread~A \qquad \qquad Thread~B$$
$$while(x == 0)~y = 1; \qquad \qquad \qquad while(y == 0)x = 1;$$

(a) Assuming that MESI is used, is it true that both threads will never be in an infinite loop?

(b) Assuming that MESI is used, is it true that when one thread exits its loop, the other thread must also be out of its loop?

(c) If not, what can be done to impose these two conditions?

(d) Of what potential use is this code?

3. Consider the following two pieces of advice given to a user:

- Using busy waiting loops on a shared flag will cause the cache line holding the shared flag to ping-pong between the caches of the cores executing the busy-waits.

- Scanning large array segments by one core can invalidate large portions of the caches in many cores. Here one should work with small tiles of arrays to reduce the cache hit-ratio.

Analyze these two pieces of advice. If the advice is not good, create an example showing how to correct them.

4.12 Bibliographic Notes

General discussion on multicore machines can be found in Geer (2005) including multicore explanation and multicore advantages over single core. Memory Cache, Basic cache terminology can be obtained from Smith (1982). A web-based Cache Tutorial, including four different tools to explore cache structure and mapping can be obtained at http://www.ecs.umass.edu/ece/koren/architecture/Cache/frame0.htm. Cache Simulators can be obtained from http://myweb.lsbu.ac.uk/~chalkbs/research/CacheApplet.htm. Data prefetch mechanisms (Vanderwiel and Lilja 2000), including: Software Data Prefetching, Hardware Data Prefetching, Sequential Prefetching, Prefetching with Arbitrary Strides, Integrating Hardware and Software Prefetching, Prefetching in Multiprocessors.

Multicore terminology is explained in Khan (2009) including: caches, data locality of caches and spatial Locality, temporal locality and hardware prefetching. False sharing and spatial locality in multiprocessor caches is discussed (Torrellas et al. 2002). Farther material on false sharing and its effect on performance of shared memory programs can be found in Bolosky and Scott (1993). Possible ways to optimize shared memory programs for multicore are also surveyed in Khan (2009).

Similar to the material presented in this chapter, Khan (2009) evaluates the impact of Data Splitting, Data Replication, Memory Pooling, Grouping Related Data, Software Prefetching and Loop Fusion as a way to improve the execution of shared memory programs over the cache coherency mechanism used by multicore machines. Some interesting hardware considerations regarding interconnections in multicore architectures are presented in Kumar et al. (2005). These aspects can be used to better understand multicore architectures. A general survey on different types of multicore architectures can be found in Blake et al. (2009). Using trace-based simulation, Bolosky and Scott (1993) present experimental evidence to its potential impact on performances.

The original description of the MESI protocol can be found in Papamarcos and Patel (1984). The equivalence of several MESI variants, Berkeley protocol, the Dragon protocol, the Firefly protocol and the Write-Once protocol is shown in Sweazey and Smith (1986). Shasha and Snir (1988) developed a compile-time analysis to identify memory operations that can be reordered without violating sequential consistency, possibly improving execution times of shared memory programs. Adve et al. (2002) contain several types of hardware optimizations that can be used to speedup MESI. Adve et al. (2002) also discuss the following issues:

- The possibility of using more relaxed types of consistency models (less restricting than sequential consistency).
- Effectiveness of hardware prefetching.
- Speculative load/store operations.
- The effect of branch prediction.
- The overhead of synchronization versus the overhead of maintaining cache consistency.
- Use of volatile registers.
- The role of the compiler in maintaining the underlying consistency.

References

Adve, S.V., Pai, V.S., Ranganathan, P.: Recent advances in memory consistency models for hardware shared memory systems. Proc. IEEE **87**(3), 445–455 (2002)

Blake, G., Dreslinski, R., Mudge, T.: A survey of multicore processors. IEEE Signal Process. Mag. **26**(6), 26–37 (2009)

Bolosky, W.J., Scott, M.L.: False sharing and its effect on shared memory performance. In: USENIX Systems on USENIX Experiences with Distributed and Multiprocessor Systems, vol. 4, p. 3. USENIX Association, Berkeley (1993)

Geer, D.: Chip makers turn to multicore processors. Computer **38**(5), 11–13 (2005)

Khan, M.A.: Optimization study for multicores. Technical report, The University of Uppsala (2009)

Kumar, R., Zyuban, V., Tullsen, D.M.: Interconnections in multi-core architectures: Understanding mechanisms, overheads and scaling. In: Proceedings of 32nd International Symposium on Computer Architecture (ISCA'05), pp. 408–419. IEEE, New York (2005). ISBN 076952270X

Papamarcos, M.S., Patel, J.H.: A low-overhead coherence solution for multiprocessors with private cache memories. Comput. Archit. News **12**(3), 354 (1984)

Shasha, D., Snir, M.: Efficient and correct execution of parallel programs that share memory. ACM Trans. Program. Lang. Syst. **10**(2), 282–312 (1988)

Smith, A.J.: Cache memories. ACM Comput. Surv. **14**(3), 473–530 (1982)

Sweazey, P., Smith, A.J.: A class of compatible cache consistency protocols and their support by the IEEE futurebus. In: Proceedings of the 13th Annual International Symposium on Computer Architecture, pp. 414–423. IEEE Computer Society Press, Los Alamitos (1986). ISBN 081860719X

Torrellas, J., Lam, H., Hennessy, J.L.: False sharing and spatial locality in multiprocessor caches. IEEE Trans. Comput. **43**(6), 651–663 (2002)

Vanderwiel, S.P., Lilja, D.J.: Data prefetch mechanisms. ACM Comput. Surv. **32**(2), 174–199 (2000)

Chapter 5
Improving the Performance of Parallel Programs: The Analytical Approach

5.1 Introduction

In this chapter we will examine the gap between the expected execution time of a parallel algorithm and the actual running time achieved by executing its encoding as a *ParC* program in an actual shared memory machine. Though there is such a gap for sequential programs, it is more problematic with parallel programs where users often encounter cases of parallel programs that fail to run fast enough or as fast as expected. In particular, a parallel program that runs on a parallel machine with P processors is expected to run about P times faster than its sequential version. There are two issues involved with this problem:

- Determining the execution time of a parallel program and comparing it with a desired execution time.
- If there is a significant gap between the two, we need to identify which factors in the parallel program should be corrected so that the performance is improved.

In general, there are two approaches to the problem of closing the gap between parallel algorithms and their actual runs as parallel programs on real machines:

Simulation This simulation is the common method of solving efficiency gaps. It is accomplished by executing the program in a simulation environment, and collecting the events and statistics relating to the execution. The events and the statistics allow the user to locate the inefficient parts of his or her program. The main problem with this method is the lengthy and often impractical simulation times. For example, a simulator can display the idle times of each processor, allowing the user to visually observe that some processors are relatively overloaded compared to others.

Performance models This is the approach discussed in this chapter. It is based on the development of a formula that can predict the expected execution time of a parallel program when executed by a specific parallel machine. By analyzing the time formula we can determine if the expected time is sufficient. If it is not, we can identify the factors that limit the performance. This approach is faster than

Y. Ben-Asher, *Multicore Programming Using the ParC Language*,
Undergraduate Topics in Computer Science,
DOI 10.1007/978-1-4471-2164-0_5, © Springer-Verlag London 2012

simulations but is likely to be less accurate. The formula is used to define the "speedup" of a program, namely, how well the program uses the parallelism of the machine in comparison to a sequential execution.

In this section, we develop a model of a virtual parallel machine (VPM), through which the user can evaluate the effect of changes made to the program. This model includes not only the structure of a virtual parallel machine, but also a speedup equation and the characteristics of efficient programs. The second element is a set of high level constructs of the programming language relating to different aspects of efficiency (such as the distinction between local and non-local memory references). The third element is a set of transformations that the user applies to the code of an initial program, resulting in an efficient program that exploits different aspects of the underlying machine.

5.2 A Simple Model of a Virtual Machine

The virtual parallel machine (VPM) is a model of a schematic parallel machine that describes the parallel execution of a program in that language. The VPM model is therefore a generalization of all of the practical aspects involved in the execution of parallel programs. The model we present here reflects two practical aspects in the realization of PRAM-like programs:

- The overhead involved in the creation of new threads.
- The different access times to local memory and to remote (global) memory, which is accessed through some sort of network.

The virtual machine hides minor aspects of the physical hardware and software that executes *ParC*. Thus, the programmer can ignore questions such as, how exactly does the operating system execute the program, or does the machine overcome barriers using busy-waits. Moreover, the virtual machine connects important aspects of the hardware (such as the number of processors) with the program's parameters and syntax (such as the number of threads spawned by the program). This connection results in a formula and a model through which the execution time of any program can be evaluated.

A "true" model will be able to fully predict the execution time of a given program. However, such a model might be too complicated as a program development tool. The model is, therefore, a compromise between the need to include as many low-level factors as possible, and the need to create a simple tool that a programmer can use to develop applications.

The realization that the model cannot provide an exact prediction of the execution time leads to the consideration of weaker requirements. The first consideration deals with an important and desirable property of the model. We say that a VPM model is *useful* if any change in a program $R \rightarrow R'$ such that R' uses fewer resources than R improves the time prediction of R' in the model. For example, if R' uses fewer network accesses than R, we require that $VPM(R') \leq VPM(R)$ (where $VPM(R)$ is the prediction of the amount of time it will take the virtual machine model to execute R). In other words, a model is useful if the user can predict and evaluate the effect (or usefulness) of any possible modification to his or her program.

The second consideration deals with the desirable property of realizations we would like the VPM to have, such as the implementation of the language. We say that the realization of a parallel programming language (*ParC* in our case) on physical hardware is *fair* if for any two programs $R1$, $R2$, if $VPM(R1) \leq VPM(R2)$ then $RM(R1) \leq RM(R2)$ (where $RM(R)$ is the actual time it takes to execute R on the above hardware). Clearly, the validation that a given model satisfies such weaker requirements is obtained via experiments and actual usage (i.e., it cannot be proven theoretically because we argued that a complete model is impossible to construct).

These two definitions imply that, once a VPM model has been accepted as the *standard model* of a parallel language, a minimal set of requirements from any possible realization of that language is devised as well. Note that the above definitions are the weakest possible, because they demand only that any improvement in the program should yield an improvement in its execution time. A stronger requirement might require a constant relation between improvements in the model and the execution time: $c_1 \frac{VPM(R1)}{VPM(R2)} \leq \frac{RM(R1)}{RM(R2)} \leq c_2 \frac{VPM(R1)}{VPM(R2)}$.

Finally, we will discuss the type of equations to use for the proposed model. This is a meta-discussion whose goal is to prompt the mathematical formulation of the proposed model. Assume that we are to estimate the value of a function $f(x)$ without really knowing the exact formula of $f(x)$. The idea is to find a sequence of lower bounds $\Omega_1(x), \Omega_2(x), \ldots$ each bounding the value of $f(x)$ by considering a different aspect of $f(x)$. For example, if $f(x) = 3x^{2.5} + zx + 3$, we may a priori know that $f(x) > x^2$, thereby obtaining $\Omega_1(x) = x^2$. Thus, if we are able to find a sequence of two lower bounds, we can write that $f(x) > \max(\Omega_1(x), \Omega_2(x))$. The proposed model will then argue that $f(x) \approx \Omega_1(x) + \Omega_2(x)$. Note that it is always true that

$$\max\big(\Omega_1(x), \Omega_2(x)\big) < \Omega_1(x) + \Omega_2(x) < 2 \cdot \max\big(\Omega_1(x), \Omega_2(x)\big),$$

so we have some justification for assuming that $f(x) \approx \Omega_1(x) + \Omega_2(x)$. A stronger justification would be to say that if $f(x) < \Omega_1(x) + \Omega_2(x)$, then we can always find another factor of $f(x)$ that bounds a different aspect of $f(x)$ (e.g., $\Omega_3(x) = 2x$) and add it to the equation, obtaining $f(x) \approx \Omega_1(x) + \Omega_2(x) + \Omega_3(x)$. Eventually, we will sum enough lower bounds to overestimate the value of $f(x)$. Note that because we have used only lower bounds, we know that in the worst case our estimation is at most k the actual size of $f(x)$, where k is the number of lower bounds we used. For example, if $f(x) < \Omega_1(x) + \Omega_2(x) + \Omega_3(x)$, then since $\Omega_1(x) + \Omega_2(x) + \Omega_3(x) < 3 \cdot \max(\Omega_1(x), \Omega_2(x), \Omega_3(x))$, we get that $3 \cdot f(x) > \Omega_1(x) + \Omega_2(x) + \Omega_3(x)$.

5.3 The *ParC* Virtual Machine Model

The previous section presented the notion of the VPM model and its goals. In this section we introduce a specific VPM model for the execution of *ParC* programs.

Fig. 5.1 The VPM model

global representative and activity queue

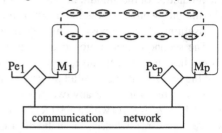

communication   network

This model is also suitable for other parallel programming languages that spawn explicit threads, and use shared memory.

The execution of a parallel program is a dynamic thread in which new threads are created and terminated. Moreover, the execution of one thread may be dependent on the execution of another thread (e.g. one thread waits for a value to be computed by another thread). This fact implies that threads cannot be run to completion, but rather one should execute threads alternately. In addition, a real parallel machine should be able to manipulate more threads than the number of physical processors. This manipulation is accomplished through one or more queues of thread records. Every processor then picks a thread from a queue and executes it for a while, then returns it to the queue and picks another one (see Fig. 5.1). The model observes the following rules:

- When a thread needs to spawn new threads, it puts one representative record with a description of these threads in the global queue.
- The spawning thread can resume its operation only when all of its children have terminated (the last child should wake the parent).
- We assume parallel access to the global queue. Moreover, many processors can access the same representative record simultaneously (e.g. using the faa() instruction). Thus, initializing $parfor(int\ i = 0; i < 1000; i + +)$ requires one step, not 1000 steps.
- Processors are never idle as long as the global queue is not empty.

Although our primary goal is to examine multicore machines, the proposed model can be used for other types of shared memory machines. In general, the distinction between the local and global memories deserves some elaboration. Some shared memory machines put the processors on one side of the communication network, and the memories on the other side. However, we claim that at least some local memory is essential to ensure optimal performance. Given that access to local memory is always faster than access to memory through the network, the program, at least, should be stored locally. Note that this dichotomy is not equivalent to the distinction between private and shared memory. Indeed, the local memories may be globally accessible to the rest of the processors. We indicate only that it is reasonable to assume that any shared memory machine will allow the processor to access a portion of the memory as its local memory. The "global memory" in the model is a conceptual entity, capturing the concept of memory that has to be accessed through the network and therefore degrades performance. It does not necessarily match any specific hardware component.

The VPM model connects these two sides (machine and program) and calculates the execution time to be the total work and overhead (of a program) divided by the number of processors. For a given program R, a specific input (which, for reasons of convenience, is omitted) and a fair realization, the execution time on the VPM model is defined using the following parameters. Some of the parameters depend on the program R, while others are constants.

P the number of physical processors that the machine has.

C the overhead needed to spawn a new thread and then to delete it, including its share in the coordination required to wake the parent thread.

c the overhead or time needed to synchronize N threads, using the sync statement. Note that $C > c$ because C contains the allocation of thread resources besides synchronization.

$N(R)$ the total number of threads spawned by the program.

$D(R)$ the longest path in the execution graph (see Fig. 5.2), which is defined recursively on R:

$$D(R) = \begin{cases} 1 & R \text{ is an atomic statement} \\ \sum_1^k D(S_i) & R = \{S_1; \dots; S_k\} \\ \sum_{i=1}^k (D(S_i) + 2) & R = \text{for } (i = 0; i < k; i++) \ S; \\ 1 + \max\{D(S_1), D(S_2)\} & R = \text{if } (exp) \ S_1; \text{ else } S_2; \\ 1 + D(S_{f(x)}) & R = f(x); \\ C + \max_1^k D(S_i) & R = \text{parfor int } i; 1; k; 1; \ S_i; \ \textbf{epar} \\ C + \max_1^k D(S_i) & R = \text{parblock } S_1 : \dots : S_k \ \textbf{epar} \end{cases}$$

where $S_{f(x)}$ is the body of the function f after substituting the parameters. Note that the $i < k$; and the $i++$; instructions are counted in the case of the sequential *for* statement.

In the case of a *sync* instruction, the longest path should include the waiting times that result from waiting for the sync instruction. Sync waiting times are inserted into the graph by adding edges between any sync instruction and all of the sync instructions executed by the threads spawned by the current parallel construct. Consider, for example, the recursive parallel program of Fig. 5.2. Before adding the extra sync edges, the longest path in the execution graph is 65, containing only the loop of the first thread. However, by adding the sync edges between suitable sync instructions, the longest path now contains all of the loops and its value is 71 (as depicted in Fig. 5.3's broken line).

$W(R)$ the total number of instructions executed by R. $W(R)$ is computed in the same way as $D(R)$, except that $C + \max$ is replaced by $\sum$ in the case of the parallel constructs. $W(R)$ is the time it would take us to simulate the sequential execution of R.

```
f(n){

    PB[

        SYNC;

        for(i=0;i<n*n;i++);

        :

        if(n>2) f(n/2);

        SYNC;

    ]

}

f(8);
```

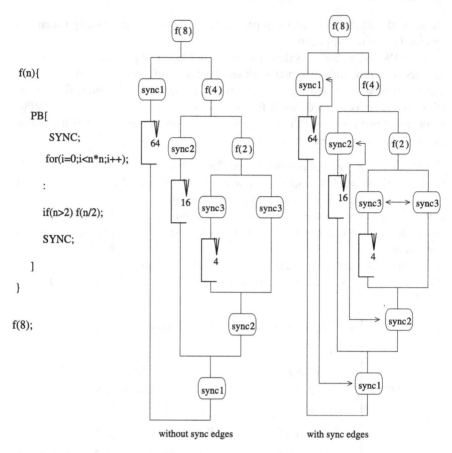

without sync edges   with sync edges

Fig. 5.2 The effect of *sync* on the longest path in the execution graph

$S_s(R)$ the sequential part of R. This counts all of the instructions that are not within the scope of any parallel construct (including indirect scopes through function calls).

$S_l(R), S_g(R)$ the total number of accesses to local and global memory, respectively. S_l is computed in the same way as $W(R)$, except that for every atomic instruction that does not belong to S_s, we count the number of accesses to local variables. A local access is any reference to a variable declared in the same block wherein the access occurred (e.g. accessing parameters and local variables in a function body). S_g is defined in a similar way, except that we count the accesses to non-local variables. For example, in the code of Fig. 5.4, $S_l = 3$ and $S_g = 6$.

$F_m(P, S_g, S_l)$ F_m is used to estimate the delay caused by each global access in the execution of R. F_m takes into account the number of processors (the maximal number of references through the communication network) and the relationship between the local and global accesses. Let $Z = \frac{S_g}{S_g+S_l}$ be the relative weight of the global accesses. At any given time, there are at most P accesses to the memory.

Fig. 5.3 The longest path passes through the sync edges

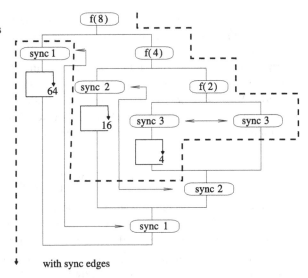

with sync edges

When Z is small compared to $\frac{1}{P}$, we estimate that most of the accesses are local and the network is not loaded. This is a simplified model but it captures the intuition that

if for every global access through the underlying communication network there are $P - 1$ local references that can be executed concurrently, then no two global accesses occur at the same time. Hence, the network is not a bottleneck.

	local	global
`int   g;`		
`f( x, y )`		
`int   x, y;`		
`{`		
`    int   k;`		
`    k = g + x;`	k, x	g
`    parblock`		
`    {`		
`        int   l;`		
`        l = k + g;`	l	k, g
`    }`		
`    :`		
`        k = x + y;`		k, x, y
`    epar`		
`}`		

Fig. 5.4 Example of counting local and global memory references

Thus, F_m is a lower bound because it assumes the best possible scheduling order of global memory references, minimizing the number of global memory references that attempt to use the communication network at any given time. This is, of course, a very optimistic assumption. It may be that all of the global accesses are executed first, saturating the communication network. Only later are all of the local accesses executed. When $Z \geq \frac{1}{P}$, we estimate that a fraction, Z, of the time the network is loaded and $\frac{1}{Z}$ of the accesses are delayed by the network. For multicore machines, the communication network is a bus. Assuming a bus can service one processor at a time, we get that

$$F_{bus}(P, S_g, S_l) = \max\left\{ \frac{S_g \cdot P}{S_g + S_l}, 1 \right\}.$$

Multicore include a caching mechanism, therefore, some of the global read accesses of *ParC* become local accesses to the cache. The cache efficiency is represented by a factor $0 \leq \alpha \leq 1$ (the "hit ratio"), such that $S_l^{eff} = S_l + \alpha S_g$ and $S_g^{eff} = (1 - \alpha)S_g$. Note that α should not be confused with the cache efficiency in a single core machine, which is usually high 0.95. The reason for this difference is that when a *ParC* program is executed, the underlying MESI/MOESI coherence protocol will invalidate more cache lines than in the case of a sequential program executed by a single core. The expected cache efficiency α is reduced when the shared memory is used extensively and is subject to experimental evaluation for each program separately. Since we model the effect of bus transactions by a constant that is experimentally determined, we can, for the time being, ignore it, assuming that $\alpha = 1$.

Using the above parameter set, the execution time of a program R and a given input is calculated in the VMP model by the following expression. This expression is, in a sense, a more elaborate version of the formula used to express Amdahl's Law (see related exercise).

$$T(R) = \max\left\{ D, S_s + \frac{N \cdot C + W - S_s + S_g \cdot F_m(P, S_g, S_l)}{P} \right\}$$

Two lower bounds are used as a basic motivation to construct $T(R)$. Clearly, the parallel time is bounded by $D(R)$ because it is the longest path in the execution graph. No matter how many processors the machine has, $D(R)$ is a lower bound. On the other hand the total amount of work divided by the number of processors $\frac{W(R)}{P}$, is another lower bound to the execution time of R (Otherwise, there would have been a better sequential algorithm). The overhead of a parallel construct with explicit sync instructions is $C + c$, and the total time should be computed accordingly.

In many practical cases, the user can express D, S_s, N, W, S_s and S_l as a function of the input size. In this case the user can derive an explicit formula that describes the parallel execution time of the program for any given input. For example, consider the recursive program in Fig. 5.5. Let n be the number that is given as an argument to f. Then

- $D(n) = (C + 2) \log n$. The depth of a binary tree wherein each node takes C instructions to be created and then executes one if statement and a function call.

Fig. 5.5 Code segment used
in an example of calculating
expected execution time

```
f(x)
int   x;
{
      if (x > 1) {
          parblock
              f(x/2);
          :
              f(x/2);
          epar
      }
}
```

- $S_s(n) = 1$. There is only one sequential statement: the first if.
- $N(n) = 2n$. The number of nodes in a binary tree.
- $W(n) = 6n$. There are $2n$ nodes each executing an if statement and two function calls.
- $S_g(n) = 2n$. Each function call f(x/2) accesses x, which is declared a local parameter of the outer function.
- $S_l(n) = 2n$. In the if(x > 1) the x is a local variable (a parameter).
- On a multicore bus machine

$$F_{bus}(P) = \max\left\{\frac{2n \cdot P}{2n + 2n}, 1\right\} = \max\left\{\frac{P}{2}, 1\right\}$$

The final expression (assuming $P > 1$) is then

$$T(R) = \max\left\{\log n(C+2),\ 1 + \frac{2n \cdot C + 6n - 1 + n \cdot P}{P}\right\}$$

Consider, for example, some specific values of $n = 1000$, $C = 100$, $P = 10$ for the execution of the above program. It follows that the most dominant factor is $\frac{2n \cdot C}{P} = 20{,}000$. The sequential execution time for $n = 1000$ is 2000. Thus, using the above formula allows us to determine that this is an extremely inefficient program that runs ten times slower than a naive sequential version. Moreover, it is clear that unless we use $P > 100$ processors, the above program will never be speeded up to the point that its execution time will compare with that of a sequential execution. Note that this thread took place before running or debugging, thereby saving considerable effort and debugging.

5.4 Speedup Notion for Programs

Using the VPM model, we can define the notion of *speedup* for parallel programs in a similar manner to the well known theoretical speedup for parallel algorithms

$$SP(R) = \frac{W(R)}{T(R)} = \min\left\{\frac{W}{D},\ \frac{1}{\frac{S_s}{W} + \frac{N \cdot C}{W \cdot P} + \frac{W - S_s}{W \cdot P} + \frac{S_g \cdot F_m(P, S_g, S_l)}{W \cdot P}}\right\}$$

Both $W(R)$ and $T(R)$ are defined only for a specific input to R. However, a speedup notion that varies from one input to the other is not useful, because it does not characterize the program. For example, consider a program that for odd input sizes has a speedup of P, while for even input sizes it has a speedup of 1. The speedup notion is therefore valid only if it is defined independently of the program's specific inputs. Thus, we assume that the user is able to express all of the factors of $W(R)$ and $T(R)$ by symbolic expressions of the input size n.

The importance of the speedup notion is that it allows us to discuss the efficiency of parallel programs. For example, we may say that a parallel program R is considered *efficient* (in the sense that it exploits the parallelism of the machine) if there is an input size N_0, such that for any $n > N_0$ the speedup is $\frac{P}{2} \leq SP(R)$.

Note that this definition is different than the theoretical one. The theoretical definition compares the execution time of a parallel algorithm with P processors to the time of the best-known sequential algorithm. Had we attempted to use this notion for parallel programs, we would have had to determine the best sequential program, which is not practical. Therefore, we compare the sequential execution time of a parallel program to its parallel execution, where the sequential execution time of a parallel program is the total number of instructions executed by that program. Hence, the speedup definition for programs is made to be less than P only as a result of non-optimal coding and execution, not the incorrect selection of the algorithmic aspects.

The ratio between sequential and parallel execution actually gives the efficiency in terms of the amount of time that the processors are active and executing useful code. The difference between the notion of a program speedup and an algorithm speedup is that in the case of the former, the algorithm has already been determined. The remaining question is how well the algorithm's implementation exploits the parallel machine.

The proposed definition identifies efficient parallel programs as those that have a linear speedup with a constant between $\frac{1}{2}$ and 1. This definition can be refined further by dividing the speedup equation into "speedup factors," which can be considered necessary conditions for efficiency. If any one of these conditions is violated, the program cannot be efficient. The equations lead to the identification of four such conditions:

Large optimal speedup: $SP^o(R) \equiv \frac{W}{D} \geq \frac{P}{2}$. In terms of the execution graph a program R should be as "wide" as possible (i.e. each parallel construct should spawn as many threads as possible). In order to correct $SP^o(R)$ the critical path D must be shortened, possibly by executing parts of it in parallel. This goal can be accomplished by, for example, joining consecutive independent parallel constructs into one construct. Clearly, SP^o is an optimal speedup because no matter how many processors we add, the speedup of a program cannot exceed SP^o.

Short sequential code factor: $seq(R) \equiv \frac{S_s}{W} \leq \frac{2}{P}$. This is actually a restatement of Amdahl's Law.

Large average size of a thread: $grain(R) \equiv \frac{W}{N} \geq \frac{C}{2}$. $\frac{W}{N}$ is the average size of a thread. This implies that the threads should be made large enough, or that not all threads can be fine-grained.

Small global access factor: $glob(R) \equiv \frac{S_g \cdot F_m(P, S_g, S_l)}{W} \leq 2$. Usually, $W \approx S_g + S_l$ (the number of instructions corresponds to the number of memory references). Thus, the condition may be rewritten as $\frac{S_g(F_m - 2)}{2} \leq S_l$, leading to the intuitive coarse approximation $S_g \cdot F_m \leq S_l$. This condition indicates that on average, a global or external access occurs every F_m local accesses. Thus, there are no delays caused by the network (see definition of F_m).

Note that the fifth factor of the speedup equation, $\frac{W - S_s}{W \cdot P}$, is always $\leq \frac{2}{P}$. Therefore, it does not limit efficiency.

The most important factor in the above list is SP^o because it is the only factor that does not relate to the hardware parameters. Thus, SP^o characterizes the program, while the other factors characterize its execution by the parallel hardware. Recall that SP^o provides an upper bound on the speedup. Thus, in cases where $SP^o > P$, we can define the *effective* speedup to be $SP^e(R) = \frac{W \cdot P}{S_s \cdot (P-1) + N \cdot C + W + S_g \cdot F_m}$, i.e. the other parts (besides SP^o) in the speedup definition. In these cases, $SP(R) = SP^e(R)$.

The discussion so far has assumed that the hardware characteristics are fixed and the user should adapt his or her program to the hardware in order to reach optimal performance. However, the opposite situation is also worth considering: the user has a specific program or application to which parallel hardware should be adapted. More specifically, for a given program and input, what is the optimal number of processors that the user needs? Simple algebraic manipulation shows that the optimal number of processors P_{opt} is obtained when $SP^o = SP^e$, and is given by:

$$\frac{W}{D} = \frac{W}{S_s + \frac{N \cdot C + W - S_s + S_g \cdot F_m}{P}}$$

$$\frac{1}{D} = \frac{P}{P \cdot S_s + N \cdot C + W - S_s + S_g \cdot F_m}$$

$$P = \frac{P \cdot S_s}{D} + \frac{N \cdot C + W - S_s + S_g \cdot F_m}{D}$$

But F_m is also a function of P. Taking that $F_m = \frac{S_g \cdot P}{S_g + S_l}$ yields:

$$P = \frac{P \cdot S_s}{D} + \frac{N \cdot C + W - S_s}{D} + \frac{S_g^2 \cdot P}{D(S_g + S_l)} \tag{5.1}$$

Thus, after simplifications we get that

$$P_{opt} = \frac{(N \cdot C + W - S_s) \cdot (S_g + S_l)}{D \cdot (S_g + S_l) - (S_s \cdot (S_g + S_l) + S_g^2)}$$

In many cases, it is reasonable to assume that $D \geq S_g$, and since $S_l + S_g > S_g$, then $\frac{S_g^2}{D(S_g + S_l)} < 1$ and its corresponding factor in Eq. (5.1) can be ignored.

$$P = \frac{P \cdot S_s}{D} + \frac{N \cdot C + W - S_s}{D}$$

Hence:

$$P_{opt} = \frac{N \cdot C + W - S_s}{D - S_s}$$

Taking $S_l > 2 \cdot S_g$ makes the above condition become $D \geq \frac{S_g}{3}$. Otherwise, $D \leq \frac{S_g}{3}$ and we get that:

$$P_{opt} = \frac{N \cdot C + W - S_s}{D - S_s - \frac{S_g^2}{S_g + S_l}}$$

Note that the optimal number of processors is usually (assuming $D > \frac{S_g}{3}$) not dependent on F_m. This lack of dependence reflects the fact that changing the number of processors does not help the delay caused by external accesses. As in the case of the speedup, P_{opt} can be expressed as a function of the input size.

5.5 Using the Speedup Factors

The speedup factors can be used to analyze the program, determine its efficiency, and then decide which factors should be improved and how. The programmer is free to modify his or her program and optimize it as long as he or she does not change the semantics of the underlying program, as expressed in the following definition:

Definition 5.1 Let $E(R, I)$ denote all possible execution orders of a program R (as described earlier). R' is a legal, efficient version of R if $E(R', I) \in E(R, I)$ for every I, and $SP(R') > SP(R)$.

Typically, the optimization threads of a given program are iterative threads, wherein a sequence of legal, efficient versions of the original program are created. The programmer attempts to isolate a group of execution orders that have a better speedup than the original program.

For example, consider the code segment in Fig. 5.6, executed on a 10 processor bus machine with $C = 10$. In this program $N = 100$, $D = 303$, $W = 603$, $S_g = 500$, $S_l = 501$ and $S_s = 2$. Using the expression for F_m we obtain that $F_{bus} = 5.0$. The speedup factors for R are:

$SP^o(R) = 1.93$;, which should be at least 5
$seq(R) = 0.003$;, which is indeed less than 0.2
$grain(R) = 6$;, which is above 5, as it should be
$glob(R) = 4.15$;, which is rather higher than 2, as it should be

The speedup equation is

$$SP(R) = \min\left\{1.93, \frac{1}{0.003 + 0.166 + 0.1 + 0.415}\right\} = 1.46$$

and $P_{opt}(R) = 13$.

Fig. 5.6 Code used in
example of speedup
calculation

```
int  g, x, A[100];
g = 0;
x = 0;
parfor( int i= 0;i<101;i++)
{
    int  j;
    if (i == 100)
        for (j=0 ; j<100 ; j++)
            g = j;
    else {
        A[i] = x;
        x = g/2;
    }
}
```

The above program is clearly inefficient, because instead of a speedup between
5 and 10, it achieves a speedup of 1.46. If the user wants to improve the speedup,
he or she can add three additional processors to reach the optimal number of 13.
However, the speedup will still not exceed 1.93.

Using the speedup factors, the user can evaluate the program as follows. It is
not balanced, as there is one thread that is longer than the total length of the rest
of the threads. This lack of balance is the dominant factor that limits the optimal
speedup. In addition, there are too many global references. A reasonable approach
for working on this program is to try to improve $SP^o(R)$ and glob(R), and hope for
a speedup of 5.

In order to improve the performance, the new version Fig. 5.7 presents the following changes:

- The number of threads has been reduced from 100 to 12. The first 10 threads
  simulate the 99 previous threads.
- The instruction $x = g/2$ is executed outside the parallel construct. This change
  does not affect the results of this program because updating a global variable 99
  times in parallel is usually equivalent to updating it once. Note that in this case
  the value of x has been determined to be 49 or 99, which are only two out of the
  $0 \ldots 99$ possible values for x in the program of Fig. 5.6.
- In order to balance the execution graph, the "long" thread $i = 100$ is divided into
  two threads $i = 11$, $i = 12$, each executing 50 assignments out of the original
  100.
- The number of processors has been reduced to 5, i.e., $P = 5$.

In this version $N = 12$, $D = 165$, $W = 415$, $S_g = 300$, $S_l = 731$ and $S_s = 3$. Using the expression for F_m, we obtain that $F_{bus} = 1.16$. The speedup factors for R
are:

$SP^o(R) = 2.67$;, which is above 2.5, as required

```
int   g, x, A[100];
g = 0;
x = 0;
parfor( int i= 0;i<13;i++)
{
    int   j;
    if (i == 11)
        for (j=0 ; j<50 ; j++)
            g = j;
    else if (i == 12)
        for (j=50 ; j<100 ; j++)
            g = j;
    else
        for (j=i*10 ; j<(i+1)*10 ; j++)
        A[j] = x;
}

        x = g/2;
```

Fig. 5.7 Improving the speedup of the program in Fig. 5.6

$seq(R) = 0.007$;, which is indeed less than 0.4
$grain(R) = 34.5$;, which is above 5, as it should be
$glob(R) = 0.8$;, which is less than 2, as it should be

The speedup equation is

$$SP(R) = \min\left\{2.67, \frac{1}{0.007 + 0.057 + 0.2 + 0.08}\right\} = 2.9$$

and $P_{opt}(R) = 3.54$, which is close to the new choice $p = 5$. Hence, the new version of Fig. 5.7 satisfies the efficiency criteria presented so far.

Another simpler approach is to observe that the instructions $g = j$; are independent and can be executed in parallel. Hence, every $g = i$ instruction can be appended to $A[i] = x$; $x = g/2$; as described in Fig. 5.8, creating a balanced program that can be further optimized (extracting $x = g/2$; outside the parallel loop). The previous optimized version is more complicated, and is used to illustrate a broader set of optimization techniques.

Next, we consider the use of mapped light parfor as a way to improve the speedup factors. For example, consider the code segment in Fig. 5.9, executed on a 10 processor bus machine with $C = 10$ and $n = 10^6$. Due to the use of light parfor, the number of threads is reduced to $N = 10$. In this case $D = n/P + P \approx 10^5$ the work is $W \approx 10^6$, $S_g = 2 \cdot 10^6$, $S_l \approx 5 \cdot 10^6$ and $S_s = 0$. For a bus or a multicore machine $F_{bus} = 2/7 \times 10 = 2.85$.

The speedup factors for this version are:

$SP^o(R) = 10$;, which is indeed greater than $P/2 = 5$

Fig. 5.8 A simple balanced
program

```
int   g, x, A[100];
g = 0;
x = 0;
parfor( int i= 0;i<101;i++)
{
                g = i;
      if (i < 100){
            A[i] = x;
            x = g/2;
      }
}
```

$seq(R) = 0$;, which is indeed less than 0.2

$grain(R) = W/N = 10^5$, which is above 5, as it should be

$glob(R) = \frac{2 \cdot 10^6 \cdot 2.85}{10^6} = 5.7$, which is higher than the required 2

The speedup equation is

$$SP(R) = \min\left\{10, \frac{1}{0 + \frac{10 \cdot 10}{10^6 \cdot 10} + \frac{10^6}{10^6 \cdot 10} + \frac{2 \cdot 10^6 \cdot 2.85}{10^6 \cdot 10}}\right\} \approx 2$$

The program in Fig. 5.9 is clearly inefficient, because instead of a speedup between 5 and 10, it achieves a speedup of 2. The main limiting factor is the relatively
large number of global memory references.

This problem can be corrected by using the mapped version of light parfor, as
depicted in Fig. 5.10. In this case $D = n/P + P \approx 10^5$ the work is still $W \approx 10^6$,
$S_g = 50$, $S_l \approx 7 \cdot 10^6$ and $S_s = 0$. For such small values of S_g compared to S_l, the

```
int   A[P], B[P];
int   res=0, loc_sum[P];

lparfor( int i= 0;i<P;i++){
      int   sum=0,k,t1,t2;

      t1 = i*n/P;
      t2 = t1 + n/P-1;
      for(k=t1; k<t2 ; k++)
          sum += a[k]*b[k];
      loc_sum[i] = sum;
}
/* its inner product is the sum of the parts */
for(i=0 ; i<P ; i++)
      res += loc_sum[i];
```

Fig. 5.9 Initial version of the inner product

```
#define MAPPED -1

int   *A[P], *B[P];
int   res=0, loc_sum[P];

mapped lparfor( int i= 0;i<P;i++){
    A[i] = (int*) malloc(N/P);
    B[i] = (int*) malloc(N/P);
    /* initialize A and B */
}
/* multiply and sum */
mapped lparfor( int i= 0;i<P;i++){
    int  sum=0,k, *a=A[i], *b=B[i];
    for (k=0 ; k<N/P ; k++)
        sum += a[k]*b[k];
    loc_sum[i] = sum;
}
/* inner product is the sum of the parts */
for (i=0 ; i<P ; i++)
    res += loc_sum[i];
```

Fig. 5.10 Inner product using partitioned arrays

Fig. 5.11 Modified VPM
model supporting locality of
the ready queue

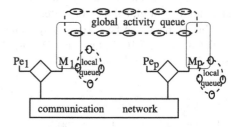

speedup is bounded by $SP^o = 10$, which is optimal. It is evident that using more processors $P = 100$ will not affect this result.

Note that thread management (i.e., access to the ready queue) should not be counted as a source for global memory references. Local variables should be allocated in the local memory of the processor that executes that thread wherein they are defined. As indicated earlier, this implies that a thread should always reside in the processor that has started to run it. Thus, *ParC* requires that threads should not migrate. Otherwise, the notion of a local variable as defined here has no meaning. Since threads cannot leave the processor, and one still needs to access the ready queue, a logical solution is to maintain a local queue of threads in every processor (see Fig. 5.11). Activities are created in the global queue, but when they are picked by a processor, they stay in the local queue of that processor.

To conclude, there are three speedup notions that are useful to a user developing a parallel application: $SP(A)$, the speedup of the algorithm, which uses the best sequential solution as a reference point, $SP^o(R)$, the maximum speedup of the program compared to a sequential execution of the program itself, and $SP^e(R)$, the effective speedup that takes hardware aspects into account. The other speedup factors can be used to check the efficiency of a parallel program. For a given program, the user should attempt to improve each factor to the maximum. The factors also indicate the barrier that offers the better performance, and where it is best to invest effort.

5.6   The Effect of Scheduling on $T(R)$

The time equation of the VPM model is actually a lower bound, in that it states the minimal execution time possible for all possible execution orders. It still remains to bound the execution time from above. Clearly, it is pointless to improve (reduce) the execution time of a program from below when the upper bound remains high. In other words, improving the lower bound of the time execution of all possible execution orders of a program does not exclude the possibility that some execution orders will still remain at the same execution time. Hence, in this section we will develop an upper bound for the execution time such that improving the speedup factors will improve both the lower and the upper bounds of the execution time.

Note that $T(R)$ smooths out delicate factors such as the effect of memory access patterns on bus contention and the overhead of cache misses in the MESI algorithm. It also ignores the fact that the overhead C contains global access to the ready queue and may depend on variable synchronization costs. Similarly, we ignore the fact that the time needed to create n threads in a queue might be a function of n, where n is the number of threads in $PF\ i = 1 \ldots n\ [R]$ or $PB\ [R1|\ \ldots\ Rn]$ statements. For example, the operating system can use a representative record, indicating that n threads need to be spawned. Thus, the creation of the representative is fast, but an inherent delay is caused when several processors attempt to extract threads from the same representative. An upper bound for the execution time can be developed only if the effect of at least one of these factors is bounded from above. In this section, the effect of possible schedulings (different mappings of threads to processors) is used to bound the execution time from above.

An important aspect ignored by the VPM model is the change in time caused by different possible orders in which the system can assign processors to threads. For example, consider the program in Fig. 5.12, executed on a machine with 2 processors. Since the machine has only two processors, one thread will be executed alone after the first two have been terminated. One order of execution is to start with A and B, and when B has terminated, use its processor to execute C, yielding $T = 100$. Another order of execution is to start with C and B, and when B or C has terminated, use one processor to execute A, yielding $T = 150$. Thus, different orders of execution may lead to different time calculations.

Fig. 5.12 A program
demonstrating the effect of
scheduling

```
parblock{
        int i; /* thread A */
        for(i=0;i<100;i++) a();
        :
        int i; /* thread B */
        for(i=0;i<50;i++) b();
        :
        int i; /* thread C */
        for(i=0;i<50;i++) c();
}
```

The delays caused by poor scheduling may be improved if context switches are used by the operating system. The following discussion describes some of the properties of preemption or context switches.

- The system halts the execution of a thread $T1$ while it is being executed by a processor $P1$. $P1$ records its current state (using a program counter, stack-pointer and registers) and saves it in the ready queue. Another thread $T2$ that is not currently being executed by a processor is selected from the ready queue by $P1$. Finally, $T2$'s state is restored in $P1$ (using a program counter, stack-pointer and registers)and $T2$'s execution is resumed.
- Context switches are initiated by one of the following events:
  - A time interrupt (e.g., every 10 milliseconds).
  - Explicit instructions that have been inserted in $T1$'s code by the compiler or manually inserted by the user.
  - A system call such as read/write operations that suspends the current thread until the operation (read/write) completes.
  - Synchronization operations between threads.
  - Spawning new threads.

  As will be explained later on, *ParC* favors inserted context switches over time interrupt context switches.
- Note that preemption switches the processors among the ready threads. Thus, it is essential in guaranteeing the "fair" execution of $n > p$ threads, where p is the number of processors. Fairness can be defined as simulating the execution of n threads by $p < n$ processors obtaining the same results as if these threads were executed by $p = n$ processors. If preemption is not used, thread $T1$ may loop forever, executing a "busy-wait" *while*(*flag*); and waiting for the reset operation *flag* $= 0$ of another thread $T2$. This reset operation is never executed because there is no processor to execute $T2$.
- Since $T1$ and $T2$ use the same set of shared variables whose memory address are distinct, there is no need to save or invalidate the cache lines of $T1$ when switching to $T2$. Similarly, there is no need to restore the cache lines used by $T2$ when its execution is resumed. Hence, context switch operations need not involve

Table 5.1 Fair scheduling with context switches

Processor	$t = 20$	$t = 40$	$t = 60$	$t = 80$	$t = 100$	$t = 120$
1	a_1	c_1	b_2	a_3	a_4	a_5
2	b_1	a_2	c_2	$b_3; c_3$	–	–

the cache. However, context switches increase the probability that the cache lines used by $T1$ will be evicted from the local cache by $T2$'s load/store operations.

- Context switches are expensive and may require about 100 clock cycles to complete. They need this amount of time because they include the operations of: (1) saving the state/context of a thread, (2) allocating a new/empty space in the ready queue, (3) saving the state of $T1$ in the ready queue, (4) restoring $T2$, and switching the stack pointer between the two threads.
- Special care must be given to interrupts that are received while a context switch is being executed, because interrupts may be received on $T1$'s stack but handled on $T2$'s stack.
- Context-switches are usually combined with a first-in-first-out (FIFO) policy of selecting threads from the ready queue. This is an important aspect because it ensures some sort of fairness and prevents the starvation of threads. *ParC* allows the user to change the FIFO policy and replicate it with another random selection, last-in-first-out or any other selection rule.

We will now consider how scheduling and preemption interact. Consider the program in Fig. 5.12, executed with a quantum time of $q = 20$ statements between every context switch. The operating system also uses a round robin policy (FIFO), for a **fair** selection of threads from the queue. Let $A = a_1; a_2; a_3; a_4; a_5$ be a division of the first thread $/ * A * /$ into a sequence of five units where each unit corresponds to 20 instructions of the loop. Similarly, let $B = b_1 = 20; b_2 = 20; b_3 = 10$ and $C = c_1 = 20; c_2 = 20; c_3 = 10$ be a division of threads $/ * B * /$ and $/ * C * /$ into the corresponding units. Then, (for the program in Fig. 5.12) any fair scheduling will achieve an execution time of 120 instructions (see Table 5.1). This scheduling improves the previous scheduling of 150 instructions, but it is still longer than the optimal scheduling of 100 instructions. Note that this scheduling satisfies the first-in-first-out fairness policy and processors select the next thread from the ready queue based on this criterion.

If the arbitrary selection of threads is allowed, **unfair** schedulings can result. Here, both the optimal scheduling of 100 instructions and the poor scheduling of 150 instructions are possible. These schedulings are demonstrated in Table 5.2 and Table 5.3. Note that the scheduling in Table 5.2 does not preserve the FIFO policy, nor does the optimal scheduling of Table 5.3.

Our model should hide this from the programmer because we do not expect that the programmer will calculate all of the possible orders of execution. Hence, we can no longer use an estimation but rather give upper and lower bounds to the execution time of a program. The execution time should be bounded below by the best execution order, and from above by the worst execution order.

Table 5.2 Unfair poor scheduling with context switches

Processor	$t = 20$	$t = 40$	$t = 50$	$t = 70$	$t = 90$	$t = 110$	$t = 130$	$t = 150$
1	b_1	b_2	b_3	a_1	a_2	a_3	a_4	a_5
2	c_1	c_2	c_3	–	–	–	–	–

Table 5.3 Unfair optimal scheduling with context switches

Processor	$t = 20$	$t = 40$	$t = 60$	$t = 80$	$t = 100$
1	a_1	a_2	a_3	a_4	a_5
2	b_1	c_1	b_2	c_2	$b_3; c_3$

Let a scheduling of a parallel program R be an assignment of a time and processor values to every instruction executed by this program. Finding the optimal scheduling (i.e., the scheduling with the minimal execution time) with a fixed number of processors is an *NP-complete* problem. However, using a known result an approximation scheduling can be defined such that $T(R)$ is less than twice the optimal time possible:

Claim 5.1 *Let T be a set of n threads executed by $P < n$ processors such that the sequential execution time of each thread is arbitrarily determined by an adversary when that thread starts. The execution time of each thread is thus fixed and does not depend on other external events such as a busy-wait. In addition, a thread ends either by termination or when it spawns new threads. Assume that the scheduling used by the P processors is to place all threads in a ready queue, letting each processor that completed a thread immediately select another thread from the ready queue. For any choice of the execution times by the adversary, the scheduling time obtained by the non-idle-processor scheduling is at most twice as bad as the best possible scheduling of these threads.*

Proof of this claim trivially follows from a stronger result that we will prove next.

Since the execution model of *ParC* explicitly demands that processors are never idle, it is actually implementing the above rule of scheduling and thus obtains up to twice the optimal execution time possible. Hence, $T(R)$ can be estimated as follows:

$$T(R) = 2 \cdot \max\left\{D, S_s + \frac{N \cdot C + W - S_s + S_g \cdot F_m(P, S_g, S_l)}{P}\right\}$$

This estimation can be improved by a closer examination of the effect of scheduling of a parallel program. Let S_i, $i = 1 \ldots P$ denote the number of instructions (including overheads) executed "with i processors" and let $S = \sum_{i=1}^{P} S_i$ be the total number of instructions. An instruction is executed with i processors if there were i processors working at the time that this instruction was executed. Since in our model a processor will take work from the queue when it runs out of work, an instruction is executed with $i < P$ processors only if the queue is empty and the rest of the processors are idle. In order to avoid referring to the execution order, we can say that the execution time T is equal to:

$$T = \frac{S_P}{P} + \frac{S_{P-1}}{P-1} + \cdots + S_1 = \frac{S_P}{P} + \sum_{i=1}^{P-1} \frac{S_i}{i}$$

Let $S_M = \max_{i=(P-1)}^{1} S_i$ then we can bound T as follow:

$$\frac{S}{P} \leq T \leq \frac{S}{P} + \log P * S_M$$

The $\log P$ is obtained by a recursive process wherein we can bound the sum of every two consecutive fractions in the sum as follows:

$$\left(\frac{1}{2} + \frac{1}{3}\right) + \left(\frac{1}{4} + \frac{1}{5}\right) + \left(\frac{1}{6} + \frac{1}{7}\right) + \left(\frac{1}{8} + \frac{1}{9}\right) + \cdots$$
$$< (1) + \left(\frac{1}{2}\right) + \left(\frac{1}{3}\right) + \left(\frac{1}{4}\right) + \cdots$$

This method, however, dose not solve the problem, because in several cases, computing S_M requires that we compute all S_i. Since the addition to $\frac{S}{P}$ results from instructions that were executed with $i < P$ processors, we might try to bound its direct effect on T rather than using the total sum of these instructions. Basically, we want to bound T by $T < \frac{S}{P} + T^{\text{inf}}$, where T^{inf} is the time needed for a machine with an unbounded number of processors (actually T^{inf} is equal to the longest path D from the previous section). The proof and the definitions of the above claim use the concept of "the execution graph" of a parallel program.

The execution graph (defined earlier but presented here in a more convenient form) of a program $G(R)$ is defined by the composition of the graphs of the threads spawned by R to form $G(R)$. Note that the execution graph can be determined if the programmer knows the exact sizes of the number of threads spawned at any point or the number of iterations of every loop. Usually, these sizes are a function of the input, and may be known by the programmer in advance. Hence, the programmer can compute $G(R)$ as a function of N, the input size. More formally and graphically, the execution graph is defined as follows (the '|c' denotes an overhead of 'c' instructions):

```
G(PF i=1..n [R])        ==>                          *
                                                     |
                                 -------------------------
                                 |c         |c          |c
                                 G(R1)      G(Ri)       G(Rn)
                                 |          |           |
                                 -------------------------
                                                     |
                                                     *
```

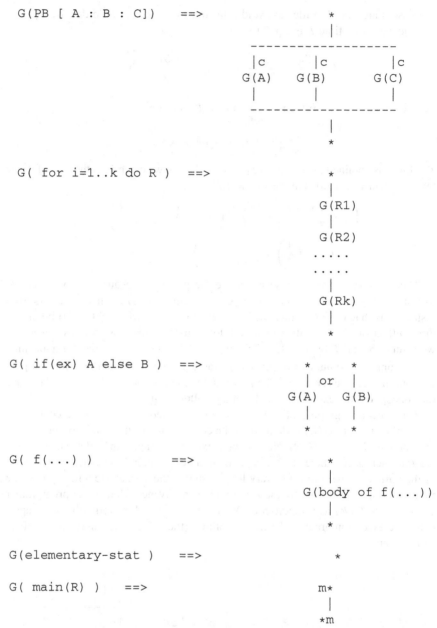

```
G(PB [ A : B : C])      ==>                            *
                                                       |
                                 --------------------
                                |c          |c            |c
                                G(A)       G(B)          G(C)
                                |           |             |
                                 --------------------
                                                       |
                                                       *


G( for i=1..k do R )    ==>                            *
                                                       |
                                                     G(R1)
                                                       |
                                                     G(R2)
                                                     . . . . .
                                                     . . . . .
                                                       |
                                                     G(Rk)
                                                       |
                                                       *


G( if(ex) A else B )    ==>                 *          *
                                            |  or      |
                                          G(A)       G(B)
                                            |          |
                                            *          *


G( f(...) )             ==>                            *
                                                       |
                                                G(body of f(...))
                                                       |
                                                       *


G(elementary-stat )     ==>                           *

G( main(R) )            ==>                          m*
                                                      |
                                                     *m
```

Note that G is a DAG beginning and ending with one node. G also satisfies the rule that any "split" (PF or PB) must be joined eventually to one node. After establishing the notion of $G(R)$, we can determine the necessary definition for the upper bound of T. For a given program R and an instance of its execution graph $G(R)$ (now referred to as G) and a parallel machine with P processors, we use the following definitions:

S: The total number of nodes in G or the instruction executed.

Deletion: A node can be removed from G if its in-degree is zero, meaning that all of its fathers have been removed. Note that the only case in which a node has more than one father is the node following $G(PF)$ or $G(PB)$. Every node that is removed corresponds to an instruction being executed by some processor.

Candidate-Group: All of the nodes that can be removed. Initially, the candidate group contains 'm*'.

Full-Step: Remove P nodes from the candidate group. Such a step corresponds to a step in the parallel machine where each processor executes one instruction. One cannot remove a node covered in this step.

Bounded-Step: The candidate group may contain fewer than P nodes (as in the case of a sequential program). In that case, some processors are idle and have no work to do.

Execution Order: By removing the upper node of $G(PF)$ or $G(PB)$, many new nodes can join the candidate group. The order in which the nodes are removed by full or bounded steps until G becomes empty determines an execution order.

T: The number of steps needed to delete all nodes in G, or the length of an execution order.

G_t: For a given execution order, G_t is the remaining graph that is left after the first t **bounded steps**.

$MLP(G_t)$: One of the longest paths in G_t. Note that the $MLP(G_t)$ starts from nodes in the candidate group and ends in '*m'.

T^{inf}: is the length of $MLP(G_0 = G)$. If $P = \text{inf}$, then there is an execution order of size T^{inf}. Hence, T^{inf} is the fastest execution time for a given program and its execution graph.

Theorem 5.1 *For a given program R and its execution graph, the time (or the number of steps) needed by **any execution order** with P processors to execute R is bounded by*:

$$\text{MAX}\left(\frac{S}{P}, T^{\text{inf}}\right) \leq T \leq \frac{S}{P} + T^{\text{inf}}$$

Clearly, any execution order needs at least $\frac{S}{P}$ steps to remove all nodes in G. However, bounded steps may prolong this process. Clearly, no program can be executed faster than T^{inf}, because any node in $MLP(G)$ can be removed only in the next step after its father has been removed.

Claim 5.2 *Let M^{ex_i} and R^{ex_i} denote the number of full and bounded steps executed by an execution order ex_i. Then, for any execution order ex_i $M^{ex_i} \leq \frac{S}{P}$ and $R^{ex_i} \leq T^{\text{inf}}$.*

Intuitively, this follows from the fact that each unbounded step must remove one node from every path that belongs to the group of paths with the maximal length in G. Since $T^{ex_i} = M^{ex_i} + R^{ex_i}$ Claim 5.2 yields Theorem 5.2. The first part of

Claim 5.2 is thus trivial but for the second part of the claim we use the following lemma:

Lemma 5.1 *The length of MLP(G_t) is less equal to $T^{\text{inf}} - t$.*

This lemma shows that the length of $MLP(G_{T^{\text{inf}}})$ is zero. Hence, in the next step, all nodes are removed, and the above claim follows. The proof of Lemma 5.1 results from the fact that there are fewer than P $MLP(G_t)$ in the current graph. Hence, all of them are removed at the t'th bounded step.

This claim is tight in that it can be shown that a simple improvement of the upper bound for T is tight. In other words, let us find a $G(R)$ that cannot be scheduled with fewer than $\frac{S}{P} + T^{\text{inf}}$ steps. Let the new bound be:

$$T \leq \left\lfloor \frac{S - S_s}{P} \right\rfloor + T^{\text{inf}}$$

where S_s is number of nodes in $G(R)$ that are not in the scope of any PF or PB. Clearly, all of the nodes in S_s belong to the longest path in $G(R)$ and therefore should not be counted twice (i.e., in $\frac{S}{P}$). The $\lfloor \ldots \rfloor$ can be justified as follows:

$$gap = \left\lceil \frac{S - S_s}{P} \right\rceil - \left\lfloor \frac{S - S_s}{P} \right\rfloor \leq 1$$

If the *gap* is one, then there is at least one bounded step that was counted in the $\frac{S - S_s}{P}$ term and in T^{inf}. This can be avoided if $\lfloor \ldots \rfloor$ are used.

Let $G(R)$ be ⊞ with $S - S_s = 5 - 2 = 3$ and $T^{\text{inf}} = 3$, then for $P = 2$ the upper bound yields $T \leq \lfloor \frac{3}{2} \rceil + 3 = 4$. Clearly, $G(R)$ cannot be scheduled with fewer than 4 steps using two processors.

In the above formalism, processors were able to switch from one thread to another through the granularity of an instruction. This is not practical. Common solutions allow context switching every pre-defined quantum time.

Corollary 5.1 *Let q be the quantum time for context switches, and c the overhead for context switches. If we insert the overhead c in G every q nodes along any path from the root of G, then the new size of G is increased by at most $(1 + \frac{c}{q})$ and so is the length of every path in G. The execution time for a given program and its graph G is bounded (regardless of any execution order) by:*

$$\text{MAX}\left(\frac{S}{P}, T^{\text{inf}} \right) \leq T \leq \left(\frac{S}{P} + T^{\text{inf}} \right) \cdot \left(1 + \frac{c}{q} \right)$$

The effect of this kind of context switch can be included by simply adding the overhead of the context switch as nodes in the graph. The nodes of the context switches should be added at a distance proportional to the quantum time.

Claim 5.3 *Let M^{ex_i} and R^{ex_i} denote the number of full and bounded steps executed by an execution order ex_i. Then, for any execution order ex_i $M^{ex_i} \leq \frac{S}{P}$ and $R^{ex_i} \leq T^{\inf}$.*

Hence, the effect of scheduling and preemption (context switches) on $T(R)$ can be stated as follows:

Theorem 5.2 *Let q be the scheduling time quantum, and c' the overhead for a single preemption. The execution time $T(R)$ is bounded (regardless of any execution order) by:*

$$T(R) \leq \left(D + S_s + \frac{N \cdot C + W - S_s + S_g \cdot F_m(P, S_g, S_l)}{P} \right) \cdot \left(1 + \frac{c'}{q} \right)$$

Practically, this implies that the effect of non-optimal scheduling (with a reasonable choice of q) can only double the execution time.

5.7 Accounting for Memory References for Multicore Machines

In this section we consider how to expand the time formula of the previous section to account for the bus transactions made in multicore machines. A closer look at the structure of the virtual machine in Fig. 5.1 shows that a processor has direct access to its local memory as opposed to access through a network to the global memory (as noted in Sect. 5.3. In addition, parts of the global memory may be local to other processors). The time formula

$$T(R) \leq \left(D + S_s + \frac{N \cdot C + W - S_s + S_g \cdot F_m(P, S_g, S_l)}{P} \right) \cdot \left(1 + \frac{c'}{q} \right)$$

accounts only for multiple accesses to the bus caused by non-local memory references. For multicore machines this is unsatisfactory because it does not account for the overhead generated by the MESI protocol (as described in the earlier Sect. 4.5). In this section we attempt to port the above time formula to account for the MESI's bus transactions.

Consider the following two programs executed over MESI. Which one is better? Which one minimizes the number of bus transactions generated by MESI? Assuming that x and y are allocated to two different cache lines, it is likely that the mixed case will generate more bus transactions than the homogeneous case. In the mixed case, after a true synchronous execution of both threads there will be two transitions of x/y between the threads, while in the homogeneous case there will be only one transition of x/y.

`int x,y;`
`parblock`
`{`
`    x++;`
`    y++;`
`    x++;`
`    y++;`
`}: {x++;`
`    y++;`
`    x++;`
`    y++;`
`} epar`
	`parblock`
	`{`
	`    x++;`
	`    x++;`
	`    y++;`
	`    y++;`
	`}: {y++;`
	`    y++;`
	`    x++;`
	`    x++;`
	`} epar`

Mixing order of assignments versus	homogeneous order

The proposed model is called the transitions model. It counts the number of "transitions" of a shared variable between different threads. Each transition is a possible bus transaction (BusRdX or BusRd) of the MESI protocol where a cache line moves from one cache to another cache. The following assumptions are used in deriving the proposed model:

- It will be hard to track transactions based on the CPU location of shared variables. We can approximate them by considering the transactions between threads. By doing so, we assume that any two threads that are updating a shared variable are not executed by the same CPU and hence will lead to some cache misses and a MESI bus transaction.
- The way that variables are allocated to the cache lines may affect the resulting number of transactions. For example, in the above program if both x, y are allocated to the same cache line, then the number of bus transactions may increase. In order to avoid tracking the mapping
- All data dependencies must be exposed. For example, we should know whether or not $*p$ and $*q$ may point to the same variable in order to determine if the execution of $*p$ followed by $*q$ will result in a bus transaction. Given that tracking data dependencies through pointers is difficult, we will assume that concurrent access through pointers is not likely to occur and that data dependencies are due to shared variables and array references only.
- Different schedulings can affect the number of bus transactions that are generated.

The transactions are computed syntactically using the following procedure:

- Each $PF = i = 1 \ldots n \; do \; S_i$ is replaced by $PB \; [S_i | S_{i+1} | \ldots S_{i+k}]$ where k is a constant sufficiently large enough to expose array backward dependencies. An array backwards dependency is formed when an array element used in iteration

i was updated in a previous iteration, e.g., a recurrence of the form $t1 = A[i - 1]; \ldots A[i]+ = t1;$. Formally, let d be the maximal loop-carried dependency of a for-loop; then, $k = d^2$. The number of arrows that this PF contributes is $arrow(PB [S_i | S_{i+1} | \ldots S_{i+k}]) * (n - l)/k$.

- Sequential for-loops $for(i = l; i < n; i++)S_i$ are similarly transformed into block statements $\{S_i | S_{i+1} | \ldots S_{i+k}\}$.
- If two variables are likely to be in the same cache line, they are replaced with the same name.
- The execution graph G is constructed for the resulting program.
- Arrows are placed following some topological order of visiting the nodes in G.

5.8 On the Usage of a Simulator

In here we briefly discuss the use of simulations to optimize the execution of parallel programs. In this respect optimizing speedups depends on isolating and understanding the effect of several parameter of the execution times as measured by a simulator for a given program. These parameters are the input size, number of cores, context-switch overhead, context switch quantum time and the scheduling policy. By the term simulation of a parallel program we refer to a sequential execution of an instrumented version of the program such that after each step of the program (execution of an assignment, evaluation of an expression or memory reference) the control is transfer to a routine that accumulates different statistics. Controlled execution of an instrumented version allow the simulator to do the following operations:

- The simulator can control or determine which instruction will be executed next, thus it has full control over the execution order of the program's code. Thus the simulator can execute the scheduling model of Fig. 1.16 computing the theoretical executions time for the case of infinite number of processors and it can also compute the execution time for a fix number of processors P by simulating the virtual machine model of Fig. 5.1 computing execution times of processors/cores and other relevant statistics.
- In particular, since the simulator actually executes the program by selecting a possible scheduling of its threads it can also measure the effect of executing the context switch operations occurred during the selected scheduling. Thus it can compute execution times for different values of the context-switch overhead C and the time duration between context-switch operations q. Thus we distinguish between the simulator considered here
- The simulator can also simulate the MESI algorithm and measure the overhead of the resulting cache misses and its effect on the resulting scheduling and the execution time.
- We can use the ability of the simulator to measure execution times with different values of C, P, q, n (n is the input size) to evaluate how sensitive a given program is to the execution order. Following the approach in Ben-Asher and Haber (1996)

we say that a program can be called "practically optimal" if for a reasonable number of cores P, and a reasonable context switch overhead C, there is a minimal input size n_0 and a choice of a context switch quantum time q, such that for every $n > n_0$ the gap between ideal execution times $Tinf$ is relatively small and stays fix. By the term small we mean that it is proportional to the ratio between the optimal number of cores (the maximal width of the execution graph) and P is the actual number of cores used in the simulations.

Consider the PRAM algorithm (following code) computing Strongly Connected Components of sparse graphs described in Jaja (1992), p. 213. This algorithm use the fact that the graph is sparse, (i.e. the number of edges is $m < O(\frac{n^2}{\log n})$) where n is the number of nodes in the graph) to compute the connected components in $O(\log n)$ parallel steps, compare to $\Omega(\log^2 n)$ needed by a transitive closure type of algorithm.

```
#define n 20
#define E 50
int M[E][2]; /* edges array */
int D[2*n]; /* list of trees transforming to stars*/
int star[2*n]; /* check star */
int e; /* number of edges */
isstar() {
parfor( int i=0;i<n;i++){ star[i] = 1; }
parfor( int i=0;i<n;i++){
    if(D[i])
        if(D[i] != D[D[i]]){
            star[i] = 0; star[D[i]] = 0; star[D[D[i]]] = 0; }
}
parfor( int i=0;i<n;i++){ star[i] = star[D[i]]; }
}

scc(){
int b=1;
while(b){
    /* graft tree i to node j */
    parfor(int k=0;k<e;k++)
    { int i,j;
        i = M[k][0]; j = M[k][1];
        if((D[i] == D[D[i]]) && (D[j] < D[i])) D[D[i]] = D[j];
    }
    /* Graft rooted stars onto other trees if possible*/
    isstar();
    parfor(int k=0;k<e;k++)
    { int i,j;
        i = M[k][0]; j = M[k][1];
        if((star[i]) && (D[j] != D[i])) D[D[i]] = D[j];
    }
```

```
        /* pointer jumping */
        parfor( int i=0;i<n;i++){
            if(D[i]) D[i] = D[D[i]];
        }
        /* check if all nodes are in a star */
        b = 0;
        parfor( int i=0;i<n;i++){
            if(D[i])
                if(D[i] != D[D[i]]) b = 1;
        }
} }
```

A program computing strongly connected components of a graph.

The program was executed by the simulator on a graph of random chains with the following parameters: n the size of the graph (actually matches the width of the execution graph), and P the number of cores. For each n and P there where two sets of experiments: in the first we measured $Tinf$ as a function of q (the context switch delay), and in the second we measured T_P. Our results Fig. 5.13 show that an for $n = 80$ and $P = 30$ $Tinf \leq T_P$, however for $P = 50$ we get that $Tinf > T_P$. When we increased n (width of the graph) to 200, we got the same phenomenon however the change happens between $p = 50$ and $p = 100$.

Note that the execution times of this program can vary according to the actual scheduling that took place. This explains the minimum points of some curves (around $Q = 80$ and $Q = 100$). Hence, based on the simulation results, a proper choice of Q may yield a better scheduling of a given program. As for the gap between effective T_P and ideal times $Tinf$, we see that there are optimal combinations of Q and P, where this gap is minimal. Thus, if P is fixed (actual number of available cores), there are cases where we can close this gap by proper choice of Q, otherwise (as is the case for $n = 200$ and $p = 50$) we can not close this gap and should attempt to modify the program.

5.9   Conclusions

Efficient execution of parallel shared memory programs (such as those written in *ParC*) requires optimized scheduling, context switching, allocation of threads to processors and load balancing. An important factor in efficiency is the ratio between local and global memory references. When this ratio is smaller than the underlying network bandwidth, the global memory references collide and cause delays. This ratio is particularly important when the network bandwidth is small, as in cases with bus machines where only one memory reference is carried out in a step.

A simple model that bounds the process of executing a parallel program in a shared memory machine has been presented. The model incorporates overheads for creating threads, context switching, scheduling, and the local/global ratio of memory references into a basic speedup formula. The formula actually predicts or mea-

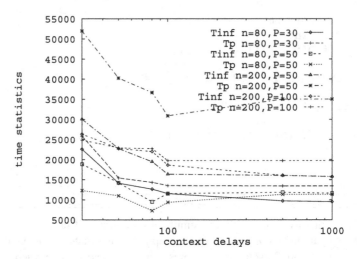

Fig. 5.13 Simulation results for the *scc()* program

sures the expected efficiency of executing a given program. Using a simple calculation, the user is able to determine how well his or her program exploits the hardware.

If the prediction is negative, the user can analyze the program (*R*) and determine the main cause for its lack of efficiency. Possible causes include one (or more) of the following factors:

- The optimal speedup factor (SP^o) bounds the amount of parallelism possible for this program regardless of any hardware limitations.
- The length of inherent sequential code segments (*seq*(*R*)).
- The average size of the threads (*grain*(*R*)). If the average size is too large, the operating system's overhead can dominate the execution times.
- The ratio between global memory references and local ones (*glob*(*R*)). If this ratio is greater than the bandwidth of the communication network, communication latency will slow down the execution. We believe that determining this ratio is also useful for multicore machines where shared memory is simulated via a cache coherency protocol.

Given that the user cannot change the hardware, he or she has to modify the program so that it will achieve better performances. Each of the above factors is matched with a transformation that reduces its effect whenever possible. This methodology can lead to efficient versions of parallel programs.

5.10 Exercises

5.10.1 Optimizing Speedup Factors

Consider the following program with $P > 5$ and $C = 10$:

```
#define N n;

int y=0,g=0;

parfor(int i=1;i<=N;i++) {
    int x;
    x = i;
    if((i % sqrt(N))==0) {
        parfor(int j=1;j<=sqrt(N);j++){
            int l;
            for(l=j;l<100+j;l++)
                faa(&x,l+i);
        }
        faa(&y,x);
    } else g = x;
}
```
A non-efficient program

1. Compute the speedup and the speedup factors for this program (as functions of *n* and *P*).
2. What are the limiting factors for this program?
3. What is the optimal number of processors (as functions of *n* and *P*) for this program? (Check the condition for *D*).
4. What is the maximal value for *P*?
5. Describe potential improvements for this program.
6. What observations can be made regarding the use of *faa*()? Is it possible to use *faa*() to reduce the number of global references?
7. Provide a new, final, optimized version of this program.
8. Compute the new speedup and its factors and evaluate the results.
9. What types of parallel programs inherently have efficiencies equal to one?
10. For the matrix multiplication program in Fig. 3.9, find the minimal *N* for which the parallel execution becomes slower than a sequential one.

5.10.2 Amdhal's Law

Amdhal's Law states that the speedup of a program (be it a sequential or parallel one) is always restricted by the fraction of its inherent sequential part. Determine which of the following claims is incorrect. For each incorrect claim, write a small parallel program showing that this claim is really false.

1. Let β (a rational number) denote the fraction of the inherent sequential part of a program. Thus, $1 - \beta$ is the part of the program that is or may be subject to parallelism. Clearly, β characterizes every possible program.

2. Let $T(i)$ denote the execution time of a program executed by a parallel machine with i processors. The speedup of a program executed with n processors is $SP = \frac{T(1)}{T(n)}$.

3. The inherent sequential part of the program cannot be parallelized. Hence, $T(n) = T(1) \cdot \beta + \frac{T(1)(1-\beta)}{n}$.

4. The speedup for $n > \frac{1}{\beta}$ is always

$$SP = \frac{1}{\beta + \frac{(1-\beta)}{n}} \approx \frac{1}{2\beta}$$

Thus, no matter how many processors we use, the speedup of a program will always be less than $\frac{1}{2\beta}$. Given that every program must have some substantial fixed fraction of the inherent sequential code, there is no point in using large parallel machines.

5.10.3 Scheduling

A parallel machine with three processors that does not perform context switches is provided. The machine executes the following "unbalanced" program:

```
parfor(int i=1;i<6;i++) {
    int k,j;
    if(i == 5) k = 200;
        else k = i*100;
    for(j=0;j<k;j++);
}
Unbalanced program.
```

Let the running time of a program be the maximal number of instructions executed by one of the three processors.

1. Provide a mapping of the threads to processors (schedule) that achieves minimal running time, and justify its optimality.
2. Provide a mapping of the threads to processors that achieves maximal running time.
3. Is there a possibility that, for some program and a parallel machine, there is a mapping/schedule whose execution time is less than the average? (assume that the sum of all threads' time is divided by P).
4. Which of the two features (context switch or thread migration) is needed to guarantee optimal running time? (Give examples justifying your claims).
5. Is there a possibility that, for some program and our standard machine model, there is a mapping/schedule where the gap between the most loaded processor and the least loaded processor is greater than the longest execution time of a thread?

6. In general, can the difference between the minimal and maximal running time, over all possible schedulings, exceed the execution time of the longest thread? Discuss this issue for machines with different scheduling policies (i.e., context switch and migration).

5.10.4 Two-Processor Machines

A parallel machine with two processors that does not use migration (i.e., the threads cannot move from processor to processor during execution) is provided. The machine executes the following program:

```
int g=0;

f(x,y)
int x,y;
{
    int L;
    for(L=0;L<y;L++) y=y;
    if(x > 1) parblock{
        f(x/2,y+1);
          :
        f(x/2,y-1);
    }
    faa(&g,1);
}
main(){
    f(4,3);
    printf("g=%d",g);
}
```
Recursive calls plus faa.

1. Draw the execution graph and number each thread, leaving some space between the instructions in the execution graph. Loops should be inserted as a sequence of instructions, as follows:

```
                                   |
                                  L=1
                                   |
                                  y=y
for L=1..y do x=y;      ==>         |
                                  L=2
                                   |
                                  y=y
                                   |
```

2. What is the final value of g?
3. What will happen if the assignment $y = y$ is replaced by $x = y$?
4. Find a scheduling for the execution graph by adding a time/processor index to every instruction in the execution graph (recall that threads are not supposed to migrate). What is the execution time for this program?
5. Add a thread index i to all of the variables (x_i) in the execution graph (including parameters). Map the variables to processors such that x_i will be mapped to a different processor than y_i. Mark accesses to variables in the execution graph as local or external. What is the ratio between local and external accesses in this program?
6. Let E denote the maximal number of simultaneous external accesses that a parallel machine allows (e.g., 1 for a bus machine). What is the maximal value of E that this program needs in order to minimize the overhead due to multiple accesses? For a given program execution, let L/G be the maximal number of local/external memory accesses that a processor executes. What is the optimal ratio between L, G and P, such that the program execution is not necessarily slowed down? (Check the case where $P = 3, L = 2, G = 3$).

5.10.5 Sync-Based Exercises

A parallel machine that does not perform context switch and thread migrations is provided. The machine executes the following sync-based program:

```
int g,N;
f(n)
int n;
{ int k=0;
    if(n < N) sync;
    parblock {
        int j;
        for(j=0;j<100;j++);
        k = k+1;
        sync;

        :

        int j;
        for(j=0;j<50;j++);
        sync;
        k = k-1;

        :

        int j;
        for(j=0;j<50;j++);
        if(k != 0) g = g+1;
```

```
        if(n >= 2) f(n/2); else sync;
    }
    faa(&g,k);
}
main(){
    g = 0;
    scanf("%d",&N);
    f(N);
    printf("g=%d",g);
}
```

A sync-based program

1. Extend the scheduling rules to include sync instructions.
2. Draw the execution graph of the program for $N = 8$; use a node [50] to mark a loop of 50 instructions. Give the same index to every group of *sync* nodes that are executed together.
3. What is the minimal and maximal value for g?
4. Using the scheduling rules to mark the nodes of the execution graph for the case when $P = 3$, what is the execution time?
5. Using the scheduling rules to mark the nodes of the execution graph for the case when $P = 1$, what is the execution time?
6. What will be changed in the conclusions obtained so far if we replace 100 with 4, and 50 with 2 in the program?
7. What is the minimal running time for the case $P = 2$ (Justify your answer).
8. Compute $T(R)$; note that D is affected by the execution of the sync.

5.10.6 The Effect of Sync on the Execution Time

The following program uses address passing in order to communicate between recursive parallel calls:

```
int t=0,g=0;

f(x,z)
int *x,z;
{ int y;
    parblock {
        y = 1;
        if(z > 0) f(&y,z-1);
        sync;
```

```
            *x = y + 2;
      } : {
          int i;
          sync;
          for(i=0;i<y;i++) g = g+1;
      }
  }
  f(&t,4);
```
A program demonstrating address passing.

1. Draw the execution graph $G(f)$ for the execution of $f(\&t, 4)$ (leave enough space for adding marks and instructions). Add g, t in the beginning of $G(f)$ to indicate their declaration. Also, add $G(f)$ to the variables (x_i, z') y_i whenever a call to $f(x, z)$ took place, where i is the thread index and z' is the value of z at the call.

2. Use an arrow to show to which variable x_i points. Add all *sync* instructions to $G(f)$, followed by $*x_i = y_i + 2$; when needed. Use a broken line to join *syncs* that are synchronized.

3. Add the value of y_j after the execution of the $*x_i = y_i + 2$; that modified it, next to y_j. Inside every loop in $G(f)$ mark the number of iterations it executed. What are the values of g and t at the end? Explain why there is no need to replace $g = g + 1$ by $faa(\&g, 1)$ in order to avoid the overwriting effects caused by the fact that $g = g + 1$ is not atomic.

4. For a general execution of $f(\&t, n)$; with $p = 3$ and $C = 50$ compute all of the parameters $N, D, W, S_s, S_g, S_l, F_{bus}$, and the speedup factors. Evaluate the results and give a short explanation of the connection between $f()$'s execution structure and the results.

5. The following rules can be adopted as a policy by a parallel operating system:
   (a) An idle processor should take threads from the queue whenever possible.
   (b) The thread queue is managed as a FIFO queue.
   (c) The thread queue is managed as a LIFO queue.
   (d) Context switching (preemption).
   (e) Activities migration.
   (f) Local variables of a thread are mapped in the local memory of the processor that started to execute this thread.
   (g) The first son of a thread is mapped to the same processor that started to execute this thread.
   (h) The last son of a thread is mapped to the same processor that started to execute this thread.
   (i) A partial group of sons (greater than one) of a thread are mapped to the same processor that started to execute this thread.

   Which combination of the above rules or their negation is best suited to execute $f(\&t, n)$? (Explain why). Which combination of the above rules or their negation is worst suited to execute $f(\&t, n)$? (Explain why). Which of the above rules contradict one another, in the sense that any one of them might speed up execution, but using both of them together will neutralize their intended effect?

5.11 Bibliographic Notes

Analytical study of speedup of parallel programs has been widely studied since the early days of parallel processing. Eager et al. (1989) establish some relations between speedup and efficiency showing that there is a bound as to how much both can be poor. Kruskal et al. (1990) developed a theory of parallel algorithms that emphasizes speedup over sequential algorithms, and efficiency in a form of complexity classes. This differs from the method presented here which is focused on the ability to bound the speedup. Reference to the NP-completeness of finding optimal schedulings for parallel programs can be found in Johnson (1983). Approximating the optimal scheduling can be done in polynomial times as is described in Papadimitriou and Yannakakis (1990). Williams and Bobrowicz (1985) obtained speedup predictions of scientific parallel programs for different number of processors using simulation techniques. Eager et al. (1989) showed that:

- The speedup is bounded by the average parallelism.
- The speedup and efficiency cannot both be bad (i.e. low efficiency guarantees high speedup).
- For static allocation of processors, a number of processors that matches the average parallelism is near optimal.

An elementary result regarding speedup of parallel programs is 'Amdahl's law" (Amdahl 1967), namely that the serial part of a program limits the speedup that may be achieved by parallelism. Kruskal (1985) argues with Amdahl's law and claims that linear speedup is almost always possible for large enough problems. Karp and Flatt (1990) proposed a new metric measuring the serial fraction which is calculated from the number of processors p and the measured speedup s as $\frac{1/s - 1/p}{1 - 1/p}$. Flatt (1991) showed that scaling up the problem size may improve efficiency and defy Amdahl's law, but may also increase the total execution time to such an extent that it would not be practical.

Sun and Gustafson (1991) show that the speedup notion is unfair in that it favors slow processors and poorly coded programs proposing two new performance metrics that are more fair. Several practical works considered measuring real speedups. For example, Wieland et al. (1992) expose a large difference in measuring speedup relative to parallel code running on one processor, or relative to an independent optimal sequential program. Sun and Ni (2002) proposed three new models of parallel speedup along with their speedup formulations. Zhang (1991) proposed a performance model to estimate the effect of factors such as sequential code, barriers, cache coherence and virtual memory paging on the execution time.

Many parallel programming languages use thread system that is similar to the VPM model described here, e.g. Gehani and Roome (1986), Kuehn and Siegel (1985) and Rose (1987). Using fetch and add instructions is described in Gottlieb et al. (1983).

References

Amdahl, G.M.: Validity of the single processor approach to achieving large scale computer capabilities. In: AFIPS Spring Joint Comput. Conf., vol. 30, pp. 483–485 (1967)

Ben-Asher, Y., Haber, G.: On the usage of simulators to detect inefficiency of parallel programs caused by bad schedulings: the simparc approach. J. Syst. Softw. 33, 313–327 (1996)

Eager, D.L., Zahorjan, J., Lazowska, E.D.: Speedup versus efficiency in parallel systems. IEEE Trans. Comput. 38(3), 408–423 (1989)

Flatt, H.P.: Further results using the overhead model for parallel systems. IBM J. Res. Dev. 35(5/6), 721–726 (1991)

Gehani, N.H., Roome, W.D.: Concurrent C. Softw. Pract. Exp. 16(9), 821–844 (1986)

Gottlieb, A., Lubachevsky, B., Rudolph, L.: Basic techniques for the efficient coordination of very large numbers of cooperating sequential processes. ACM Trans. Program. Lang. Syst. 5(2), 164–189 (1983)

Jaja, J.: An Introduction to Parallel Algorithms. Addison-Wesley, Reading (1992)

Johnson, D.S.: The NP-completeness column: An ongoing guide. J. Algorithms 4(2), 189–203 (1983). (about parallel scheduling)

Karp, A.H., Flatt, H.P.: Measuring parallel processor performance. Commun. ACM 33(5), 539–543 (1990)

Kruskal, C.P.: Performance bound on parallel processors: An optimistic view. In: Broy, M. (ed.) Control Flow and Data Flow: Concepts of Distributed Programming. NATO ASI Series, vol. F-14, pp. 331–344. Springer, Berlin (1985)

Kruskal, C.P., Rudolph, L., Snir, M.: A complexity theory of efficient parallel algorithms. Theor. Comput. Sci. 71(1), 95–132 (1990)

Kuehn, J.T., Siegel, H.J.: Extensions to the C programming language for SIMD/MIMD parallelism. In: Intl. Conf. Parallel Processing, pp. 232–235 (1985)

Papadimitriou, C.H., Yannakakis, M.: Towards an architecture-independent analysis of parallel algorithms. SIAM J. Comput. 19(2), 322–328 (1990)

Rose, J.R.: C*: A C++-like language for data parallel computation. In: USENIX Proc. C++ Workshop, pp. 127–134 (1987)

Sun, X.H., Gustafson, J.L.: Toward a better parallel performance metric*. Parallel Comput. 17(10–11), 1093–1109 (1991)

Sun, X.H., Ni, L.M.: Another view on parallel speedup. In: Proceedings of Supercomputing'90, pp. 324–333. IEEE, New York (2002). ISBN 0818620560

Wieland, F., Reiher, P., Jefferson, D.: Experiences in parallel performance measurement: The speedup bias. In: Symp. Experiences with Distributed & Multiprocessor Syst., pp. 205–215. USENIX, Berkeley (1992)

Williams, E., Bobrowicz, F.: Speedup predictions for large scientific parallel programs on Cray X-MP like architectures. In: Intl. Conf. Parallel Processing, pp. 541–543 (1985)

Zhang, X.: Performance measurement and modeling to evaluate various effects on a shared memory multiprocessor. IEEE Trans. Softw. Eng. 87–93 (1991)

Chapter 6
Compilation Techniques

Compiler technologies are crucial for the efficient execution of sequential programs, a statement which is also true for parallel programs. For parallel programs its the operating system performs most of the work. As a result, the overhead for scheduling and distributed shared memory simulation increases. In this chapter we present simple compilation techniques that can be used to guarantee efficient execution of shared memory parallel programs and in particular for multicore machines. We address the difficulties involved with supporting preemption/context-switch of threads in compiled code. Note that preemption is crucial for fair execution of shared memory programs but not necessarily every thread should be preempted repeatedly.

We present a comprehensive approach for compilation, where efficiency is guaranteed whenever preemption is not really needed. The compiler is used to insert explicit context-switch instructions, so that preemption is supported only where it is required. In addition, the proposed compilation scheme guarantees that the set of stacks of each thread (called "cactus stack") is embedded in the regular stack of each core, such that most of the threads are spawned as regular function calls or loop iterations. Finally, the efficiency of the MESI/MOESI protocols is enhanced by inserting "special" code before "heavy" loops. This code samples the iteration space of these heavy loops before they are executed, so that most of the memory pages that are used by the loops can be prefetched. Consequently the number of cache-misses is reduced. Finally the virtual memory mechanism of the multicore machine is used to get rid of the unused frames ("holes") that are left on the local stack of every core. The page-table is managed using special assembler instructions inserted by the proposed compilation scheme.

6.1 Introduction

In general, we wish to compile a parallel ParC program into a sequential program (one that does not contain parallel constructs) that will be executed concurrently by every core. Typically, parallel systems are characterized by the fact that they are

Y. Ben-Asher, *Multicore Programming Using the ParC Language*,
Undergraduate Topics in Computer Science,
DOI 10.1007/978-1-4471-2164-0_6, © Springer-Verlag London 2012

mainly managed in an operating system mode, so that all the decisions are made during execution in an "on-line" mode. Using a compiler for parallel programs means that most of the decisions are made "off-line" before the execution begins. It is not surprising that most of the existing systems for parallel-processing work in an operating system mode, since making optimal choices during run-time is easier than doing so at compilation time. An advantage of compilers versus operating systems is that the low level code produced as output can handle the machine's resources more efficiently, e.g. changing the stack pointer in a context-switch operation (compared to the use of system calls in the "on-line" approach).

Our goal is to obtain a comprehensive method for compilation of parallel programs, such that all the **basic compilation** techniques for shared memory parallel programs have been addressed. The proposed techniques implements such a compiler that can be used for parallel execution of shared memory on any multicore machine.

Following is a list of basic requirements that should be addressed by the compiler:

Activity creation and termination. Usually, the number of threads generated during execution of parallel programs is significantly larger than the number of available cores or processors. Had we unrolled the execution and obtained a full trace of the execution we could have discovered that many of the threads were "falsely" spawned. For example, we could find out that two threads were executed one after the other and hence there was no need to actually spawn the second thread. It is likely to assume that most of these threads could have been generated using regular function calls or loop iterations. Such a technique is called *Lazy Threads* and is used to save the overhead involved in the creation of threads on a remote core (including the overhead for allocating a new stack). Similarly the termination of a thread can (in some cases) be realized by a `return` instruction or simply the end of a code segment.

Preemption. Switching between threads is crucial for maintaining the fairness requirement of *ParC*, so that while loops whose termination depends on shared variables will eventually terminate. Preemption is usually realized using interrupts from the clock; a compiler can analyze the program and insert explicit context-switch instructions in suitable places in the code; saving the overhead of unnecessary context-switches and the overhead of the interrupt handler.

Cactus or loose stack. The fact that *ParC* supports dynamic creation of threads and preemption requires that the operating system should maintain a set of separate stacks, one for each thread that is currently being executed or waiting in the ready queue. This set of stacks is called "cactus stack" since it can be viewed as a tree of stacks, starting with the stack of "main()" and then splitting for every thread that is spawned. This increases the overhead of the execution as many instructions are wasted in allocating/deallocating and maintaining the separate of stacks. In addition, as the stack allocated to each thread must be of a fixed length, some protection mechanisms are needed to detect stack overflow, which adds to the general overhead. The proposed compiler should be able to embed the cactus-stack directly into the regular stack of the core without increasing the overhead of maintaining the cactus stack compared to a regular stack. The main difficulty of using such an embedding is to reallocate the "holes" left on the stack by threads that have terminated. In the proposed compilation scheme the compiler uses the page-table mechanism of the underlying machine to move such holes to the top of the stack so that their physical pages can be reused.

Referencing non-local variables. Nesting of parallel constructs in *ParC* requires that direct reference of nonlocal variables (those defined in external constructs) should be made fast. We argue that if a thread is represented by a function then it is clear that referencing a non-local variable by a thread requires two memory references even for multicore machines that support a shared memory space. The reason is that the addressing modes supported by CPU vendors allow either a direct access to global variables through absolute addresses or a direct access to local variables of functions through an offset from the stack pointer. Consequently the nesting structure of parallel constructs in ParC implies that addressing non local shared variables declared outside the current scope requires:

- One memory reference to reach the local address space of the external thread.
- Another memory reference to reach the local variable of the external thread.

Originally, we used C-functions to represent threads whose arguments are pointers to the external shared variables used by that thread (as depicted in Fig. 2.21). Thus, each access to a non local variable may involve up-to two memory operations as it is implemented through a pointer. This concept was suitable for the cactus stack that is managed as a loose set of stacks that are allocated separately for every thread. The only possible way to implement a direct access to non-local variables is to dedicate a set of registers that will point to the nested scopes of other threads. This type of code generation is also not likely to be used since it may severely restrict the use of registers. This situation resembles the need to access nonlocal variables in a language permitting nesting of function declarations. hence we will discuss this issue later on, however, the reader should bear in mind that though typically an access to a shared variable is usually implemented with two memory references, it can be made with one memory reference if direct addressing schemes are used.

Scheduling and load-balancing. Usually the operating system performs this task by maintaining a global FIFO queue of threads that are ready to run, where, when a machine runs out of work it fetches its next thread from that queue. It is well known that using a global queue guarantees optimal load-balancing (as the gap between the loads of any two cores can not exceed the maximal length of an thread). However it requires extra overhead for maintaining this queue and synchronizing the accesses to that queue. Using a compiler implies that the scheduling should be determined at compilation time.

A simple scheme, in which the compiler generates code that equally divides the new threads between the cores can be used. This is based on the assumption that threads generated by the same parallel construct have equal "length" (i.e., perform the same amount of work in each iteration, e.g. multiplying rows and columns in matrix multiplication). As a result, each core gets an equal part of threads that can be executed one after the other as regular iterations of a loop. Only in the case that the current thread spawns new threads or performs a context switch, is it inserted into a ready-queue.

6.2 Inserting Explicit Context Switch Instructions

An important aspect of executing parallel code is to overcome the problem of choosing the correct execution order for threads whose termination depends on the execution of other threads. Typically, this can happen when shared memory is used, and one thread waits for the results of another thread. Consider for example the following two loops with mutual dependence (left side):

```
int x=0,y=1;
parblock
{
  while(y){
    while(x%2 == 0);
    x++; if(x>1000)y=0;}
} : {
  while(y){
    while(x%2 == 1);
    x++; }
}
```
Mutual dependence

```
int x=0,y=1;
parblock
{ int k=0;
  while(y){
    k++; if(k%100 == 0)csw();
    while(x%2 == 0) {
      k++; if(k%100 == 0)csw();}
    x++; if(x>1000)y=0;}
} : {
  int k=0;
  while(y){
    k++; if(k%100 == 0)csw();
    while(x%2 == 1)
      k++; if(k%100 == 0)csw();
    x++; } }
```
inserting explicit CSW instructions.

Clearly, the only way for the above threads (left-side) to terminate, is if we execute them concurrently. However, it may happen that both threads will be allocated to the same core. In this case, we must stop the execution of at least one thread, and continue with the next, so that preemption or context-switch must be used. Operating systems use interrupts from the clock, in order to perform context switch between threads. Interrupt driven context-switches increase the overhead of the execution compared to a compiler that can insert calls for context-switch at the right places in the code. This is depicted in the above figure (right-side) where context-switch is executed every 100 iterations. The idea is not to perform context-switch too frequently, thus saving the overhead involved in this operation. The optimal choice of where and when to insert explicit context-switches is a complex subject, however some simple heuristics can be used. For example, explicit context-switch instructions can be inserted only inside `while loop`. Moreover, the quantum time for executing the context switch can be set proportionally to the number of iterations executed so far. The following code gives two alternatives for inserting context-switch instructions. The left-side code uses a counter and performs the context-switch every fixed amount of iterations. This type of solution is useful if the number of iterations executed by the loop is relatively small compared to the total number of steps in the program. The code in the right-side doubles the quantum time (`cstime`) between two consecutive context-switch instructions, every time the number of iterations executed so far equals $cstime^2$. This is useful if the while loop is "heavy" and we do not want to use too many context-switch instructions.

| `k++; if(k%100 == 0)csw();` | ```k++;
if(k%cstime == 0){
if(k > cstime*cstime)
cstime+=cstime;
csw(); }``` |
|---|---|
| Fixed quantum time for csw() | proportional increase of the quantum time |

Not every while-loop is used for synchronization, hence the compiler need not insert context-switch instructions in such loops. This requires special analysis to check that the condition of a given while-loop is not depending on shared variables that are modified by another thread. We remark that there is no need to insert a context switch in for-loops since they are executed for a fixed number of iterations and can not be used to "wait" for an update made by another thread.

Note that spinning on shared variables could also occur by using recursive calls. However, since the memory of a parallel system is finite, then any program that uses such a recursion might be halted by the system without violating the sequential consistency condition of the execution. Thus there is no need to insert context-switches in recursive calls. Another reason for not using context-switches in recursive calls is that it will lead to "breadth-first" scheduling, which might blowup the memory compared to "depth-first" scheduling which is more efficient.

6.3 Using Function Calls to Spawn Threads

In this section we discuss the basic ideas involved in spawning threads using function calls or loop iterations. A more comprehensive scheme which takes into account preemption will be presented in the next section.

As described in the introduction, one of the goals of a compiler for a parallel language is to guarantee that most of the threads will be created locally using function calls or loop iterations. In this way the overhead for spawning new threads is minimized. Actually, this includes two goals:

- Reduce the number of memory operations needed to distribute new threads, i.e., use $p = \#cores$ operations to spawn n threads instead of one operation for every new thread.
- Use fast mechanisms to create new threads on the current core, once the spawning operation has been "received". By this we assume that it requires at least p memory operations to spawn n threads on a multicore with p cores. This follows from the fact that each core should at least read the range $1, \ldots, n$ of threads that need to be generated, hence at least p memory references must be made.

Another related task involved with creating efficient code is the efficient addressing of local or external variables inside threads. This task is well performed by conventional compilers, using fixed offsets from the frame-pointer to address local variables/parameters of functions and procedures (Wilhelm 1995).

The above goals are easily realized if the compiler will represent a thread (say A) by a "thread function" $f_A(\ldots)$, such that spawning A is realized by calling $f_A(\ldots)$. We have briefly described this idea in Sect. 2.3, and now elaborate it in the context of creating an efficient compilation scheme. In this way the variables that are defined in A, will be realized as local variables of f_A, allowing fast access to local variables defined inside threads. However, since *ParC* allows arbitrary nesting of parallel constructs, A may reference external shared variables, that are defined in outer parallel constructs. This situation resembles the case of Pascal like languages, where nested definitions of functions are allowed. External references to global variables are usually realized in two ways:

1. An auxiliary array called the "display" is constructed in the activation record of every function, containing offsets to the frame-pointers of all the relevant outer nested functions. The display is generated every function call, by copying and modifying the display array of the caller. Consequently function calls become inefficient, however external references can be made faster using 2–3 instructions (Pittman 1992).
2. A chain of "static link" pointers or offsets is constructed on the stack, such that each static link points to the frame of the function where the current function is defined. The calling sequence is efficient, however, a reference to an external variable requires a sequence of instructions that follows the chain of static links to get the right frame-pointer.

External references are very common in ParC programs, mainly since ParC supports nesting of parallel constructs as a way to obtain a mapping of local variables to local memories. It is therefore important to efficiently address global variables. Both the display and the static link methods can be used. However, we have chosen the following option. Let $v_1, \ldots, v_k$ be the set of external variables that are referenced by a thread A. The compiler will replace every reference to v_i by a reference to a pointer $*pv_i$, and pass the addresses of $v_1, \ldots, v_k$ through $pv_1, \ldots, pv_k$ as arguments to f_A. The definition of f_A is therefore $f_A(int * pv_1, \ldots, *pv_k)\{\ldots\}$. It is invoked by calling $f_A(\&v_1, \ldots, \&v_k)$. Thus, external references are realized using parameters that point to the right variables. This method is useful if the number of external variables that are used by a thread is small. However their nesting distance is not negligible. This, we believe, is a common case in *ParC* programs.

Other argumentation for not using the Display or the Static-link methods in our case is as follows. It is desirable to implement the compiler such that the target code is C and not assembler, so that we only have to deal with the additional parallel constructs. Clearly both Static-link and Display work with offsets and require that the target code will be in assembler level. Another crucial point is that both Static-link and Display assume that the stack segment is continuous. However in a parallel execution, some of the addresses of external variables will be to stack segments that are allocated separately in different parts of the memory (e.g., using *malloc()* to allocate a new stack for a new thread). What is the meaning of offsets in this case? It might be possible to extend the Static-link and the Display methods to work with parallel execution, however passing parameters is extremely simple and therefore more natural to use. In any case since the scoping rules imply nesting then the two memory operations used to accesses an external shared variable must be performed anyway.

Consider the following translation of a parblock that spawns two threads, such that the first thread has one external variable i, and the second thread references two external variables i, j. Each thread is translated into a function that gets a pointer to i as its argument. In the spawning sequence, the function name f_A and its arguments $\&v_1, \ldots, \&v_k$ are passed as parameters to a send() instruction whose first argument is core *id* where the thread should be executed. The rest of send(pid, f, ...)'s arguments include the function address, number of parameters, and the parameters of $f()$ themselves. Using send(pid, f, ...), allows us to put the calling sequence for $f1$ and $f2$ on the message-stack of each core. In general, the allocation of threads generated by a parblock to cores can be done in random as a simple way to guarantee load-balancing. The idea behind random distribution is that if we assume that threads' lengths are random variables then there is a theorem due to Hoeffding that can be used to prove that:

- Let p be the number of cores and $n > p^2$ number of threads spawned by a program.
- The number of instructions executed by each thread X_i is a random variable with average size E.
- The probability that some core executed more than $k \cdot \frac{n}{p} \cdot E$ instructions is less than $\frac{1}{p}$.

Thus, if the number of threads spawned by a program is sufficiently large load balancing is achieved just by randomly distributing them between the cores.

| ```
f(int n)
{ int  i,j;
   parblock
   { int  x;
       x = i;
       if(n> 1)
       f(n-1);}
      :
      { int  y;
        j = y+i; } epar
``` | ```
f(int n)
{
    int  i,r;
    r = rand()%PNUM;
    send(1,f1,&i,&n,r);
    r = rand()%PNUM;
    send(2,f2,&i,&j,r);
}
``` |
|---|---|
| nested parblock example | the spanning sequence |
| ```
f1 (i,n)
int *i,*n;
{ int  x;
   x = *i;
   if(*n > 1)
      f(*n-1);}
f2 (j,i)
int *j,*i;
{ int  y;
   *j = y+ *i; }
``` | |
| thread functions | |

Note that the compiler can detect if, in the scope of a thread, an external shared variable is "read-only". In this case, the compiler does not have to pass a pointer to this variable, and instead it can use a copy of that variable. For example, i is "read-only" in both functions so that the compiler need not use the indirection $*i$.

Another optimization that could be used, is not to pass shared global variables as parameters, since global variables have one absolute address that can be computed at compile time. Passing pointers to external variables is necessary only if the address can not be computed at compile time, which is the case with shared variables that are stored on the stack, i.e., defined in the scope of some thread.

Another important issue in generating efficient code for parallel programs is to determine the scheduling that will occur during the execution, i.e., determine the allocation of threads to cores and the order of their execution. As explained in the introduction, the operating system usually uses a global queue to solve this problem, combined with context switches and thread-migration. This method obtains an optimal ratio of load-balancing since an ideal core will take a thread from the global queue and export newly spawned threads to this queue. However, it is very costly in terms of overhead. A compiler can determine the scheduling at compile time, sim-
```

ply by determining where to send new threads that are generated by a spawn. As explained in the introduction, the proposed scheduling uses a simple rule, namely:

- threads spawned by a parblock construct are randomly distributed between the different cores.
- threads generated by parfor, are divided into #*cores* chunks, that are distributed between the different cores. Each chunk is represented by a thread function (called "selector function") that will locally execute an equal part (given by the parameters fr, to in the following code) of the parfor's threads as loop itera-tions. We assume that the amount of computations involved with each iteration of a parfor is the same. Thus, an equal distribution of these iterations between the different cores is a reasonable strategy to preserve load-balancing.

In addition, the realization of the above scheduling should guarantee that the next instruction after spawning will be executed only after the last spawned thread has terminated. The spawning sequence of parfor contains a counter (mcounter) that is set to the number of cores minus one (the local chunk that is executed directly by the spawning thread). The address of mcounter is passed to every invocation of the selector function along with mid, the core-id of the spawning thread. Before terminating, the selector function checks if its core-id is equal to mid. If the answer is yes then the spawning thread waits until mcounter becomes zero, otherwise, it sends a done() message to mid that will decrease mcounter by one. The waiting itself is done by busy-wait or by receiving and executing new messages.

Consider for example the translation of a program to multiply two matrices in parallel $C_{N,N} = A_{N,N} \times B_{N,N}$:

```
parfor int i;0;N-1;1;
   parfor int j;0;N-1;1;{
   int k;
   for(k=0;k<n;k++)
    C[i][j]+=A[i][k]*B[k][j];
   } epar
epar
done(int *cn){ (*cn)-; }
selector_2(int mid,*mc,
    fr,to,**A,**B,**C,*i){
int k,j;
for(j=fr;j<to;j++)
   for(k=0;k<n;k++)
   C[*i][j]+=A[*i][k]*B[k][j];
if(core_id == mid)
   while(*mc > 0) wait();
else send(mid,done,mc);
}
matrix multiplication, done
```

```
selector_1(int mid,*mc,fr,to,**A,**B,**C){
int i,p,b=N/#cores;
for(i=fr;i<to;i++){
  int mcounter=#cores-1;
  for(p=0;p<#cores;p++)
    if(p != core_id)
      send(p,selector_2,core_id,&mcounter,p*b,
           (p-1)*b,A,B,C,&i);
    selector_2(core_id,&mcounter,core_id*b,
      (core_id-1)*b,A,B,C,&i);
    if(core_id == mid)
      while(*mc > 0) wait();
    else send(mid,done,mc);
} }
/* spawning sequence of the first parfor */
int p,b=N/#cores,mcounter=#cores-1;
  int mcounter=#cores-1;
  for(p=0;p<#cores;p++)
    if(p != core_id)
      send(p,selector_1,core_id,&mcounter,p*b,
           (p-1)*b,A,B,C);
    selector_1(core_id,&mcounter,core_id*b,
      (core_id-1)*b,A,B,C);
```
selector functions and spawning sequences

In this example, *core_id* identifies the current core. The spawning sequence works by distributing #cores − 1 selector functions; each will execute a chunk of $N/\#cores$ iterations of the original parfor one after the other. Clearly, one chunk can be executed locally by the current core thus saving a self message. Note that array names (A, B, C) are read-only variables and need not be passed as pointers. The total number of threads is $\#cores^2 + \#cores$ compared to $N^2 + N$ had we spawned every iteration of the parfor.

An alternative way of spawning threads of a parfor is through a recursive scheme. Initially we spawn two threads on two remote cores. Each thread will spawn two more threads until each core has only one thread, which then can be executed as a function call. As a result the spawning time is reduced to logarithmic time (in the number of cores) instead of linear time. This is a most useful technique if the number of cores is relatively large and the communication distance between some of the cores is large. In this case, the compiler can generate an optimal spawning sequence, which is adapted to the topology of the underlying network. This resembles the broadcasting tree developed for the LogP model (Culler et al. 1993).

Finally, note that all the threads have been executed as regular function calls or loop iterations using the stack in a normal way. So that there was no need to allocate separate stacks for new threads.

6.4   Scheduling and Supporting Context-Switch

The scheme proposed in the previous section allows threads to be generated on the stack as regular function calls. In particular, the scheduling order inside every core is determined by the function calls, thus it becomes fixed and is equivalent to a depth-first scheduling. This scheme ignores the need to support preemption, since it assumes that there are no dependencies between the threads, and that every thread-function returns to its caller. Otherwise, we must maintain a queue of ready-to run threads, so that after a thread has suspended (as a result of a context-switch or a spawn) we can chose the next thread to be executed out of the set of threads on which it might be dependent. It follows that preemption requires us to maintain some sort of a ready-queue structure. The reason is that the order of preemption and terminations of threads can not be fully determined during compile time, as it might depend on input values and intermediate results. Hence, we are obliged to use an "on-line" solution and realize a ready-queue in each core.

However, the compiler can detect which threads do not execute a context switch and spawns them as regular function calls or in the case of parfor as regular iterations of loops. Moreover, the code to insert the current thread into the ready queue should be activated only if the current thread actually executes a context-switch. Thus using a compiler yields that in many cases, threads (even those which contain a busy wait) will not necessarily be inserted into the ready-queue. Consider for example, two threads spawned by parblock, such that the first thread reset a flag $x = 0$, while the second waits for x to become zero by executing $while(x)$ $csw()$;. Clearly if the first thread have been executed first, then the second thread will terminate immediately, and there is no need to insert it into the ready-queue.

The ready-queue itself can be made efficient using compiled code compared to its realization by the operating system. First, the compiler can try to insert context-switch instructions only between consecutive statements (i.e., after ';'). In this way, we do not have to store condition bits and temporary values of registers every time we perform a context-switch. In addition memory allocation for the ready-queue's records is avoided, since the compiler automatically saves space for these records on the stack using the frames of the threads. The ready-queue itself is realized as a double linked list using two global pointers prev and next to insert and delete elements from the ready-queue (as described in Fig. 6.1).

A thread that performs a context-switch inserts itself into the tail of the ready-queue, and resumes a thread from the head of the ready-queue. Upon termination, the current thread removes itself from the ready-queue (using the prev and next pointers).

Fig. 6.1 An activation record
including a record for the
ready-queue

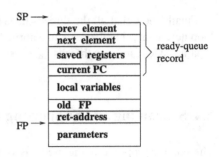

A special treatment should be given to the spawn operation. Recall, that so far, a spawn was realized by sending chunks of iterations to the rest of the cores, executing one chunk locally and waiting for the termination of all other chunks. This produces a **depth first** evaluation order, i.e. let A_i be the ith thread in a chunk $[fr \ldots to]$, then, if A_i spawns new threads, then the remaining iterations $[i + 1 \ldots to]$ will be executed only after all threads that were spawned by A_i (called descendants) have terminated. However, there may be some threads that are dependent (through shared memory) on the execution of the remaining iterations $[i + 1 \ldots to]$. Thus, in order to support preemption the compiler should allow the remaining iterations $[i + 1 \ldots to]$ a chance to be executed concurrently with the descendants of A_i. This can be done by inserting the remaining iterations as a new thread to the ready-queue or sending it as a self-message that will be executed by some "stacked" descendant of A_i later on.

The compilation scheme for spawning new threads that supports preemption works as follows:

Remaining iterations Let A_i be the current thread executed as an iteration by $selector_f(\ldots, fr_f, to_f, \ldots)$ and assume that A_i spawns new threads through messages with

$$selector_g(\ldots, fr_g, to_g, \ldots).$$

The remaining iterations $[i + 1 \ldots to]$ that are left after the ith thread starts to execute the new local chunk $selector_g(\ldots, fr_g, to_g, \ldots)$ are sent as a self-message to the current core, using $send(p, fselector_f, i + 1, to_f, \ldots)$. The reason for doing so is that there might be dependencies between the remaining iterations and some descendant of A_i. Pushing the remaining threads as a self-message makes their execution by future threads possible. Clearly, sending this self message should be done before we continue with the spawning operation of the new parfor.

Returning from a spawn In case that A_i has terminated (returned to the main loop of $selector_f(\ldots, fr_f, to_f, \ldots)$) and the self message containing the remaining iterations $[i + 1 \ldots to]$ have not been executed yet, then the self-message should be discarded and the main loop of $selector_f(\ldots, fr_f, to_f, \ldots)$ can continue with the remaining iterations (as usual).

Preemption A thread (say A_i) that performs a context-switch, is suspended and its state is inserted into the ready-queue. The execution of the main-loop continues with the remaining $[i + 1 \ldots ub]$ iterations. Thus the code for context-switch contains a *longjump*() to the beginning of the main-loop of the last *selector$_f$*($\ldots, fr_f, to_f, \ldots$). This operation requires a global variable to hold the label of the last main loop, and a way to restore the label of the previous main loop once the current selector function terminates. We remark that *longjump/setjump(buffer)* are two instructions that are used to record a current state of execution (program-counter, registers, stack-pointer, etc.) and restore it at a later stage of the execution. These instructions can be used to implement a scheduler at user level where a context switch is realized by a *addqueue(buf =* *setlump*()) of the current thread, selecting a new thread T from a queue and then switching to this thread using *longjump(T.buf)*.

Stack changes due to preemption When a thread performs a context-switch the stack size used so far by it remains and the next iteration continue right after. Thus when this thread terminates it will leave a "hole" on the stack. The problem of re-allocating these holes is discussed in the next section.

After the main loop The code after the main-loop of each invocation of

$$selector_f(\ldots, fr_f, to_f, \ldots)$$

waits until all the threads of this chunk that performed a context-switch terminate. The reason for doing so, is to guarantee that all the threads that were executed by the current chunk have been terminated, and the execution of the chunk has been completed.

In addition to that busy-loop, if the current chunk is a "master-chunk" (the chunk that is executed directly by the spawning thread), then a second loop is executed. This loop waits until all the chunks that were spawned by the current thread are done. The waiting is performed by a busy-wait until the number of remaining threads is reduced to zero.

The busy-wait alternates between receiving new jobs by spawning messages and resuming threads from the ready-queue.

Returning from a context switch Upon termination, a thread that was inserted into the ready-queue should decrease a counter indicating how many threads have performed a context-switch.

In addition, such a thread should return to its caller, namely the last thread that took it out from the ready-queue. So that the execution of the busy-wait loop that resumed this thread will continue.

Schematically, the code of *selector$_f$*() is as follows:

```
selector_k(lb...ub){
  initialize csw_counter=0; mcounter=p-1; lastM=MLOOP;
            MLOOP=main-loop;
  main-loop: i=lb .. ub do {
    beginning of iteration i:
    code of the parfor body
    in-case of a spawn: {
      send self message with 'fselector_k(i+1...ub)';
      send each core a message with a suitable chunk
      fselector_j(...);
      fselector_j(1...n/p);
      if the remaining iterations have been executed
      then exit main-loop;}
    code of the parfor body
    in-case of a context-switch executed
    by the current thread: {
      increase csw_counter;
      insert current thread to the ready-queue;
      goto MLOOP the beginning of the main-loop; }
    code of the parfor body
    end of iteration i.
  }
  while (csw_counter > 0)
    receive active messages and threads
    from the ready-queue;
  if master-chunk then
    while (mcounter > 0)
      receive active messages and threads
      from the ready-queue;
  else send a done message to the master-chunk;
  restore previous MLOOP, MLOOP = lastM;
}
```

The benefit of this compilation scheme is that all the threads are spawned as regular functions or loop iterations and only in the case that they perform a context-switch or spawn do they enter the scheduling cycle.

It is still left to show why this scheme is correct. In particular, showing that the execution order produced by our scheme is fair, i.e., any program which (under all possible scheduling orders) terminates on a shared memory core with preemption, will also terminate had it compiled using the above scheme. The following chain of deductions is used:

- Assume that every core is "stacked", i.e., there are no new threads that are being inserted into the ready-queue, no spawning and no new messages. Otherwise there

Fig. 6.2 A "stacked" situation in one of the cores

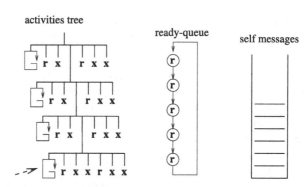

is some progress and at least one of the cores is not stacked and by induction can execute the program.

- If no progress is made then the situation at each core is as described in Fig. 6.2, where all the threads are either in the ready-queue ('r' in the figure) or have terminated ('x' in the figure). The core is stack on the while-loop of the last invocation of *fselector*() and keeps fetching threads from the ready-queue, however all these threads are blocked and constantly perform a context-switch.
- Clearly the threads in the ready-queue are not dependent on each other nor on threads that have already terminated. As in that case, some threads would have made progress in the next round of resuming all the threads from the ready-queue.
- It is therefore evident that the threads in the ready-queue are dependent on future threads from up-coming spawns. However in this case, the scheduling executed so far is also possible for a shared memory core that uses preemption. Hence, the program could also "get stack" using an equivalent schedule that is using a global-queue and preemption.

6.5 Memory Management of Stacks

In this section we discuss techniques for memory management that are needed in order to realize the imbedding of the Cactus stack on the core stack as described earlier. The main difficulty in using function calls to realize spawns on the same stack is that stack segments of different threads might be mixed. This might happen when a thread A_i performs a context switch, allowing the stack segment of another thread A_j to begin right above its current segment. A_j might be a new thread spawned by a message, or an existing thread which is resumed by a context-switch of A_i. Thus, when A_i is resumed, future function calls of A_i will form a new stack segment above the stack segment of A_j. The fact that the stack segment of a thread is not continued requires that the following problems should be addressed:

- The termination of a thread that has performed a context switch might leave unused stack segments ("holes") on the stack, that need to be reallocated.

- Recursion might cause a problem, as after a sequence of "pops", frames of new recursive function calls of A_i might fill the current stack segment of A_i and over run the frames of A_j.

Next we discuss how to reuse holes on the stack, provided that an explicit manipulation of the page tables is possible. The proposed method reallocates the physical pages of holes to new virtual addresses needed for extending the stack. Virtual addresses that were made free by the termination of preempted threads will not be reused; instead their physical pages will be reallocated. In this way, the stack may grow almost infinitely, since it is unlikely that the total stack size used by a parallel program will exceed the virtual address space (between 2^{32}–2^{64}). Clearly, in order to reallocate physical pages of holes we must require that stack segments will fill up a sequence of pages, i.e., start and end in units of pages.

Note that in the proposed scheme, physical pages of "holes" can be reused however the virtual addresses of these holes **must** remain part of the stack. Consider the case of three stack segments that belong to different threads A_i, A_k, A_j on top of each other, and assume that A_k terminates leaving a hole on the stack. Now, if A_j terminates then the top of stack should be reset to the end of A_i, however if the virtual address segment of A_k is not valid, then we can not let the stack grow into A_k. It is therefore necessary to re-allocate physical pages back to the holes once the stack pointer is reduced below the hole. This can be easily done using the virtual memory mechanism, simply by marking the pages of holes as swappable. In this way, when the stack increases the physical pages of the holes will be reallocated, by the operating system or by the underlying abstract core. When the stack decreases and passes through a hole, physical pages will be reallocated to the suitable segment. Note that these operations are usually supported by current operating systems, e.g. the virtual locking mechanism of Windows-NT. If the compiler controls the page-table, then reusing of physical pages must be handled explicitly by the code, so that a list of holes should be kept as a separate data-structure. Thus, imbedding of the Cactus stack on the core's stack is fully realized by the virtual memory mechanism.

Another important problem is related to the gap between the size of a function frame (usually around 20 bytes) compared to page-size (around 1000–8000 bytes). It is therefore desirable to store several function calls in one page, so that memory can be saved. Moreover, it is desirable that stack segments will contain as many pages as possible, so that the overhead of allocation/de-allocation of stack segments is reduced. This can be done only if the maximal stack size needed by a thread is known at compilation time. In the proposed solution, stack size estimations are combined with dynamic test or stack size and are inserted into the generated code.

Estimating the stack size of a thread that does not include recursion can be easily done considering the maximal static calling sequence. In this calling sequence, the size of the frame needed for every function call is statically computable, since it depends only on the number of arguments, local variables, and the maximum stack frame size of any function that might be called. A solution for recursive calls requires that a new stack segment must be allocated during execution, as the size needed for a stack can no longer be determined by the compiler. We insert explicit code to check the size of the stack that has been consumed so far.

The proposed scheme uses a "calling graph". This is a directed graph, whose nodes correspond to functions (with their frame size) and the edges to possible function calls, i.e., an edge $\langle f, g \rangle$ indicates that f () may call g () during execution. This calling graph is then used to estimate expected stack sizes as follows:

1. The calling graph is partitioned into cycles, and a **test** for dynamic stack allocation is inserted in one of the edges of every such cycle. The stack size allocated by every test is set to the maximal length to the next test, namely to the size of the appropriate calling sequence between the two tests.
2. If possible, each cycle should have a unique allocation-test. Otherwise the same test will serve several cycles and should use their maximum size.
3. Once the tests in the calling graph have been determined, they are inserted in the source code. A test on the edge $\langle f, g \rangle$ is inserted before the call to g () in f ().
4. Three global variables are used by the tests: current_stack points to the last address on the stack of the current thread; stack_size is the stack size estimation for the current thread (its initial value is estimated by the compiler as described before); next_size is the maximal stack size needed to "move" from the test of the current cycle to the next possible test (including the one resulting from repeating the cycle).
5. The stack size allocated for the current thread is doubled every time the execution passes through the current test. In this way, only $\log n$ allocations of stack fragments will be executed if a recursive function calls itself n times. At the worst case we have wasted twice than what is really needed.
6. The amount of stack allocated by a test is at least next_size, so that there will be enough stack size to reach the next test in the graph.
7. The allocation tests are conditional, such that a new request should be issued only when the amount of stack needed to reach the next test exceeds the amount of available stack.

The code for reusing memory pages works as follows (see Fig. 6.3). The system starts by allocating a fixed amount of physical pages used to construct a list of free pages. In addition the virtual address space is logically divided between the different cores, so that each core will use only a fraction of the virtual address space. In this way the variables allocated on the stack of each thread have unique addresses. The result is that the memory is shared. Referencing a virtual address which is not in the current page table will cause a page fault. This allows the virtual core to bring the correct page from the remote core where the virtual address resides. Finally, we assume that we have bypassed the protection mechanism of the underlying operating system such that we can update the entries of the page table.

- The allocation of stack space is performed in the main loop of fselector_k (), before it starts a thread. A global variable (denoted by vadd) contains the last virtual address used for the stack in every core.
- There is no need to use special allocation if the thread does not contain a csw() instruction, as the thread will return to the main-loop.
- An additional stack segment right above the current SP will be allocated for a thread that might perform a context-switch.

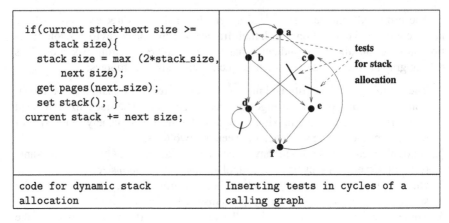

| code for dynamic stack allocation | Inserting tests in cycles of a calling graph |

```
if(current stack+next size >=
    stack size){
  stack size = max (2*stack_size,
    next size);
  get pages(next_size);
  set stack(); }
current stack += next size;
```

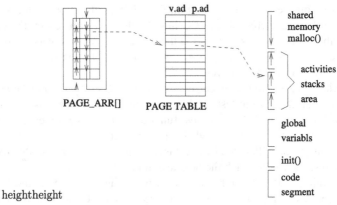

heightheight

Fig. 6.3 Memory configuration

- The amount of physical pages for a preempted thread as determined by the static analysis is allocated and a linked list containing the description of these pages is produced. The page-table is updated such that the stack-frame that will be used by this thread will start in the next page after vadd. This procedure is repeated every time control passes an allocation test. Thus the list of pages used for the stack-frames of the current thread expands and the page-table is updated.
- When the thread terminates, the list of physical pages used for its stack is added to the list of free pages so that they can be reused. Since the stack of every thread starts a new page, no two threads share the same page, and the pages can be safely reused.

Note that a deadlock may occur if none of the existing threads can allocate enough pages for their stacks. However such a deadlock is an indication that the amount of physical pages allocated for the program is not sufficient, and a suitable request for allocating more physical pages should be sent to the operating system.

6.6 Bibliographical Notes

The compilation scheme presented here is a variant of "lazy threads" (Goldstein et al. 1996) promoting the idea of executing threads as sequential function calls forming "Lazy Thread" execution. In addition, a lazy thread might later on be forked as a real thread if it needs to suspend. Unlike the scheme presented here, lazy thread does not handle busy-wait (while-loops depending on shared variables) which will cause a deadlock if used. Few limited forms of lazy thread are widely used. OpenMP (Addison et al. 2009) suggests several keywords that allow the programmer to control the way parfor iterations are executed:

static Iterations are divided into fixed-size chunks, each chunk is executed sequentially.
dynamic Each core requests a chunk of iterations from a common queue.
guided Chunk sizes are decreasing dynamically.
auto chunk sizes are determined by the compiler.

Fixed scheduling of loop iterations to fewer threads can sometimes reduce the performance of a parallel program. Ayguade et al. (2003) study cases where an optimized scheduling may depend on architectural characteristics, different inputs or need to be dynamically changed through the execution of the program. Hummel et al. (1992) describe a scheduling technique related to lazy threads that is designed to reduce the bottleneck of using a shared ready-queue. The method (called factoring) lets each core take a chunk of threads rather than just one, where the chunk size decreases in steps as less threads are left.

An interesting direction is to consider scheduling techniques for asymmetric multi-core architectures, where cores in the same processor can have different performance (see Li et al. 2007). Theoretical tools and scheduling techniques can be found in Brucker (2007).

Preemption in concurrent systems (Berry 1993) Burdorf and Marti (1990) considers scheduling without preemption or context-switch obtaining load-balancing by scheduling those processes that lag behind. Krueger and Livny (1988) compare preemptive and non-Preemptive load distributing showing that migration of threads can improve performance significantly, even if initial placement is already balanced. Preemption can also affect cache performance, Mogul and Borg (1991) studies the effect of the increased miss ratio after a context switch operation. Context switch operations are now used in modern multicore architectures in hardware mode such that each core executes several hardware threads and switch between them to improve the scheduling. Weber and Gupta (1989) proposed to overlap memory latencies by switching to another hardware thread every cache miss. Since then many works studied different aspect of using hardware threads also known as Simultaneous Multi-Threading (SMT) or hyperthreads (e.g., Tullsen et al. 1995; Ungerer et al. 2003 or Reddy et al. 2002).

Basic stack management and its use in sequential programming languages can be found in Advanced compiler design and implementation (Muchnick 1997). Cactus stack (also known as Spaghetti stack) has been studied to a limited degree. Hauck and Dent (1968) studied hardware support for a cactus stack. Hummel and Schonberg (1991) describe a VPM that uses a shared thread-queue for load balancing including the implementation of a cactus stack. Kearns et al. (1982) evaluates performance of coroutines using different stacks structure. Among of the structures the article is benchmarking is the spaghetti stack which is a different name for cactus stack used in ParC.

The scheduling scheme where a chunk of parfor iterations is equally partitioned between the cores can be found in Polychronopoulos's book (Polychronopoulos 1988) describing a variety of optimization techniques for scheduling. This techniques forms a simple variation of the *stacklet* technique used in Goldstein et al. (1995). The idea of using random allocation of threads to cores to guarantee load-balancing has been proposed in Ben-Asher and Sibeyn (1995).

References

Addison, C., LaGrone, J., Huang, L., Chapman, B.: Openmp 3.0 tasking implementation in Openuh. In: Open64 Workshop at CGO 2009 (2009)

Ayguade, E., Blainey, B., Duran, A., Labarta, J., Martìnez, F., Martorell, X., Silvera, R.: Is the schedule clause really necessary in Openmp? In: Proceedings of the International Workshop on OpenMP Applications and Tools 2003. Lecture Notes in Computer Science, vol. 2716, pp. 69–83 (2003)

Ben-Asher, A.S.Y., Sibeyn, J.F.: Load balancing: A programmer's approach or the impact of task-length parameters on the load balancing performance of parallel programs. Int. J. High Speed Comput. 7(2), 303–325 (1995)

Berry, G.: Preemption in concurrent systems. In: Foundations of Software Technology and Theoretical Computer Science, pp. 72–93. Springer, Berlin (1993)

Brucker, P.: Scheduling Algorithms. Springer, Berlin (2007). ISBN 354069515X

Burdorf, C., Marti, J.: Non-preemptive Time Warp scheduling algorithms. Oper. Syst. Rev. 24(2), 7–18 (1990)

Culler, D., Karp, R., Patterson, D., Sahay, A., Schauser, K.E., Santos, E., Subramonian, R., von Eiken, T.: LogP: Towards a realistic model of parallel computation. In: Symp. Principles & Practice of Parallel Programming, pp. 1–12 (1993)

Goldstein, S.C., Schauser, K.E., Culler, D.E.: Lazy threads, stacklets, and synchronizers: Enabling primitives for compiling parallel languages. In: Third Workshop on Languages, Compilers, and Run-Time Systems for Scalable Computers (1995)

Goldstein, S.C., Schauser, K.E., Culler, D.E., Lazy threads: Implementing a fast parallel call. J. Parallel Distrib. Comput. 37, 5–20 (1996)

Hauck, E.A., Dent, B.A.: Burroughs' B6500/B7500 stack mechanism. In: AFIPS Spring Joint Comput. Conf., vol. 32, pp. 245–251 (1968)

Hummel, S.F., Schonberg, E.: Low-overhead scheduling of nested parallelism. IBM J. Res. Dev. 35(5/6), 743–765 (1991)

Hummel, S.F., Schonberg, E., Flynn, L.E.: Factoring: A method for scheduling parallel loops. Commun. ACM 35(8), 90–101 (1992)

Kearns, J.P., Meier, C.J., Soffa, M.L.: The performance evaluation of control implementations. IEEE Trans. Softw. Eng. 8(2), 89–96 (1982)

Krueger, P., Livny, M.: A comparison of preemptive and non-preemptive load distribuing. In: Intl. Conf. Distributed Comput. Syst., pp. 123–130 (1988)

Li, T., Baumberger, D., Koufaty, D.A., Hahn, S.: Efficient operating system scheduling for performance-asymmetric multi-core architectures. In: Proceedings of the 2007 ACM/IEEE Conference on Supercomputing, pp. 1–11. ACM, New York (2007)

Mogul, J.C., Borg, A.: The effect of context switches on cache performance. In: Intl. Conf. Architect. Support for Prog. Lang. & Operating Syst., pp. 75–84 (1991)

Muchnick, S.S.: Advanced Compiler Design and Implementation. Morgan Kaufmann, San Mateo (1997). ISBN 1558603204

Pittman, T.: The Art of Compiler Design. Prentice Hall, New York (1992)

Polychronopoulos, C.D.: Parallel Programming and Compilers. Kluwer Academic, Dordrecht (1988)

Reddy, V.K., Sule, A., Anantaraman, A.: Hyper-threading on the Pentium 4. ECE 792E Advanced Microarchitecture (2002)

Tullsen, D.M., Eggers, S.J., Levy, H.M.: Simultaneous multithreading: Maximizing on-chip parallelism. In: Proceedings of the 22nd Annual International Symposium on Computer Architecture, pp. 392–403. ACM, New York (1995). ISBN 0897916980

Ungerer, T., Robič, B., Šilc, J.: A survey of processors with explicit multithreading. ACM Comput. Surv. **35**(1), 29–63 (2003)

Weber, W.-D., Gupta, A.: Exploring the benefits of multiple hardware contexts in a multiprocessor architecture: Preliminary results. In: Ann. Intl. Symp. Computer Architecture Conf. Proc., pp. 273–280 (1989)

Wilhelm, R.: Compiler Design. Addison-Wesley, Reading (1995)

Chapter 7
Working with Sequential Versions

In here we propose a programming methodology for developing efficient parallel programs. We basically advocate the idea that the parallel program is obtained from its sequential version by a sequence of gradual changes as follows:

- Most of the developing stages are made sequentially and in gradual stages.
- Each stage can be debugged sequentially, such that many bugs are found and removed before the parallel program is tested. Clearly, debugging a parallel program is harder than a sequential one, due to the fact that for a parallel program all possible execution orders must be tested.
- Dependence analysis of the sequential program can reveal potential ways to invoke more parallelism to the desired parallel program.

Hence, the proposed methodology consists of the following stages:

Initial sequential version → *potential parallel version* → *parallel version*

where the "potential parallel version" is a modification of the initial version such instructions which can be executed in parallel are now grouped together in a loop. Note that the "potential parallel version" is a sequential program, which has the same semantic as the initial version, however can be made parallel by replacing sequential loops by a parallel ones. The "potential parallel program" is obtained by a dependence analysis of statements in the initial sequential version, which reveal potential parallelism.

The speedup equations developed previously together with the *ParC* language are used to derive a set of transformations. The set, when applied to a sequential *C* program, results in an efficient and practical parallel program. The transformations therefore provide a programming methodology that enables the user to develop an application to fit a specific parallel machine.

The programming concept that we suggest here is to start with a sequential version of the algorithm we wish to parallelize. Since *ParC* is an extension of *C*, the sequential version is a *C* program. This *C* program can be compiled and executed in many cases to ensure "sequential correctness". Gradually, taking into account different efficiency factors of programming in *ParC*, the user will refine the sequential

Y. Ben-Asher, *Multicore Programming Using the ParC Language*,
Undergraduate Topics in Computer Science,
DOI 10.1007/978-1-4471-2164-0_7, © Springer-Verlag London 2012

version to create an efficient parallel version. This refinement thread is carried out through a set of transformations, that the user applies to the initial program. Using the virtual machine model the user can evaluate the effect of every transformation on the parallel performance. These transformations depict both the crucial limiting factors of the underlying machine, and some optimizations on the parallel code. The optimizations we have in mind resemble some compiler optimizations, such as extracting invariants from a loop body.

The first step of expressing our parallel algorithm as a sequential C program needs further clarifications. The idea is based on the fact that in many cases, parallel programs can be directly transformed to sequential ones without significant changes to the structure of the parallel program. For example, a parfor may be replaced by a sequential for loop, a parblock by a sequence of blocks, etc. While many parallel algorithms present a simple structure, that is easily expressed with sequential code, this is not the general case. The main problem lies in PRAM algorithms that rely on the synchronous nature of the PRAM model. In *ParC*, which supports an asynchronous model, explicit measures are needed to ensure that the required synchronization conditions are met. Programs that contain busy-waits or implicit synchronization must be written directly in *ParC*. They cannot be executed to test sequential correctness. However, the performance enhancing transformations are still applicable.

This programming methodology enjoys the following advantages:

- The programmer starts with a sequential C version of its program. Hence some of the debugging and testing can be done sequentially.
- The transformations direct the programmer to different possibilities of how to parallelize and improve the program. In some cases a different order of applying the transformations can lead to different parallel programs.
- Using the transformations the programmer is guaranteed to take into account all the limiting factors relating to the execution of the program.
- The debugging task can follow the gradual order of applying the transformations, thus debugging, testing and coverage are applied after each change at a time.
- Maybe the most important benefit of such a concept is that it supplies a paradigm of teaching parallel programming. This is similar to the techniques of abstraction, recursion, etc. that are used to teach sequential programming.

Special care must be given to the case of creating sequential versions to a parallel code that synchronizes via while-loops and shared variables. For example the code:

```
int A[N],B[N];
int fa=1,fb=1;
parblock {
    compute(A);
    while(fa == 1) fb=0;
    fb = 0;
    use(B);
```

```
} : {
    compute(B);
    while(fb == 1) fa=0;
    fa = 0;
    use(A);
}
```
Synchronization through while-loops

In a correct implementation of barrier synchronization each thread can reach its *use()* instruction only after the other thread executed one iteration of its while-loop. Note that executing both threads sequentially will always yield an infinite loop:

```
int A[N],B[N];
int fa=1,fb=1;
{
    compute(A);
    while(fa == 1) fb=0;
    fb = 0;
    use(B);
} {
    compute(B);
    while(fb == 1) fa=0;
    fa = 0;
    use(A);
}
```
Wrong way to sequentialize

A correct way to sequentialize this code is to mix or merge the two while-loops as follows:

```
int A[N],B[N];
int fa=1,fb=1;
{
    compute(A);
    compute(B);
    while(fa == 1 || fb = = 1){
        fb = 0;
        fa = 0;
    }
    use(B);
    use(A);
}
```
Correct way to sequentialize

Thus the general rule for creating sequential versions of a parallel code is to select a sequential order in which the instructions of the threads can be executed and merge the statements from all threads following this order.

Selecting a sequential order and then merging assignments accordingly can sometimes "hide" a bug that exists in a parallel code. Consider sequentializing the following parallel code for computing the maximum of n numbers: In this code, every thread compares one element of an array to the current maximum (S), and attempts to update S if its value is greater than S. Replacing the parallel-for by a sequential for-loop yields a correct version that always halts with S being the maximal value in $A[]$.

$$
\begin{array}{ll}
S = 0; & S = 0; \\
parfor(int\ i, i < n; i++)\{ & for(int\ i, i < n; i++)\{ \\
\quad while(A[i] > S) \qquad \Longrightarrow & \quad while(A[i] > S) \\
\quad\quad S = A[i]; & \quad\quad S = A[i]; \\
\} & \}
\end{array}
$$

Indeed, the sequential version (next figure right side) proves that there is at least one execution sequence where the algorithm finds the maximum. However the parallel version contains a bug that is not revealed by the above sequential version. In order to allow the bug to manifest one has to apply a different form of transformation that better simulates the parallel execution:

$$
\begin{array}{ll}
 & int\ F[N]; \\
 & S = 0;\ B = 1; \\
S = 0; & while(B)\{ \\
parfor(int\ i, i < n; i++)\{ & \quad for(int\ i, i < n; i++)\ F[i] = 0; \\
\quad while(A[i] > S) \qquad \Longrightarrow & \quad for(int\ i, i < n; i++) \\
\quad\quad s = A[i]; & \quad\quad if(A[i] > S)\{\ F[i] = 1;\ B = 1;\ \} \\
\} & \quad for(int\ i, i < n; i++) \\
 & \quad\quad if(F[i])S = A[i]; \\
 & \}
\end{array}
$$

Thus it is better to select several different sequential orders when merging different threads of a parallel code.

7.1 The Transformation Set

In this section we introduce the transformation set, using the following scheme: a short description, necessary pre-conditions, the syntactical form (initial structure facing the transformed structure), and the parallel time of each version. In all the time calculations we assume that N and P are such that the depth of the execution graph is less than the total work divided by P.

7.1.1 *parfor Transformation*

Description: transform for loops to parallel loops.
Conditions: iterations should be made independent.

`for (i=0 ; i<N ; i++)`
`{`
    `stmt`
`}`
	`parfor int i; 0; N-1; 1;`
	`{`
	    `stmt`
	`} `**`epar`**

$T = N \cdot |S|$	$T = (N(|S| + C))/P$

Where $|S|$ is the time to execute `stmt`.

7.1.2 *parblock Transformation*

Description: transforms a sequence of blocks or function calls to parallel blocks.
Conditions: function calls or blocks should be made independent.

`f(...);`
`g(...);`
`h(...);`
	`parblock {`
	    `f(...);`
	  `:`
	    `g(...);`
	  `:`
	    `h(...);`
	`}`

$T = |f| + |g| + |h|$	$T = (|f| + |g| + |h|)/P$

Where $|f|$ is the time to execute `f(...)`, etc.

7.1.3 *Privatization Transformation*

This transformation complements the first two. It moves variables into parallel constructs to make them local. A variable that is left out of a parallel construct will be shared and might be used simultaneously by several threads which in turn can imply multiple BusRd/BusRdX transactions of MESI.

Description: Move variables declarations inside parallel constructs, to ensure correctness and make the threads independent.

Conditions: The variables should be logically private, and not used for synchronization.

```int i, k;for (i=0 ; i<N ; i++) { k = ...; if (k) stmt}```	```parfor(int i=0;i< N;i++){ int k; k = ...; if (k) stmt}```

This transformation is necessary for correctness, and does not change the performance. The localization transformation deals with the use of local variables to enhance performance.

7.1.4 Chunk Transformations

In the cases where $N \gg P$, we might use chunking to spawn only P threads, each of which will sequentially execute $\frac{N}{P}$ of the original threads. The chunking transformation reduces the overhead of spawning N threads. The lparfor statement in *ParC* is based on this idea, so in simple cases (such as initializing an array) the user can realize chunking by transforming a parfor to an lparfor. However, chunking can appear in more sophisticated forms. For example, the sorting algorithms using the Baudet & Stevenson principle can be viewed as a chunking transformation.

Description: transform parallel loops of N threads to P threads.
Conditions: iterations should be made independent of execution order.

```parfor(int i=0;i< N;i++){ stmt}```	```int np = N / P;parfor(int J=0;J< N;i+=np){ int i; for (i=j ; i<j+np; i++) { stmt }} epar```
$T = (N(\lvert S\rvert + C))/P$	$T = (N \cdot \lvert S\rvert)/P + C$

In certain cases, chunking can also be applied to parallel blocks. For example, recursive divide-and-conquer algorithms may create far too many threads. The overhead may be reduced by stopping when P have been generated.

Description: limit number of threads created by recursive function calls.
Conditions: parallel calls should be made independent of execution order.

```f(...)```
 ``` { ```
 ```   if (cond)```
 ```   return();```
 ```   else```
 ```   parblock {```
 ```   f(...);```
 ```   :```
 ```   f(...);```
 ```   }```
 ``` } ```
	```f(p, ...)```
	 ```int p; {```
	 ``` if (cond)```
	 ``` return();```
	 ``` else if (p > 1)```
	 ``` parblock {```
	 ``` f(p/2, ...);```
	 ``` :```
	 ``` f(p/2, ...);```
	 ``` }```
	 ``` else {```
	 ``` f(1, ...);```
	 ``` f(1, ...);```
	 ``` }```
	 ``` } ```

$T = (N(|f| + C))/P$	$T = (N \cdot |f|)/P + C$

Where N is the number of recursive calls to `f(...)`.

7.1.5 Loop Reorder Transformation

Often the user is faced with parallel programs consisting of a parallel loop nested inside a sequential loop. This is a common structure in parallel algorithms, where an iterative procedure is used to solve the problem, and each iteration includes a parallel computation. It is also a very convenient way to program in *ParC* since a parallel loop includes synchronization, and thus the threads of the next iteration cannot start until the threads of the current iteration have terminated. However, this structure is not efficient since it re-spawns new threads in every iteration. The loop order transformation handles this situation.

Description: exchange the order of a parallel loop nested in a sequential loop.
Conditions: none.

```while (cond) {```
 ```   parfor(int i=0;i< N;i++) {```
 ```   stmt```
 ```   }```
 ``` } ```
	```parfor(int i=0;i< N;i++){```
	 ``` while (cond) {```
	 ``` stmt```
	 ``` sync;```
	 ``` } }```

$T = K \cdot N(C + |S|)/P$	$T = N(C + K(|S| + c))/P$

Where K is the number of iterations in the while loop.

Note that the same idea can be applied to combine consecutive parfors appearing one after the other into one parfor:

```parfor(int i=0;i< N;i++)```
 ```{```
 ```   stmtA```
 ```}```
 ```parfor(int i=0;i< M;i++)```
 ```{```
 ```   stmtB```
 ```}```
	```parfor(int i=0;i< max(N,M);i++)```
	 ```{```
	 ``` if (i <= N)```
	 ``` stmtA```
	 ``` sync; /* if needed */```
	 ``` if (i <= M)```
	 ``` stmtB```
	 ```}```

7.1.6 Asynchronous Transformation

The loop order transformation enforces strict synchronization on every iteration. In many cases it may be beneficial to relax this requirement. This can be done by using a local estimate on the number of iterations that are needed to solve the problem. Then each thread can execute a number of iterations without synchronizing, and only then check if all the work has been done. If the problem turns out to require additional iterations, rerun the whole thread.

Description: exchange the order of a parallel loop nested in a sequential loop, and reduce the synchronization requirements.

Conditions:

- The algorithm is "monotonic", so that extra iterations cannot create invalid results, only prolong the running time.
- The threads can guess a local estimate of the number of iterations.
- There is a halting criterion which can be easily computed. Using this criterion the algorithm can determine when to rerun.

```while (cond) {```
 ```   parfor(int i=0;i< N;i++){```
 ```   stmt```
 ```   }```
 ```}```
	```do {```
	 ``` parfor(int i=0;i< N;i++)```
	 ``` {```
	 ``` int k;```
	 ``` for (k=0 ; k<estimate ; k++)```
	 ``` stmt```
	 ``` }```
	 ```} while (cond);```

$T = K \cdot N(C + |S|)/P$	$T = N \cdot L(C + K' \cdot |S|)/P$

Where K is the number of iterations that is really required, K' is the estimate, and $L = K/K'$ is the number of repetitions.

Note that the halting condition is computed in a sequential segment, as it was in the original code. In certain cases it is possible to compute the condition locally in parallel. When this is the case, the **do**-while loop may be completely nested within the parfor.

7.1.7 Localization Transformation

This transformation is applied in order to transform global accesses (usually to a global array) to local ones. This is done by copying in the global data to every thread, performing the computation locally, and then copying the results back to the global array.

Description: Copy global data to a local variable, update the local copy, and copy the results back to the global memory.

Conditions:

- Each thread updates distinct global variables (e.g. disjoint parts of an array).
- Each thread accesses (reads) global variables that it does not update. Thus the variables cannot be partitioned between the threads, but have to be copied.
- The total number of accesses to global variables is significantly larger than the number of variables. Specifically, each thread should use each variable more than once.
- The algorithm is "oblivious", in the sense that each thread is not dependent on the updates of any other thread.

```int G[N]; /* global array */``` ``` parfor(int i=0;i<N;i++) { G[i] = f(i,G[0],...,G[N-1]); } ```	```int G[N]; /* global array */``` ``` parfor(int J=0;i< N;J+= N/P) { int i, G_loc[N]; for (i=0 ; i<N ; i++) G_loc[i] = G[i]; for (i=j ; i<j+N/P ; i++) G_loc[i] = f(i,G_loc[0],..., G_loc[N-1]); for (i=j ; i<j+N/P ; i++) G[i] = G_loc[i]; } epar ```
$S_g = N^2$	$S_g = N(P+1),\quad S_l = N^2$

The usefulness of the localization transformation is enhanced by previous transformations. The above example uses chunking to create a situation in which each thread uses each global array element more than once, thus making a local copy beneficial. A similar effect can be achieved by the asynchronous transformation, as shown in the case study in the next section.

7.2 Loop Transformations

Loop transformations are well known techniques to parallelize sequential code. In here we consider the possibility to apply them to parallel-loops. We focus on loop transformations as a manual technique to improve parallel code.

7.2.1 Loop Interchange

In this transformation we switch between an external loop and an internal loop as follows. Similar to regular loop interchange we require that dependencies allow us to apply this interchange. In the following code the outer loop can not be parallelized due to the backward dependency of reading $a[i-1][j]$ which was updated on the previous $i-1$ iteration. However, in this case we can interchange the two loops reducing the number of threads significantly. Cache considerations are more complex in this case including:

- Since each inner loop now repeatedly access $a[1\ldots n-1][j]$, $b[0\ldots n-2][j]$, $c[1\ldots n][j]$ then arrays must layout in the memory such that consecutive addresses follow the first index.
- The original version re-spawns n threads every ith iteration of the external loop. Thus, since threads created by the inner loop can be arbitrarily allocated to the different cores then data items ($a[i-1][j]$ and $c[i-2][j]$) allocated to the k'th core by the threads of the $i-1$ iteration may be useless to the threads allocated to the kth core at the ith iteration.
- After loop-interchange, the arrays-parts that each thread is referencing do not overlap. Thus, there should be no overhead due to MESI cache invalidations and BusRdx operations.

| ```
for(i=1;i<n;i++){
    parfor(j=1;j<n;j++){
        if(a[i][j] > 100)
            a[i][j] =
            c[i-2][j]+b[i][j];
        else c[i][j] +=
            a[i-1][j];
    }
}
``` | ```
parfor(j=1;j<n;j++){
    for(i=1;i<n;i++){
        if(a[i][j] > 100)
            a[i][j] = c[i-2][j]+b[i][j];
        else c[i][j] += a[i-1][j];
    }
}
``` |
|---|---|
| Loop interchange: | generating n threads instead of n^2 |

7.2.2 Loop Distribution and Loop Fusion

Basically in this transformation we break a loop into two or more smaller loops. Typically, loop distribution is used to parallelize loops that have a circular dependencies. In the following example, the for-loop can not be executed in parallel due the circular dependency of $B[i-2]$ and $A[i-2]$. However, by splitting the loop into three sub-loops and reorder the resulting sub-loops it is possible to parallelize all three sub-loops.

```for(i=2;i<n;i++){ A[i] = A[i] + B[i-2]; B[i] = A[i+1]*B[i]; C[i] = B[i-2]+A[i-2]; }```	```parfor(i=2;i<n;i++){ B[i] = A[i+1]*B[i]; } parfor(i=2;i<n;i++){ A[i] = A[i] * B[i-2]; } parfor(i=2;i<n;i++){ C[i] = B[i-2]+A[i-2]; }```
Loop distribution:	allows parallel execution.

Loop distribution can be useful to reduce the amount of cache misses in multicore machines. In the following code threads repeatedly invalidate copies of $A, C, B[i-1/i+1]$ residing in different core. It thus pays off to split this loop to three parallel loops executed one after the other and so reduce cache invalidations significantly.

```parfor(i=2;i<n;i++){ while(A[i] < 100) A[i] += (B[i-1] + B[i+1])/2; while(B[i] < 100) B[i] += (C[i-1] + A[i+1])/2; while(C[i] < 100) C[i] += (C[i-1] + A[i+1])/2; }```	```parfor(i=2;i<n;i++){ while(A[i] < 100) A[i] += (B[i-1] + B[i+1])/2; } parfor(i=2;i<n;i++){ while(B[i] < 100) B[i] += (C[i-1] + A[i+1])/2; } parfor(i=2;i<n;i++){ while(C[i] < 100) C[i] += (C[i-1] + A[i+1])/2; }```
Loop distribution:	improves parallel execution.

The opposite transformation of loop fusion can be useful in reducing the number of threads that are spawned. In the following code we fuse two parfor at the cost of waiting for the two previous iterations to update their $A[i]$ value.

```
char  M[n][n]; /* the adjacency matrix */
int   t, i, j, k;
for (t=0 ; t<log(n) ; t++)
    for (i=0 ; i<n ; i++)
        for (j=0 ; j<n ; j++)
            for (k=0 ; k<n ; k++)
                if ((M[i][k]) && (M[k][j]))
                    M[i][j] = 1;
```

Fig. 7.1 A sequential transitive closure program

```parfor(i=0;i<n;i++){ A[i] = B[i] + C[i]; } parfor(i=2;i<n;i++){ B[i] = A[i-1] + A[i-2]; }```	```A[0] = B[0] + C[0]; A[1] = B[1] + C[1]; S[0]=S[1]=1; for(i=2;i<n;i++){ A[i] = B[i] + C[i]; S[i]=1; while(S[i-1]==0); while(S[i-2]==0); B[i] = A[i-1] + A[i-2]; }```
Loop fusion:	reducing #threads.

7.3 Case Study: Transitive Closure

To demonstrate the concept presented in this paper, this section provides a case study of parallelizing a sequential transitive closure algorithm. By using the parfor, chunking, asynchronous, and localization transformations, an efficient parallel program is derived.

The sequential transitive closure algorithm is shown in Fig. 7.1. Its input is an $n \times n$ adjacency matrix describing an n-node graph. Its output is an adjacency matrix of a graph, where every two nodes that were originally connected by a path are now connected by a direct edge. The method is to simply raise the input matrix to the nth power, by squaring it $\log n$ times. The expected execution time for this program is $T_{seq} = 4n^3 \log n$.

The first parallel version is obtained by using the parfor transformation on the outer loop of the matrix multiplication, and the privatization transformation to make the indexes of the inner loops private (Fig. 7.2).

Using the VPM model we can now evaluate the expected execution time for the program. We will assume that the input size is big enough so that the diameter of the execution graph is negligible compared to the other factors in the time equation. The expected execution time for this program can be evaluated as follows: $N =$

```
char   M[n][n]; /* the adjacency matrix */
int    t;

for (t=0 ; t<log(n) ; t++)
    parfor int i; 0; n-1; 1;
    {
        int  j, k;
        for (j=0 ; j<n ; j++)
            for (k=0 ; k<n ; k++)
                if ((M[i][k]) && (M[k][j]))
                    M[i][j] = 1;
    } epar
```

Fig. 7.2 Applying the parfor and privatization transformations to the sequential version

$n \log n$, $W = 4n^3 \log n$, $S_g = 3n^3 \log n$, $S_l = 8n^3 \log n$, and $F_{bus} = \frac{P}{4}$ (we assume that n itself is a constant, and therefore we do not count it). In order to test the predictions of the VPM model we use the following ratio (which is similar to the speedup notion):

$$\frac{T_{seq}}{T_{simple}} = \frac{4n^3 \log n}{\frac{Cn\log n}{P} + \frac{4n^3 \log n}{P} + \frac{3Pn^3 \log n}{4P}} \approx \frac{1}{\frac{C}{4n^2 \cdot P} + \frac{1}{P} + \frac{3}{16}}$$

This implies that in the best case the speedup cannot exceed $\frac{16}{3} = 5\frac{1}{3}$. Moreover, for $N^2 < C$ the speedup could be even smaller. Indeed the experimental results of Table 7.1 verify this prediction. In particular, as n increases the speedup increases from about 2 to about 4, compared to the sequential version. The difference between the predicted limit of $5\frac{1}{3}$ and the observed limit of 4 is due to the high level of abstraction used for the prediction; note that we do not require a thorough check of the assembler code.

The next step is to reduce the effect of the overhead C by applying the chunking transformation (Fig. 7.3). The expected execution time for this program can be evaluated as follows:

$$N = P \log n \qquad W = 4n^3 \log n + 3P \log n$$
$$S_g = 3n^3 \log n + P \log n$$
$$S_l = 8n^3 \log n + 4P \log n + 3n \log n$$
$$F_{bus} = \frac{P}{4}$$

Keeping only the dominant terms, and assuming that $P \log n$ is small compared to n^3:

$$\frac{T_{seq}}{T_{chunck}} = \frac{4n^3 \log n}{\frac{CP\log n}{P} + \frac{4n^3 \log n}{P} + \frac{3Pn^3 \log n}{4P}} \approx \frac{1}{\frac{C}{4n^3} + \frac{1}{P} + \frac{3}{16}}$$

This implies that this program will show a similar behavior to the simple parallelization. However, for small n it might be worse, due to the extra $P \log n$ global memory

Table 7.1 Simulation results of executing the different versions of the transitive closure program for a multicore with 12 cores

Size	Version	Speedup
32	sequential	1
32	simple	2.2
32	chunked	2.1
32	asynchronous	1.8
32	localized	4.5
64	sequential	1
64	simple	2.5
64	chunked	2.2
64	asynchronous	1.9
64	localized	5.5
128	sequential	1
128	simple	3.8
128	chunked	3.6
128	asynchronous	3.0
128	localized	10.1
256	sequential	1
256	simple	3.8
256	chunked	3.8
256	asynchronous	3.5
256	localized	11.5

references. For large enough n, the overhead C will be negligible and the speedup will approach the maximum value of $5\frac{1}{3}$. The experimental results of Table 7.1 verify this prediction.

Next we can apply the loop order transformation coupled with the asynchronous transformation. Note that our algorithm is a perfect candidate for the asynchronous transform, since it fulfills all the necessary conditions for the basic algorithm:

Monotonicity: The statement if ((M[i][k]) && (M[k][j])) M[i][j] = 1; can never produce wrong results, regardless of any execution order.

Local estimate: Since in a synchronous run $\log n$ iterations are enough, $\log n$ can be used for the local estimate.

Halting criterion: If there are no indexes i, j, k such that i is not connected to j, but i can be connected to j via k, then all connections have been computed. This criterion can be computed in parallel.

The program is shown in Fig. 7.4. The expected execution time for this program can be evaluated as follows: Let L denote the number of times the whole thing is repeated. Then (disregarding low-order terms, and assuming $P \ll n$)

```
char   M[n][n];  /* the adjacency matrix */
int    t, np;

np = (n + P - 1) / P;
for (t=0 ; t<log(n) ; t++)

    parfor int z; 0; n-1; np;
    {
        int   i, j, k, lim;

        lim = z + np;
        if (lim > n)
            lim = n;

        for (i=z ; i<lim ; i++)
            for (j=0 ; j<n ; j++)
                for (k=0 ; k<n ; k++)
                    if ((M[i][k]) && (M[k][j]))
                        M[i][j] = 1;
    } epar
```

Fig. 7.3 Applying the chunking transformation to the version in Fig. 7.2

$$N = LP$$
$$W = L4n^3(\log n + 1)$$
$$S_g = L\left(3n^3 \log n + 4n^3\right)$$
$$S_l = L8n^3(\log n + 1)$$
$$F_{bus} = \frac{3P}{11}$$

Which leads to the speedup prediction

$$\frac{T_{seq}}{T_{async}} = \frac{4n^3 \log n}{\frac{CLP}{P} + \frac{4Ln^3(\log n+1)}{P} + \frac{9LPn^3 \log n}{11P}} \approx \frac{1}{\frac{LC}{4n^3 \log n} + \frac{L}{P} + \frac{9L}{44}}$$

If $L = 1$, the speedup will show a similar behavior as that of previous transformations. However, as we can expect L to be larger than 1 in the general case, the speedup should be slightly *lower*. The experimental results of Table 7.1 verify this prediction.

From the analysis so far it seems that applying the chunking and asynchronous transformations only made things worse. However, the program now spawns as few threads as possible, namely no more than the P necessary. These threads are coarse-grained and hardly synchronize. Thus the next reasonable step is to use localization, and reduce S_g to the minimum.

At first glance the transitive closure algorithm is a hopeless candidate for local memory computing. In the original matrix multiplication algorithm, almost all memory references are global. However, the transformations used so far changed the algorithm so that making local copies becomes beneficial. Thus local copies of the

```
char   M[n][n];  /* the adjacency matrix */
int    not_done, np;
np = (n + P - 1) / P;
do{
    not_done = 0;
    parfor( int z= 0; Z< n-1; z+=np)
    {
        int  i, j, k, t, lim;
        lim = z + np;
        if (lim > n)
            lim = n;
        /* compute transitive closure asynchronously */
        for (t=0 ; t<log(n) ; t++)
            for (i=z ; i<lim ; i++)
                for (j=0 ; j<n ; j++)
                    for (k=0 ; k<n ; k++)
                        if ((M[i][k]) && (M[k][j]))
                            M[i][j] = 1;
        sync;
        /* check halting condition */
        for (i=z ; i<lim ; i++)
            for (j=0 ; j<n ; j++)
                for (k=0 ; k<n ; k++)
                    if ((!M[i][j]) && (M[i][k]) && (M[k][j]))
                        not_done = 1;
    }
} while (not_done);
```

Fig. 7.4 Applying the loop order and asynchronous transformations to the chunked version from Fig. 7.3

adjacency matrix are made, and used to calculate the transitive closure of disjoint parts of the graph. In effect, we have derived an algorithm that can be described as follows:

```
do {
        1. divide M into P parts: M_1, ..., M_P.
        2. calculate M_i^n in parallel.
        3. reconstruct M.
} while (not all connections found);
```

As a final optimization, the matrix can also be squared as part of the check for the halting condition. The final program is shown in Fig. 7.5.

```
#define my_M(i,j) (*(char*) loc_M+(i)*n+(j))
char  M[n][n]; /* the adjacency matrix */
int   not_done, np;
np = (n + P - 1) / P;
do {
   not_done = 0;
   parfor( int z= 0; Z< n-1; z+=np)
   {
      int   i, j, k, t, lim;
      char  *loc_M;
      /* make local copy */
      loc_M = malloc( n*n );
      for (i=0 ; i<n ; i++)
         for (j=0 ; j<n ; j++)
            my_M(i,j) = M[i][j];
      lim = z + np;
      if (lim > n)
         lim = n;
      /* compute transitive closure asynchronously */
      for (t=0 ; t<log(n) ; t++)
         for (i=z ; i<lim ; i++)
            for (j=0 ; j<n ; j++)
               for (k=0 ; k<n ; k++)
                  if ((my_M[i][k]) && (my_M[k][j]))
                     my_M[i][j] = 1;
      /* copy back my part */
      for (i=z ; i<lim ; i++)
         for (j=0 ; j<n ; j++)
            M[i][j] = my_M(i,j);
      free( loc_M );
      sync;
      /* check halting condition and square */
      for (i=z ; i<lim ; i++)
         for (j=0 ; j<n ; j++)
            for (k=0 ; k<n ; k++)
               if (((!M[i][j]) && (M[i][k]) && (M[k][j]))) {
                  not_done = 1;
                  M[i][j] = 1;
               }
   } epar
} while (not_done);
```

Fig. 7.5 Applying the localization transformation to the version from Fig. 7.4

Again neglecting all low order terms, the parameters in the timing equation are:

$$N = LP$$
$$W = L\left(4n^3 \log n + 5n^3 + 3(P+1)n^2\right)$$
$$S_g = L\left(5n^3 + (P+1)n^2\right)$$
$$S_l = L\left(11n^3 \log n + 10n^3 + 20n^2\right)$$
$$F_{bus} = \frac{P}{2\log n + 1}$$

This leads to the equation

$$\frac{T_{seq}}{T_{local}} = \frac{4n^3 \log n}{\frac{CLP}{P} + \frac{(4n^3 \log n + 5n^3)L}{P} + \frac{5n^3 LP}{2\log n + 1}}$$

$$\approx \frac{1}{\frac{CL}{4n^3 \log n} + \frac{L}{P} + \frac{5L}{4\log nP} + \frac{5LP}{8\log^2 n}}$$

The dominant factor is now $\frac{L}{P}$, thus we expect that the speedup will be about P for large enough values of n, if indeed L is small. The results of Table 7.1 shows that this is the case.

The input in every experiment is the adjacency matrix of a graph composed of two separate, randomly constructed components.

7.4 Case Study: Matrix Multiplication

The chunking of nested sequential loops, can be done in several ways. In the previous example of Fig. 7.3 only the external loop has been made parallel, and then chunked. This method is reasonable only for cases where $n \gg P$, otherwise, we may consider a more complex chunking, taking into account different relations between n and P.

We start with a simple sequential program for matrix multiplication $C = A \times B$, where each matrix has $\langle n \times n \rangle$ elements:

```
float A[n][n], B[n][n], C[n][n];

int i,j,k;

for(i=0;i<n;i++)
    for(j=0;j<n;j++){
        C[i][j] = 0;
            for(k=0;k<n;k++)
                C[i][j] += A[i][k]*B[k][j];
    }
```
Sequential matrix multiplication.

The running time of this program is $T = n^3$.

A naive programmer can use the parfor-transformation to create the parallel version of the above program:

```
float A[n][n], B[n][n], C[n][n];

parfor(int i=0; i<n;i++){
   parfor(int j=0; j<n;j++)
      {
      int k;
      C[i][j] = 0;
         for(k=0;k<n;k++)
               C[i][j] += A[i][k]*B[k][j];
   }
}
```
Simple parallel matrix multiplication.

The running time in this case is $T = \frac{n^2(C'+n)}{P}$, provided that $P < n^2$. External memory references and the depth of the execution graph, are not used in the time computations since we are interested only in the relations between P and n.

Note that the indexes i, j are now local variables, in case where the above program is executed in parallel there is no danger of collisions of these indexes. Hence, the privatization transformation is used to correct treatment of the indexes. The deceleration of k was moved to the most inner "parfor", allowing every thread to work with a different copy of k (transformation F3).

If the number of processors P is known to be less than n it is better to use the following "chancing" technique:

```
float A[n][n], B[n][n], C[n][n];

parfor(int l=0; l<n; l+=n/P)
{ int i,j,k;

   for(i=l;i< l+ n/P; i++) {
      for(j=0;j<n;j++){
         C[i][j] = 0;
         for(k=0;k<n;k++)
             C[i][j] += A[i][k]*B[k][j];
      }
   }
}
```
Parallel matrix multiplication with chunking.

The running time in this case is $T = \frac{P(C' + \frac{n}{P} * n^2)}{P} = C' + \frac{n^3}{P}$, provided that $P < n$.

In the case that we need more parallelism $P > n^2$, we can compute the inner for-loop in parallel, using a simple standard "chancing" technique: let $Pp = \frac{P}{n^2}$ denotes the number of physical processors we can assign to compute the inner for-loop. The summing operation $C_{i,j} = \sum_{k=0}^{n-1} A_{i,k} \cdot B_{k,j}$ can be split to Pp parallel summations of $\frac{n}{P}p$ elements each. Each summation will hold its result in a temporary array $tmp[Pp]$. Finally $C[i][j]$ is the sum of all the elements of $tmp[]$.

```
float A[n][n], B[n][n], C[n][n];

for(i=0;i<n;i++)
    parfor(int i=0; i<n;i++){
        parfor(int j=0; j<n;j++){
            C[i][j] = 0;
            int tmp[P];
            parfor(int l=0; l<n; l+=n/Pp {
                tmp[l] = 0;
                for(k=1; k < l+ n/P -1; k++)
                    tmp[l] += A[i][k]*B[k][j];
            }
            for(k=0; k < l; k++)
                    C[i][j] += tmp[k];
        }
    }
```

Parallel matrix multiplication with $P \geq n^2$ processors.

Note that by declaring $tmp[]$ inside the second parallel-loop every thread has its own copy of $tmp[]$. If we could not used the scoping rules to create local variables, we would have to use a more complicated data-structure and indexing system to manipulate n^2 copies of $tmp[]$.

7.5 Case Study: PDE—Partial Differential Equations

In this section we describe a well known algorithm to solve partial differential equations. The function values are stored in a two dimensional grid (var[N][N]). In each iteration every element var[i][j] take its new value to be that of the average of its four neighbors. This threads is repeated until the maximal change of values in var[i][j] (denote by delta-m) is less than a certain threshold (epsilon). (Let K denote the number of iterations needed to complete the algorithm.)

```
#define N 256
#define epsilon 0.4
float var[N+2][N+2]; /* the PDE array */
float tmp[N+2][N+2]; /* temporary array to hold the results */
float ttt[][]; /* used for the swap */

pde() {
int delta_m = epsilon*2;

while(delta_m > epsilon){
   for(i=0;i<N;i++)
      for(j=0;j<N;j++){
         float sum,delta_ij;

         sum = var[i][j] + var[i-1][j] + var[i+1][j]
         + var[i][j-1] + var[i][j+1];
         sum = sum/5; /* compute the average */
         delta_ij = abs(var[i][j] - sum);
         /* compute the maximum of delta_ij */
         if(delta_ij > delta_m) delta_m = delta_ij;
         tmp[i][j] = sum; /* assign the new value */
      }
   ttt = var; var =tmp; tmp =var;/*swap between var and tmp*/
} }
```
PDE- sequential version with $T = K \cdot N^2$.

In order to transform pde() to a parallel program, we apply the transformations described before. The first step is to apply the parfor transformation to the pde(), note that sum, and delta-ij become local as they should be according to this transformation. As a result of using the parfor transformation, delta-m may not contain the maximum of all delta-ij (since some if statements occurs in parallel). Next we can use chunking not to spawn more than P threads, we assume that $P < N$. Note that using chunking may help us finding the real value of delta-m, since still many iterations are executed sequentially. Hence, we can use "chancing" technique to compute the real value of delta-m:

```
#define N 256
#define epsilon 0.4
float var[N+2][N+2]; /* the PDE array */
float tmp[N+2][N+2]; /* temporary array to hold the results */
float ttt[][]; /* used for the swap */

pde() {
int delta_m = epsilon*2;
int delta_ar[P]; /* used to hold temporary values of delta_m */
```

```
/* initialize delta_ar[k] */
for(k = 0;k<P;k++) delta_ar[k] = epsilon*2;
while(delta_m > epsilon){
    parfor(int l=0;l<N+1;l=l+N/P {
        for(i=1; i < l+N/P-1; i++)
            for(j=0;j<N;j++) {
                float sum,delta_ij;
                sum = var[i][j] + var[i-1][j] + var[i+1][j]
                    + var[i][j-1] + var[i][j+1];
                sum = sum/5; /* compute the average */
                delta_ij = abs(var[i][j] - sum);
                    /* compute the maximum of delta_ij */
                if(delta_ij > delta_ar[l]) delta_ar[l] = delta_ij;
                tmp[i][j] = sum; /* assign the new value */
            }
    }
    for(k = 0;k<P;k++) /* compute the real value of delta_m */
        if(delta_ar[k] > delta_m) delta_m = delta_ar[k];
    ttt =var; var =tmp; tmp =var; /*swap between var and tmp*/
} }
```

$$T = K \cdot P(N^2/P + C')/P = (K \cdot N^2)/P + K \cdot C'$$

Finally we can use the loop reordering transformation to reduce the number of threads spawned by the program to P. It is reasonable that the local condition $delta - ar[l] > epsilon$ can serve as a good estimation to the number of iteration each thread should execute. The real value of delta-m has to be computed outside the main while-loop. In this case we use the asynchronous transformation, otherwise if a threads has reached it local minima it will stop computing new values, regardless if the other threads needs more iterations.

```
#define N 256
#define epsilon 0.4

float var[N+2][N+2]; /* the PDE array */
float tmp[N+2][N+2]; /* temporary array to hold the results */
float ttt[][]; /* used for the swap */

pde()
{
int delta_ar[P]; /* used to hold temporary values of delta_m */
/* initialize delta_ar[k] */
for(k = 0;k<P;k++) delta_ar[k] = epsilon*2;

parfor(int l=0;l<N+1;l+=N/P)
{
    int delta_m = epsilon*2;
    start:
```

```
while(delta_ar[1] > epsilon){
   for(i=1; i < 1+N/P-1; i++)
      for(j=0;j<N;j++)
      {
          float sum,delta_ij;
          sum = var[i][j] + var[i-1][j] + var[i+1][j]
              + var[i][j-1] + var[i][j+1];
          sum = sum/5; /* compute the average */
          delta_ij = abs(var[i][j] - sum);
                 /* compute the maximum of delta_ij */
          if(delta_ij > delta_ar[1]) delta_ar[1] = delta_ij;
          tmp[i][j] = sum; /* assign the new value */
      }
      ttt =var; var =tmp; tmp =var; /*swap between var and tmp*/
   }
   for(k = 0;k<P;k++) /* compute the final value of delta_m */
         if(delta_ar[k] > delta_m) delta_m = delta_ar[k];
   if(delta_m > epsilon) goto start;
   }
}
```

$$T = P(K \cdot N^2/P + C')/P = (K \cdot N^2)/P + C'$$

Note that the swap operation is not synchronized between the threads. Since both var[][] and tmp[][] are global, this may mean that the fastest threads will swap the arrays to all other before they have completed their iterations. One way is to use a sync command before the swap operation, such that $T = P(K \cdot (N^2 + c')/P + C')/P = (K \cdot N^2)/P + (K \cdot c')/P + C'$. A better way (and in the spirit of probabilistic algorithms) is to use localization to declare var[][] and tmp[][] inside the parfor. This will make every thread swap only at the end of its iteration. Hence, $2N$ elements out of $\frac{N^2}{P}$ elements in every threads, might compute the average with iterations ahead of their own.

The performances of the PDE algorithm is subject to delicate tuning hence the performances of the above parallel version are also depends on program and on testing, as a result the program might be modified. What is important here is that loop reordering or any other transformation can be used as a guide line to create an efficient parallel program.

One interesting observation is that the order in which we applied the transformations, and the relations between P and N', may lead to different more complicated parallel programs.

7.6 Case Study: Dynamic Chunking

One of the most important transformations is the chunking transformation, in which only P threads are spawned, each computing sequentially a "chunk" of $\frac{N}{P}$ iterations

Fig. 7.6 Parallel algorithm to
sum the elements on an array

```
int   A[N];
int   j;

for (j=lg(N)-1 ; j>=0 ; j--) {
    parfor ( i;  0;  2^j-1;  1 )
        A[i]  += A[i+2^j];
}
```

of what was parallel threads. This reflects a static assignment of parallel processors to sequential threads. Consider the basic structure of a parfor nested inside a sequential-loop as in the loop order transformation. In this case the parfor vary in every iteration of the loop. If we want to apply chunking on this structure, the P threads have to change their "chunk" dynamically.

The problem that demonstrates this dynamic chunking, is calculating the sum of the elements of an array. For simplicity, we shall assume that both the size of the array N, and the number of processors P, are powers of two.[1] The basic parallel algorithm is to sum element pairs, then pairs of pairs, and so on, resulting in a tree structure. It is easier to express this algorithm if the pairs are not taken as adjacent elements, but rather as elements that are half an array apart. In this way the used part of the array is halved in each step. A ParC version of this procedure is given in Fig. 7.6 (with relaxed notation, e.g. use of 2^j for exponentiation).

This formulation is convenient in that it includes an implicit synchronization at the end of each iteration, because a new parfor is spawned for each one. But this costs the overhead associated with the parfor, which is much higher than the overhead of synchronization alone. Therefore it is better to reorganize the code and put the sequential for loop *inside* the parfor, adding an explicit synchronization at the end of each iteration. This is shown in Fig. 7.7. Note that the number of threads must be halved in each iteration.

In many cases the array is much larger than the number of processors. It is then advisable to *chunk* the computation, i.e. to spawn only P threads and have each one take care of a number of values. This optimization is shown in Fig. 7.8. The original lg(N) iterations are now split into two phases. In the first lg(N)-lg(P) iterations, there are more threads than array elements. Each thread then loops on the array elements that are assigned to it (this is the loop with index k). The assignment changes from one iteration to the next, as the partial sums are created in the lower half of the array. In the final lg(P) iterations, the number of threads is halved with each iteration, and the assignment does not change any more, as it was in the previous example.

Up till now the dynamic chunking used a rigid concept of dividing the available number of processors between all sub-computations. Clearly if the program

---

[1]Parc provides the number of processors in a variable named proc_no. We use P here for short.

```
int   A[N];

parfor ( int i=0; i<N/2; i++ ) {

    int   j;  /* private due to scoping rules */

    for (j=lg(N)-1 ; j>=0 ; j--) {
        if (i>=2^j)
            pcontinue;  /* terminate top half */
        A[i] += A[i+2^j];
        sync;  /* explicit barrier each iteration */
    }
}
```

Fig. 7.7 Reducing the overhead of respawning new threads

```
int   A[N];

parfor ( int i=0; i<N/2; i+=N/2P ) {

    int   j, k, cnk=N/2P;

    for (j=lg(N)-1 ; j>=0 ; j--) {
        if ((j<lg(P)) && (i>=2^j))
            pcontinue;  /* terminate top half in last lg(P) iterations */
        for (k=i ; k<i+cnk ; k++)  /* loop on private chunk */
            A[k] += A[k+2^j];
        if (j>lg(P)) {  /* shift to lower part of the array in first phase */
            i = i/2;
            cnk = cnk/2;
        }
        sync;
    }
}
```

Fig. 7.8 Applying dynamic chunking to fit the program to the number of processors

executes several algorithms or sub computations in parallel, the number of available processors is dynamically changed. Thus, when one algorithm has terminated, its processors can be used by another active computation. Hence the parameter p (number of available processors) should be dynamically updated, accumulating unused available processors of terminated computations. Note that the term *available processors* does not indicate actual physical processors, but rather a virtual counter indicating the number of threads dedicated for the current computation.

This dynamic updating of p, is demonstrated in Fig. 7.9 where a global variable *GP* holds the current number of available processors. Before executing a parallel code, each thread tries to increase its number of available processors (given as pa-

```
int GP; /* available number of processors pair task*/
int prsum(A,fr,to,p)
int A[],fr,to,p; /* p is the initial number of processors */
{
int k,j,s,a,b;
    if(fr == to) return(A[fr]);
    k=0;
    while((GP > 0)&&(k == 0)) /* try to get extra processors */
        if((k = faa(&GP,-GP)) < GP) {
            faa(&GP,k);
            k = 0;
    }
    p = p+k; /* add extra processors */
    if(p <= 1) {
        s=0;
        for(j=fr;j<=to;j++) s += A[j];
    } else {
        pparblock {
        a = prsum(A,fr,(to+fr)/2,p/2);
        :
        b = prsum(A,(to+fr)/2 +1,to,p/2);
        }
    faa(&GP,p); /* return your processors to the global pool */
    return(a+b);
    }
}
```

Fig. 7.9 Recursive parallel summing, with dynamic number of processors

rameter in p). Hence whenever a thread terminates (either one spawned by $rpsum$ or by another algorithm) its processors are added to GP. This technique is demonstrated in Fig. 7.9 where the sum of N elements is computed in parallel, as long as there are available processors.

7.7 Case Study: Using Pointer Arrays

In using local arrays, as suggested before, we actually prevent one thread to access the elements of the array stored in the local memory of another thread. In cases where we wish to access local variables of another thread we can use a global pointer array, where each element points to a local part of the original array. As an example of the use of a pointer-array, we can use the sum algorithm of Fig. 7.7.

In this algorithm the addition operation is : "$A[i] = A[i] + A[i + 2^j]$", the access to "$A[i]$" is always local, while the access to "$A[i + 2^j]$" might be global. Hence in localizing the algorithm the access to "$A[i + 2^j]$" must use global pointer-array:

```
    int A[N]
    parfor(int l=0;l<N/2; l+=N/P)
    {
        for(j= log(N)-1;j >= 0;j--){
            for(i=1;i< l+N/P;i++){
                if (i < 2^j)
                    A[i] = A[i] + A[i + 2^j];
            }
            sync;
        }
    }
```
Original sum algorithm

```
int *a_p[P]; /*pointer array to the local parts of A[]*/
    parfor( int l=0; l<N/2;l+=N/P)
    {
        int A[N/P],p,z;
        a_p[P] = A; /*the local address of each A is made public*/
        sync; /*wait for every body to put their addresses*/
        for(j= log(N)-1;j >= 0;j--){
            for(i=1;i< l+N/P;i++){
            if (i < 2^j){
                /* 'p' is the local memory of A[i+2^j] */
                p = (i+2^j) / (N/P);
                /* 'z' is the place of A[i+2^j] in the local memory*/
                z = (i+2^j) % (N/P);
                A[i] = A[i] + (a_p[p])[z];
            }
            }
            sync;
        }
    }
```
Transforming sum to use local memories references

7.8 Parallelization of Sequential Loops

In addition to these transformation the programmer can use loop parallelization techniques to further transform the sequential version into a parallel one. This section promotes the idea of obtaining a parallel version of sequential loops as a way to increase the parallelism of parallel programs. So far we have considered only programs that realize parallel algorithms, however parallel code can be obtained by parallelizing sequential code and in particular loops. There are many techniques for automatic parallelization of loops by compilers, however we believe that these techniques should be part of manual parallel programming as well. The assumption is that if the programmer is familiar with these techniques she can use them in cases where a compiler will fail to do so.

Consider the following sequential loop:

```
int i,A[N],B[N],C[N],D[N+2];

for(i=0;i<N-1;i++) {
    A[i] = B[i];
    C[i] = A[i]+B[i-1];
    D[i] = C[i+1];
    B[i] = C[i]+2;
}
```
Initial sequential version

It can be separated into two loops such that the first loop can be executed in parallel. This results from the fact that $D[i]$ uses the value of $C[i+1]$ which is not yet updated inside the original loop. Thus $D[i]$ uses the "old" values of $C[]$ and can be executed in parallel. The potential parallel program is therefore:

```
int i,A[N],B[N],C[N],D[N+2];

for(i=1;i<N-1;i++) {
    A[i] = B[i];
    D[i] = C[i+1];
}
for(i=1;i<N-1;i++) {
    C[i] = A[i]+B[i-1];
    B[i] = C[i]+2;
}
```
potential parallel version

Note that the second loop can not be made parallel as it is.

7.9 Lamport's Diagonalization

The example that we use follows the hyperplane method of Lamport describing an automatic method to transform nested *for* loops into a parallel code. The underlying sequential code implements the core of Gauss-Seidel iteration method for solving a linear equation system on a grid of numbers. Such code is used to solve many numerical problems such as partial differential equations. We are mainly concerned

with the ability to derive the parallel version via a sequence of gradual changes of
the following sequential code:

```
int a[N][N],b[N];

s3()
{
int i,j,k;
for(i=0;i<N-1;i++)
    for(j=1;j<N-1;j++)
        for(k=1;k<N-1;k++)
            a[j][k] = (a[j-1][k]+a[j+1][k]+a[j][k-1]+a[j][k+1])/4;
}
```
Initial version: of finite difference method

At first glance it seems that this code is inherently sequential, since every iteration in every loop depends on the previous one. For example, $a[j][k]$ can not be
updated before $a[j][k-1]$ and $a[j-1][k]$ have been updated. Moreover, $a[j][k]$
of the ith iteration, can not be updated before $a[j][k-1]$ and $a[j-1][k]$ of the
$(i-1)$th iteration have been updated. The main attempt is to transform the initial
version into a final sequential version which can be easily parallelized. Thus we
need an equivalent sequential version where most of the do loops can be performed
in parallel.

We start with a simple one dimensional case, in which each iteration depends on
its previous one. As it will turn out, only $N/2$ iterations will be needed for the final
version of $s3()$.

```
s1()
{
int i,j;
for(i=0;i<N/2;i++)
    for(j=1;j<N-1;j++)
        b[j] = (b[j-1]+b[j+1])/2;
}
```
One dimensional finite element code

A *time/updates* diagram can be used to depict inherent dependencies in $s1()$,
revealing potential parallelism. The following table shows the updates sequence of
six elements, such that each element is updated three times. The table consists of
steps, such that all possible updates that can take place in this step (without violating
dependencies of $s1()$) are given. We use j/i to mark the ith update of the jth
element, $<$ for an element read by its right neighbor and $>$ for an element read by
its left neighbor. Note that no element is being simultaneously read and written in
the same step, nor written more than once. In addition, let $b[j]$ be an element which
is updated in a step, then both the left and the right neighbors of $b[j]$ should not be
updated at that step.

Step	b[0]	b[1]	b[2]	b[3]	b[4]	b[5]	b[6]	b[7]
0	<	1/1	>	–	–	–	–	–
1	–	<	2/1	>	–	–	–	–
2	<	1/2	><	3/1	>	–	–	–
3	–	<	2/2	><	4/1	>	–	–
4	<	1/3	><	3/2	><	5/1	>	–
5	–	<	2/3	><	4/2	><	6/1	>
6	–	–	<	3/3	><	5/2	>	–
7	–	–	–	<	4/3	><	6/2	>
8	–	–	–	–	<	5/3	>	–
9	–	–	–	–	–	–	6/3	–

Hence, all odd/even elements before the jth element of $b[]$ can be updated simultaneously. This freedom is used in the following program which is equivalent to $s1()$:

```
p1()
{
int i,j,t;
for(i=1;i<N-1;i++)
    for(j=i;j>0;j=j-2)
        b[j] = (b[j-1]+b[j+1])/2;
for(i=1;i<N-1;i++)
    for(j=i;j<N-1;j=j+2)
        b[j] = (b[j-1]+b[j+1])/2;
}
```
Final sequential version of $s1()$

Next we consider the inner iterations of $s3()$ which perform one update of $a[][]$:

```
s2()
{
int i,j,k;
for(j=1;j<N-1;j++)
    for(k=1;k<N-1;k++)
        a[j][k] = (a[j-1][k]+a[j+1][k]+a[j][k-1]+a[j][k+1])/4;
}
```
A single update of $a[][]$

Using a similar update table, one can observe that the elements of each diagonal of $a[][]$ can be updated simultaneously, yielding the following final version for $s2()$:

Fig. 7.10 Updates in a
diagonal

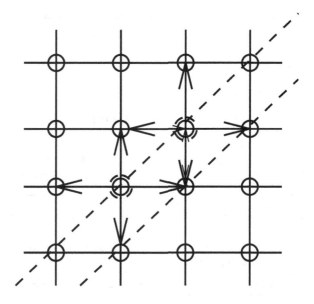

```
pp2()
{
int i,j,k,jj;
for(j=1;j<N-1;j++)
   for(k=1;k<=j;k++){
        jj=j-k+1;
        a[k][jj] =
            (a[k][jj-1]+a[k][jj+1]+a[k-1][jj]+a[k+1][jj])/4;  }
for(j=1;j<N-1;j++)
   for(k=j;k<N-1;k++){
        jj=N-2+j-k;
        a[k][jj] =
            (a[k][jj-1]+a[k][jj+1]+a[k-1][jj]+a[k+1][jj])/4;  }
}
```
Final version for $s2()$

The first loop in $pp2()$ traverses all $N - 2$ diagonals under the main diagonal of
$a[][]$, while the second loop traverses the ones above the main diagonal. Since the
updates of elements in a diagonal are independent, the diagonal can be updated in
parallel (see Fig. 7.10).

In an attempt to make the body of the two main loops similar and use a single
main loop we obtain:

```
p2p()
{
int i,j,k,jj;
for(j=1;j<2*N-3;j++)
   if(j<N-1)
      for(k=1;k<=j;k++){
         jj=1+j-k;
         a[k][jj]= (a[k][jj-1]+a[k][jj+1]+a[k-1][jj]+a[k+1][jj])/4;}
   else
      for(k=j-N+2;k<=N-2;k++){
         jj=j-k; /*here jj= N-2+j-k-N+2;*/
         a[k][jj]= (a[k][jj-1]+a[k][jj+1]+a[k-1][jj]+a[k+1][jj])/4;}
}
```
A more coherent version

Finally we can replace the inner loops with a procedure call, such that diagonals are traversed as elements:

```
diagonal(j,fr,to,z)
int j,fr,to,z;
{ int k,jj;
   for(k=fr;k<=to;k++){
      jj=z+j-k;
      a[k][jj]= (a[k][jj-1]+a[k][jj+1]+a[k-1][jj]+a[k+1][jj])/4;}
}
p2()
{
int j;
for(j=1;j<2*N-3;j++)
   if(j<N-1) diagonal(j,1,j,1);
   else diagonal(j,j-N+2,N-2,0);
}
```
Improved version of *pp2()*

Thus, *s3()* can be written such that diagonals are updated instead of raws in *a*[][]:

```
sp3()
{
int i,j;
for(i=0;i<N-1;i++)
for(j=1;j<2*N-3;j++)
    if(j<N-1) diagonal(j,1,j,1);
    else diagonal(j,j-N+2,N-2,0);
}
```
diagonalized version of *s3()*

This last program resemble the one dimensional case of $s2()$, where diagonals are updated instead of single elements of $b[]$. Hence $p1()$ and $p2()$ can be combined to form the final version of $s3()$:

```
p3()
{
int i,j,k,jj;
for(i=1;i<2*N-3;i++)
    for(j=i;j>0;j=j-2)
        if(j<N-1) diagonal(j,1,j,1);
        else diagonal(j,j-N+2,N-2,0);
for(i=1;i<2*N-3;i++)
    for(j=i;j<2*N-3;j=j+2)
        if(j<N-1) diagonal(j,1,j,1);
        else diagonal(j,j-N+2,N-2,0);
}
```
Final version of $s3()$

In $p3()$ all the elements of every diagonal can be updated in parallel and the jth iteration are also independent. Thus a parallel version of $p3()$ can be devised, by replacing $for - loops$ with $pparfor$ as follow:

```
diagonal(j,fr,to,z)
int j,fr,to,z;
{
    parfor(int k=fr;k<=to;k++){
        int jj;
        jj=z+j-k;
        a[k][jj]=(a[k][jj-1]+a[k][jj+1]+a[k-1][jj]+a[k+1][jj])/4;
} }
p3()
{
int i;
for(i=1;i<2*N-3;i++)
    parfor(int j=i;j>0;j=j-2){
        if(j<N-1) diagonal(j,1,j,1);
        else diagonal(j,j-N+2,N-2,0);
    }
for(i=1;i<2*N-3;i++)
    parfor(int j=i;j<2*N-4;j+=2){
        if(j<N-1) diagonal(j,1,j,1);
        else diagonal(j,j-N+2,N-2,0);
    }
}
```
Parallel version of $s3()$

This parallel program uses $2N$ parallel steps instead of N^3 steps used by $s3()$. This process demonstrates a possible way to develop parallel programs from an initial sequential version. This is of course not a general method, however it demonstrates, that in some cases dependencies can be overcome.

7.10 Exercises

7.10.1 Q1

Consider the following sequence of programs:

```
#define n 60
#define p 6
#define np 10
int A[n];

op(i,a,b)
int i,a[],*b;
{
if(a[i] == 1)
if(a[i-1] == 0){
   a[i-1]=1; a[i]=0; *b=1;}
}

pck()
{
int b,i;
b = 1;
while(b == 1){
   b = 0;
   for(i=1;i<n;i++) op(i,A,&b);
}
}
```

pck program

```
pck1()
{
int b,i;
b = 1;
while(b == 1){
```

```
    b = 0;
    parfor(int i=1;i<n;i+=np)
    { int j;
       for(j=i;j<i+np;j++)
          op(j,A,&b);
    }
}
```

pck1 program

```
pck2()
{
int c,k1,k2;
c = 1; k1=0; k2 = 0;
while(c == 1){
   c = 0;
   k1++;
   parfor(int i=1;i<n;i+=np)
   { int j,b,k;
      b = 1; k=0;
      while(b == 1){
         b = 0; k++;
         for(j=i;j<i+np;j++)
            op(j,A,&b);
      }
      _faa(&k2,k);
   }
   parfor(int i=1;i<n;i+=np)
   { int j;
      for(j=i;j<i+np;j++)
         op(j,A,&c);
   }
   }
printf("needed %d iterations of total %d iterations",k1,k2);
}
```

pck2 program

```
pck3()
{
int c,k1,k2;
c = 1; k1=0; k2 = 0;
while(c == 1){
   c = 0;
   k1++;
```

```
    parfor(int i=1;i<n;i+=np)
    { int k,j,b,ma[n];
        b = 1; k=0;
        for(j=i-1;j<i+np;j++)ma[j] = A[j];
        while(b == 1){
            b = 0; k++;
            for(j=i;j<i+np;j++)
                op(j,ma,&b);
        }
        for(j=i-1;j<i+np;j++)A[j] = ma[j];
        _faa(&k2,k);
    }

    parfor(int i=1;i<n;i+=np)
    { int j;
        for(j=i;j<i+np;j++)
            op(j,A,&c);
    }
}
printf("needed %d iterations of total %d iterations",k1,k2);
}
```
pck3 program

```
pck4()
{
int c,s,k1,k2;
c = 1; k1=0; k2 = 0;
while(c == 1){
    c = 0; k1++;
    if(k1%2 == 0)s=1;else s=np;
    parfor(int i=s;i<n;i+=np)
    { int k,j,b,ma[n];
        b = 1; k = 0;
        for(j=i-1;j<i+np;j++)ma[j] = A[j];
        while(b == 1){
            b = 0; k++;
            for(j=i;j<i+np;j++)
                op(j,ma,&b);
        }
        for(j=i-1;j<i+np;j++)A[j] = ma[j];
        _faa(&k2,k);
    }
    parfor(int i=1;i<n;i+=np)
    { int j;
        for(j=i;j<i+np;j++)
            op(j,A,&c);
```

```
        }
    }
    printf("needed %d iterations of total %d iterations",k1,k2);
    }
pck4 program
```

1. What is the effect of *pck*() on *A*[]?
2. Show that *op*(*i*, *A*, &*b*) operations, are independent and can be performed in parallel.
3. Show that *op*(*i*, *A*, &*b*) is monotonic, i.e show that for any sequence α of *op*(*i*, *A*, &*b*) operations there is another sequence β, such that α; β produce the correct result of *pck*().
4. Attach a transformation operation to *pck*1, *pck*2 and *pck*3. For every transformation describe how it was implemented in this case.
5. What is the improvement of *pck*4() compare to *pck*3()?
6. Assume that each *while*(*b* == 1) loop should terminate after *n* iterations. Compute $T(pck_i)$ for every *pck*() version, test all versions using the simulator, compare the results to your estimations of $T(pck_i)$.

7.10.2 Q2

Consider the following sequential program.

```
#include <stdio.h>
#define n 16
int A[n][n];

printa(){
int i,j;
   for(i=0;i<n;i++){
      for(j=0;j<n;j++) printf("%1d",A[i][j]);
      printf("/n");
   }
}

fpaint(fx,tx,fy,ty)
int fx,tx,fy,ty;
{
   int i,j,m;
   m = (tx-fx)/2;
   for(i=fx;i<tx;i++)
      for(j=fy;j<ty;j++)
         if(
```

```
           (((fx<= i)&&(i< fx+m)) && ((fy<= j)&&(j< fy+m))) ||
           (((tx-m<= i)&&(i< tx)) && ((ty-m<= j)&&(j< ty)))
         ) A[i][j]=1;
         else A[i][j]=0;
    if(m >=4) {
      fpaint(fx+m,tx,fy,fy+m);
      fpaint(fx,fx+m,fy+m,ty);
    }
}
main(){
   fpaint(0,n,0,n);
   printa();
}
```

fpaint program

1. How does $A[][]$ look after executing *fpaint*? Describe in words the operation of fpaint.
2. Which constructs can be made parallel in fpaint. Write the code for *parfpaint* obtained from *fpaint* by this direct parallelization of *fpaint*.
3. For the execution of *parfpaint* with p processors and array size n, compute the following:

   Tp direct execution time as defined in the parallel prefix example.
   $T(R)$ Estimation time. This include the computation of: $N, D, W, S_s, S_l,$ S_g, F_{bus}.
   Execute *parfpaint* on the simulator, compare the time statistics to the previous times.

4. Use the transformations to improve *parfpaint*. Compute the direct and estimate time for this version. Execute it on the simulator and compare the results.

   Reduce the number of 'IF' statements executed by fpaint, and explain in what ways this change reduces the execution time. Test the "ifless" version on the simulator, and explain your results.

7.11 Bibliographic Notes

The ability to transform sequential loops to parallel loops and sequence of function calls to parallel threaded execution has been the subject of many scientific works. OpenMP for example uses pragma comments to denote loops and statements that can be executed in parallel. A large body of work has been done on automatic compiler transformations to introduce parallelism and improve performances. The transformation method proposed here is along completely different lines: we wish to help programmers who develop explicitly parallel algorithms in the task of coding these algorithms and producing efficient parallel programs. Nevertheless, some of the transformations used are quite similar to those used in automatic parallelization.

Loop transformations are widely studied and used to automatically parallelize loops. Bacon et al. (1994) is a survey covering most of these transformations including: loop unrolling, loop interchange, loop tiling, loop skewing, loop fusion, loop peeling, loop distribution, and loop flattening. Careful and complex dependence analysis (Banerjee 1993) of array references is needed to verify the legality of applying these loop transformations. Padua and Wolfe (1986) is a comprehensive survey of what a compiler can do to increase vectorization and parallelization. Kuck et al. (1980) describe PARAFRASE, an optimizing compiler preprocessor that restructures the source code so as to increase efficiency of parallel execution. Whitfield and Soffa (1990) consider the fact that the order in which loop transformations (and other code optimizations) may effect the usefulness of each optimization. Whitfield and Soffa (1990) propose a unique method for selecting this order that is based on evaluating pre and post conditions associated with each transformation. Wolf and Lam (1991) combine loop interchange loop skewing and loop reversal in one transformation that is expressed by an unimodular matrix that is a linear combination of unimodular matrices of loop interchange loop skewing and loop reversal. Moreover it is possible to compute the unimodular transformations which best parallelize a set of nested loops by solving a suitable algebraic equation (Dowling 1990).

Loop transformations are also useful to improve locality of shared memory references. McKinley et al. (1996) use a cost model to estimate the impact of some loop transformations on the ability to reuse cached value, e.g., replacing the innermost loop by external loop can improve locality or may reduce cache hits. Wolf and Lam (1991) devised unimodular transformations that increase cache locality.

The diagonalization technique for parallelizing nested loops with back iteration dependencies caused by accessing multi-dimensional arrays was proposed by Lamport (1974).

Ben-Asher and Stein (2000) considered the opposite direction showing that parallel code can be transformed to sequential code mainly for debugging purposes.

References

Bacon, D.F., Graham, S.L., Sharp, O.J.: Compiler transformations for high-performance computing. ACM Comput. Surv. **26**(4), 345–420 (1994). citeseer.ist.psu.edu/bacon93compiler.html

Banerjee, U.: Loop Transformations for Restructuring Compilers: The Foundations. Springer, Berlin (1993). ISBN 079239318X

Ben-Asher, Y., Stein, E.: Basic results in automatic transformations of shared memory parallel programs into sequential programs. J. Supercomput. **17**(2), 143–165 (2000)

Dowling, M.L.: Optimal code parallelization using unimodular transformations. Parallel Comput. **16**(2–3), 157–171 (1990)

Kuck, D.J., Kuhn, R.H., Leasure, B., Wolfe, M.: The structure of an advanced retargetable vectorizer. In: Proc. COMPSAC '80 (1980). A revised version appeared in K. Hwang, *Supercomputers: Design and Applications*, pp. 163–178, IEEE Computer Society, 1984

Lamport, L.: The parallel execution of do loops. Commun. ACM **17**, 83–93 (1974)

McKinley, K.S., Carr, S., Tseng, C.W.: Improving data locality with loop transformations. ACM Trans. Program. Lang. Syst. **18**(4), 453 (1996)

Padua, D.A., Wolfe, M.J.: Advanced compiler optimizations for supercomputers. Commun. ACM **29**(12), 1184–1201 (1986)

Whitfield, D., Soffa, M.L.: An approach to ordering optimizing transformations. In: Symp. Principles & Practice of Parallel Programming, pp. 137–146 (1990)

Wolf, M.E., Lam, M.S.: A loop transformation theory and an algorithm to maximize parallelism. IEEE Trans. Parallel Distrib. Syst., 452–471 (1991)

Wolf, M.E., Lam, M.S.: A data locality optimizing algorithm. ACM SIGPLAN Not. **26**(6), 30–44 (1991)

Chapter 8
Performance and Overhead Measurements

The previous sections used a set of parameters (overheads, number of processors, etc) to analyze and predict the performance of parallel programs. This section addresses the problem of measuring those and other important parameters, for a given shared memory machine. These parameters are not likely to be found in the manuals, since the combination of the operating system with the hardware is not usually documented (it depends for instance, on the underlying compiler). In this section we use a specific multicore parallel machine called MC, however the proposed methods should work for other machines as well.

Seeking methodology to conduct experiments of parallel computers using only two tools: **External clock** and **Selected programs**. Thus the problem is to *isolate* one cause and effect. Hence the user can obtain vital information of various factors, which can dominate potential performances, on his specific parallel machine. The difficulty in doing so, lies in the fact that when one measures through a program, it usually the case that the program results and performances are affected by several causes. Moreover the mutual effect of several cases may produce a new effect. The experimental art is then, to devise a program whose performance is mainly affected by one cause. All other cases are negligible compared to this the cause whose effect we want to measure.

This chapter reports measurements of cache performances, bus contention effects, context-switch overhead, overhead for spawning new threads, the effectiveness of load balancing, and synchronization overhead on this system.

8.1 Introduction

When evaluating a new system, it is important to make accurate measurements of the overheads involved in various system operations. This is not always as easy as it sounds.

On the MC, and bus-based shared memory machines in general, the problem is one of isolating the measurements from irrelevant external effects. For example, the measured results depend on the following:

Y. Ben-Asher, *Multicore Programming Using the ParC Language*,
Undergraduate Topics in Computer Science,
DOI 10.1007/978-1-4471-2164-0_8, © Springer-Verlag London 2012

- Whether data structures are local or remote, and must be accessed through the bus.
- If remote accesses are made, what is the contention for the bus at that time.
- What is the contention for a specific memory module. This influences both local and remote references.
- What is the load on the PEs, i.e. how many threads are being time shared.

The methodology used is to write application programs that perform a certain operation a large number of times, and measure their execution times. The applications are written so that the transient effects at startup are negligible relative to the total execution time, thus enabling us to attribute the whole time to the repeated performance of the operation being measured. However, care must be taken that some additional operation does not "slip in" together with the one we are interested in.

8.2 Processing Rates

Each core in the MC is fairly independent, controlled by an independent clock using different L1 cache and handed out different jobs by the operation system. New cutting edge microchip manufacturing processes which integrate more than 1 million transistors per mm^2, are highly delicate in the sense that even a particle in the width of 1/1,000,000 of human hair might harm the processor and lead to the creation of asymmetric cores. Since even the proper care and use of a MC involves thermal and electrical currents flowing through the integrated circuits, over time, electrical properties might change and core symmetry might be harmed.

The first experiment set up to test performance variation across different cores of the same multicore machine.

```
for (firstProc=0;firstProc<PROC_NUM; firstProc++){
    for (secondProc=firstProc+1;
        secondProc<PROC_NUM; secondProc++){
res[firstProc][0]=res[secondProc][0]=
        res[firstProc][1]=res[secondProc][1]=0;
parfor (i= 0; i< PROC_NUM; i++){
    long j;
    if (i==firstProc || i==secondProc){
        for (j=0 ; j<ITER ; j++) {
            res[i][0]++;
            if (res[i][0]>=STOP_ITER && res[i][1]==0){
                if (i==firstProc)
                relativeResults[firstProc][secondProc]=
                    res[secondProc][0]-STOP_ITER;
                else
                relativeResults[secondProc][firstProc]=
                    res[firstProc][0]-STOP_ITER;
                res[i][1]=1;
    } } } } }
```

```
/* Print results:*/
for (firstProc=0;firstProc<PROC_NUM; firstProc++){
    for (secondProc=0;secondProc<PROC_NUM; secondProc++){
        printf("%4d ",(int)(100*((double)relativeResults
                [firstProc][secondProc])/STOP_ITER));
    }
    printf(" {1..n } ");
}
```

The above code tests all pairs of cores against each other. A pair of threads is spawned, one on each core. The thread iterates a large number of times and when it reaches half the number of iterations, it samples the progress of its competitor thread and tabulates it.

A few experiments were made with different values of iterations (2,000,000, 20,000,000 and 200,000,000 were used), both combinations of variables stored locally and variables stored in a cache line shared across the different cores were examined. The MC which were used in this experiment were AMD Phenom 9950 Quad-Core and an Intel CoreI7 also a Quad-Core, the operating system was a "light" Linux-KUbuntu. The actual code used in these experiments is a bit more complex, since it makes 100 repetitions for each pair to measure an average result, it also calculates the worst deviation of performance for each pair. Also some extra variables were used to isolate and remove the affect of time it takes for different threads to launch and start.

Results are shown in Tables 8.1 and 8.2. Each table contains the rates of all processors(cores) relative to other processor. The number in entry $a[i, j]$ indicates the relative speed (in percentages) of core j in relation to core i. A row of negative numbers indicates a relatively fast processor (core).

The relatively low processing rate differences shown in Table 8.1, indicate that the cores perform with similar speed. The discrepancy between the average processing rates (Table 8.1) and the maximal difference measured (Table 8.2) is caused by the intervention of the operating system scheduler. Thus, using the Linux operating system scheduler derives some nondeterministic interruption of the kernel scheduler. These are only fair terms for this experiment since real world software is usually executed with multi-process operating systems that interrupts some of the cores from time to time with other tasks.

8.3 The Effect of MESI/MOESI Bus Transactions on the Processing Rates

Here we use the code of Sect. 8.2 to measure the effect of MESI/MOESI bus transaction needed to update the value of a shared variable on the processing rates of the different cores/hardware-threads. We modify the code of Sect. 8.2 to once perform a parallel access by two cores to two different local variables that are placed in two different cache lines. Thus accessing these two local variables should hardly create

Table 8.1 Average Relative Rates—Percentages of relative rate for 4-cores AMD with *STOP_ITER =* 1,000,000 and all counters are in different cache lines

	1	2	3	4
1	0	0	0	3
2	0	0	0	2
3	0	−1	0	2
4	−1	−1	−1	0

Table 8.2 Maximal Difference Rates—Percentages of relative rate for 4-cores AMD with *STOP_ITER =* 1,000,000 and all counters are in different cache lines

	1	2	3	4
1	0	82	−38	82
2	51	0	52	86
3	51	−40	0	85
4	87	−55	−54	0

Table 8.3 Average Relative Rates—Percentages of relative rate for 4-cores Intel with *STOP_ITER =* 100,000,000 and all counters are located in the same cache line

	1	2	3	4	5	6	7	8
1	0	−1	0	0	0	0	0	−50
2	0	0	0	0	0	0	0	−50
3	−1	0	0	0	0	0	0	−50
4	0	0	0	0	−1	0	2	11
5	0	0	0	1	0	0	0	−49
6	0	0	0	−1	−1	0	1	−50
7	0	0	0	−3	−1	−2	0	−51
8	71	71	72	−13	69	69	73	0

any BusRd/BusRDx transactions. This is compared to the case where the two cores perform a parallel access updating a shared variable which results in multiple Bus-RDx transactions. Since both cores or hardware threads update the shared variable (as oppose to the case where one core updates and the other reads the variable) it is expected that the MESI overhead of the bus transactions will be symmetric to both active cores.

Tables 8.1 and 8.2 show acute deference between two smilingly "identical" runs of the code. Table 8.4 shows results of our experiment running on Intel core I7 with hyper threading, Table 8.3 shows the result of a similar experiment with one difference, the counters used in our experiment code (res[CoreNum][0]) reside all in the same cache line. This is achieved by redeclaring the array, *res[]*, that stores the threads' local variables to a smaller sized array. "Shrinking" the array causes the spacing between the threads' variables to reduce which ultimately causes the local variables to reside on the same cache line (formal specification of our core i7 machine points to the fact that the cache line size is of 64 bytes).

It follows that in the case of accessing local variables there was hardly any effect on the processing rates while for the case of updating a shared variable there were

Table 8.4 Average Relative Rates—Percentages of relative rate for 4-cores Intel with *STOP_ITER* = 100,000,000 and all counters are located in different cache line		1	2	3	4	5	6	7	8
	1	0	0	1	0	0	0	0	0
	2	0	0	0	0	0	0	0	−1
	3	−1	0	0	0	0	0	0	0
	4	0	0	0	0	0	0	0	0
	5	0	0	0	0	0	0	0	0
	6	0	0	0	0	−1	0	0	0
	7	0	0	0	−1	0	0	0	0
	8	0	0	1	0	0	0	0	0

significant differences in the processing rates of several cores, while core number eight suffered a significant slowdown. These findings were repeated in further experiments which we performed, with different values for the STOP_ITER. This interesting behavior can be attributed to the fact that the core is physically asymmetric to some extent. This effective asymmetry causes what seems to be a priority-based behavior. Besides bus resources access scheduling which occurs during concurrent request to multiple L1 cache that reside in different cores, there is also the influence of the MESI cache coherency protocol, which is implemented for the core i7 processors. Physical chip asymmetry derives that concurrent cache line request, will be dealt in an asymmetric deterministic manner. The MESI protocol will "favor" a cache line request for a specific core. Consequently if two cores attempts to update a cache-line simultaneously, and one of the cores is "favorable" it will suffer shorter delays than the other. Also, we can not rule-out some influence of the operating system which might also "favo" a specific core, and hand out some background task for the same core to perform. This will cause the core to perform poorly. Another interesting conclusion can be drawn by looking at the differences between the runtime of each experiment. The local version of the code performed about 1.5 times faster than the non-local version. This gives us a taste of the overhead that comes with the MESI protocol. In the non-local version, different variables of distinct threads were mapped on to the same cache line, this caused false shearing, meaning, causing unnecessary cache line invalidation to occur.

8.4 The Effect of Hardware Threads

In here we consider the possible effect of hardware threads. In our machines there are four cores and each core can execute two hardware threads. The instructions from two hardware threads $T1, T2$ that are executed on the same core are interleaved by the hardware such that the overhead for cache-misses made by $T1$'s load/store operations is overlapped with the execution of instructions from $T2$ (and vice versa). Thus, using up to four threads imply one thread per core, now adding more threads will activate the use of hardware threads at each core.

The technique we used in order to place the variables in deterministic cache lines, was to align the memory using arrays, for example: since the hardware we used for the experiment was Intel core i7 which is stated to have 64 bit cache lines, we used a two dimensional array of longs where the second dimension was a fixed size of 8 (long *localData*[*PROC_NUM*][8]). Since the rows of an array are aligned continuously inside the memory, we can assume that localData[0][0] has at 64 bit distance from localData[1][0]. Note that the cost for not carefully aligning the variables inside the memory would be "false sharing", whereas the cost for using this method is readability. Mind that the second dimension of the arrays in this experiment is redundant and is used only for the alignment, thus only 0 is used as an index for the second dimensions. The same technique, for placing the variables in deterministic cache lines, is used in all of our experiments.

Consider the following code:

```
long globalData[PROC_NUM][1],gj[PROC_NUM][1];
long localData[PROC_NUM][CACHE_LINE_SIZE];
long lj[PROC_NUM][CACHE_LINE_SIZE];
printf("measuring local access contention\n");
for (processors=1; processors<PROC_NUM+1; processors++){
  t1=clock();
  parfor (i=0; i<PROC_NUM+1; i++){
    if (i<processors){
    for (lj[i][0]=0; lj[i][0]<STOP_ITER; lj[i][0]++){
    localData[i][0]=lj[i][0]%(1+localData[i][0]);
  } }
  }
  t2=clock();
  time=t2-t1;
  printf("time for local access with %d threads: %ld, \n",
                          processors, time/processors);
}
printf("\nmeasuring global access contention\n");
for (processors=1; processors<PROC_NUM+1; processors++){
  t1=clock();
  parfor (i=0; i<PROC_NUM+1; i++){
    if (i<processors) {
    for (gj[i][0]=0; gj[i][0]<STOP\_ITER; gj[i][0]++){
    globalData[i][0]=gj[i][0]%(1+globalData[i][0]);
  }
    } }
  t2=clock();
  time=t2-t1;
  printf("time for global access with %d threads: %ld\n",
                          processors,time/processors);
```

The code above performs two measurements on the core-I7 using two separate parfors. The first parfor measures the effect of adding more hardware threads to the cores where each thread accesses a different local variable (no cache misses are expected). The second parfor also measures the impact of using more hardware threads for the case that the threads access variables that are likely to be in the same cache-line. Hence, for the second parfor there are more bus-transactions and it is interesting to see how the overlapping of instructions from hardware threads that are executing on the same core will be manifested.

The results are as follows:

time for local access with 1 threads :	1810000
time for local access with 2 threads :	1960000
time for local access with 3 threads :	1880000
time for local access with 4 threads :	1880000
time for local access with 5 threads :	2292000
time for local access with 6 threads :	2588333
time for local access with 7 threads :	2805714
time for local access with 8 threads :	3025000

The time here is measured using the clock() function, clock() returns the number of clock cycles that were actually "used" by the machine. The final time result is divided by the active threads number. When a core is idle, its clock cycles do not aggregate to the final clock() result. As noted above, the elapsed execution time was about the same for Cores 1–4, indicating that each core executes one hardware thread and all threads run in parallel. Hence, basically the execution time of each core is the same. However, adding more threads issued interleaved execution of two hardware threads per core. The Intel I7 we used has only 4 real cores, so when executing more than 4 threads at a time, performance degrades as one core must execute two hardware threads simultaneously. Note that executing two hardware threads per core did not double the execution time, possibly due to the overlapping effect of load/store latencies.

In the same manner we measure the performance degradation when the calculation is done using global variables residing in the same cache-line. As explained before, we align the variables on the same cache line using an array. The results of this second measurement are as follows:

time for global access with 1 threads :	1660000
time for global access with 2 threads :	5930000
time for global access with 3 threads :	6187500
time for global access with 4 threads :	7483750
time for global access with 5 threads :	5688000
time for global access with 6 threads :	6790000
time for global access with 7 threads :	7243333
time for global access with 8 threads :	7321666

When comparing the first 4 threads, we can see that as the number of threads rise, the performance degrades, this matches our expectation of performance slow-down caused by the MESI/MOESI protocol that causes the bus transactions to be an active bottleneck. The relatively "surprising" results are that when executing more than four threads at a time, the performance does not seem to degrade in the same manner and in one point it even seems to improve. The reason for this is that when running more than 4 threads, two threads are executed by the same core, when this happens, the MESI/MOESI does not add more overhead since for these two threads, the cache line resides in the same physical core that executes the threads. Let $T1, T2, T3, T4, T5$ be five threads such that $T1, T5$ are executed in the same core then MESI/MOESI's collisions (bus transactions) that exists between $T1, T2, T3, T4$ do not exist between $T1$ and $T5$.

8.5 Initial Measurements of MESI

Further exploration of MESI Protocol bus interaction.

In the following experiment we set out to check the performance impact of different Read/Write Bus interactions. We examined four different cases of local and global variable access. In the first experiment we performed Writes and Reads only from non shared, local memory variables. In the following three experiments we altered the location of the variables such that the second experiment will include global reads and local writes, the third experiment will include local reads and global writes whereas the forth experiment will include global reads and global writes.

The first experiment's code is as follows:

```
#define CORES_NUM 4
#define STOP_ITER 10000000000L
int main(){
long readArray[100],writeArray[100],i,output=0;
time_t start,stop;
time(&start);

 parfor (i=0;i< CORES_NUM; i++){

   // *8 will make sure each read is from a different
   // cache line
   long* reader=&readArray[i*8];

   // *8 will make sure each write is to a different
   // cache line
   long* reader=&readArray[i*8];
   long j=0,buffer[8];
        *reader=i;
        *writer=i;

        for (j=0; j<STOP_ITER; j++){
                        *writer+=*reader;
        }
        output+=*writer;
```

```
}

time(&stop);
return 0;
}
```

In order to transform variable access from local to global, we only changed the index calculation for accessing readArray and writeArray. The adjustments in the two lines below, are the only adjustments needed to be done in order to transform access from local to shared.

```
// changed from %i*8% to %i% in order to enable
// shared access
    long* reader=&readArray[i];

    long* writer=&writeArray[i];// shared access
```

Thus, these two changes in the original code of the first experiment will produce the forth experiment.

The total execution time of each experiment is as follows:

```
1. Local Reads Local Writes: 30 s
2. Global Reads Local Writes: 30 s
3. Local Reads Global Writes: 55 s
4. Global Reads Global Writes: 65 s
```

The results displayed above are average results as the execution time varied from one execution to another. Execution time of experiments 3 and 4 varied up to 5 seconds from one execution to another.

The identical results of experiments 1 and 2 indeed shows that the different caches were populated with the data and the cache line was marked as shared, but, this shared state did not involve a cache miss. All read transactions were accompanied by a cache hit.

The results of experiments 3 and 4 imply a substantial number of cache misses and also, some latency that occurred due to Bus Write Back to the main memory. As opposed to experiment 3, experiment 4 involved more intense interactions on the bus. These extra bus transactions lead more situations where variables written back from the cache to memory. From these experiments it seems that MESI's bus transactions doubled the execution time leading to the possible conclusion that the penalty for each bus transaction is twice the cost of a local read/write operation. However, the situation is more complex and the above experiment only works when we use four threads, otherwise when two cores are used there is no slowdown.

8.6 Remote Access Penalty

In previous sections, we have explained and seen that there is an overhead for multiple accesses of memory and variables that are shared among several cores. As

explained before, the majority of the overhead comes from the implementation of
the Cache Coherency Protocol MESI, such as the MESI, where a variable which is
marked as exclusive in core A, and is being modified by core B, must be transferred
to the core B cache from core A, and it's state must be modified in both caches accordingly. The experiment in this section is designed to answer the question: how
much more time does it take for this shared "global" access verses a "local" one? In
this experiment three threads are spawned; two of them (A and B) read and write to
the same "global" variable while the third thread (thread C) perform identical reads
and writes only to a local variable. Since thread A and B might read and write to the
shared variable in a non-colliding manner, which will render the variable relatively
local, we added a counter ($globalSum[0]/globalSum[1]$) which counts the number
of times where the variable was marked as "Modified" in one cache and then immediately used for read/write in the other cache. Thread C is used as a reference point.
When it completes 1000000000 iterations, it notes the number of iterations that the
other threads have completed in the same time. Then, a simple calculation is done
to see how many "global" accesses were made by the two threads, and how many
more iterations were done by the third thread. Finally we print these statistics.

The use of $globalAccCounter[0][0]/globalAccCounter[1][0]$ implies that the accesses of the threads are cache hits. The use of $((*remoteFlag) * -1) - 1$ allows us
to detect a change from the previous update made by the same thread without using
an if-statement. This is because the use of if-statements introduces variable latencies
due to branch-predictions outcomes made in hardware.

```
parblock
   { /* global access A */
     for (i=0; i<STOP_ITER; i++){
        globalAccCounter[0][0]+= ((*remoteFlag)*-1)-1;
        (*remoteFlag)=-1;
        progress[0][0]=i;
     }
   }:
   { /* global access B */
     for (j=0; j<STOP_ITER; j++){
        globalAccCounter[1][0]+= ((*remoteFlag)*1)-1;
        (*remoteFlag)=1;
        progress[1][0]=j;
     }
   }:
   { /* local access C */
     for (k=0; k<STOP_ITER; k++){
        globalAccCounter[2][0]+=((*localFlag)*1)-1;
        (*localFlag)=-1;
        progress[2][0]=k;
     }

     sum=(globalAccCounter[0][0]+globalAccCounter[1][0])/-2;
     progress1=progress[0][0];
     progress2=progress[1][0];
```

```
printf("Remote Access: %.21f%%\n",
        100.*sum/(progress1+progress2));
printf("progress: 1= %.21f%% 2= %.21f%% 3= 100%%\n",
        (100.*progress1)/STOP\_ITER,
        (100.*progress2)/STOP_ITER);
```

We conducted the experiment hundreds of times using an external loop. We verified that each of the three spawned threads was executed by a different core (as opposed to the possibility that the first two were executed as hardware threads on the same core). On average it appears that 9.5 percent of the accesses to the shared variable were actually global and involved a cache miss. We know this since we measured the number of times where a thread read a value that was written by another thread. In this case (9.5 % were not a cache hit) the slowdown of the two threads was about 42 percent (meaning the threads progress was at about 58 percent compared to the third reference thread that implemented only local accesses). This brings us to the conclusion that a global access costs 10.88 times more than a local one. The reason why only 9.5 % were clearly cache misses is due to the fact that each loop accesses several global variables not just *remoteFlag*:

- Assume that one thread (A) suffers a cache miss when accessing

$$globalAccCounter[k][0]$$

or when accessing *progress*$[k][0]$. Consequently this thread is delayed until the bus transactions that are generated due to this miss is completed.
- During this delay assume that the other thread (B) access its

$$remoteFlag, \qquad globalAccCounter[k'][0], \qquad progress[k'][0]$$

and all of them are cache hits (Exclusive or Modified states). Consequently this thread (B) can repeatedly access these variables without any cache miss until the BusRDx of the first thread A invalidates the cache entry of B.

Another effect that can explain the fact that only 9.5 % of changes were observed is the fact that "bad" sequences of the form:

$$rA; rB; \langle wArA; wB; rB \rangle; \langle wArA; wB; rB \rangle; \langle wArA; wB; rB \rangle;$$

$$\langle wArA; wB; rB \rangle; \langle wArA; wB; rB \rangle; \langle wArA; wB; rB \rangle; wA; wB$$

can occur such that neither thread-A nor thread-B observe values written by the other thread since they constantly read the values written by themselves, i.e., in this sequence $\langle wArA; wB; rB \rangle$ no thread observes any change.

It thus follows that generating repeated accesses of MESI transactions are hard to obtain and even constant loops accessing the same variables in parallel are not likely to produce many MESI transactions.

8.7 Wrapping MESI Overhead by Local Accesses

The load on the bus and the MESI transactions types and frequencies depends, of course, on the shared variables access rate from the different processors. This in turn depends on the ratio of local to global memory references. This experiment shows how a larger percentage of local references can reduce the MESI's overhead. In this experiment, each core/thread accesses global shared variables many times inside a loop. In order to have an estimation of the overhead, we first execute the same loop only with access to local variables. Next we wrap each global access with k local accesses, and again, we compare it to the case where only local accesses are executed, and so on. As the wrapping grows we observe that the MESI overhead gets smaller and smaller. Finally we see that the time needed for global accesses is negligible. This shows the importance of overlapping the overhead of global accesses by local ones. In ParC the user can use local variables declared in the current thread to realize this wrapping.

The following code was used to measure the wrapping effect:

```
#define local    localCounter[i][0]++;
#define global   globalCounter[i][0]++;
#define Duplicate5(instr)   instr instr instr instr instr
#define Duplicate10(instr)  Duplicate5(instr) Duplicate5(instr)

#define Duplicate240(instr) Duplicate120(instr)\
        Duplicate120(instr)
int main(){
int i=0,j=0;
long localI[PROC_NUM][CACHE_LINE_SIZE];
long globalCounter[PROC_NUM][1];
long localCounter[PROC_NUM][CACHE_LINE_SIZE];
clock\_t before,after;

before=clock();
parfor (i=0; i<PROC_NUM; i++){
for (localI[i][0]=0;localI[i][0]<STOP_ITER;localI[i][0]++){
local
}
}
after=clock();
printf("local time  1: %ld\n",after-before);

before=clock();
parfor (i=0; i<PROC\_NUM; i++){
for (localI[i][0]=0;localI[i][0]<STOP_ITER;localI[i][0]++){
global
}

}
after=clock();
printf("global time 1: %ld\n",after-before);

before=clock();
parfor (i=0; i<PROC_NUM; i++){
for (localI[i][0]=0;localI[i][0]<STOP_ITER;localI[i][0]++){
```

```
Duplicate5(local)
local
}
}
after=clock();
printf("local time  5: %ld\n",after-before);
before=clock();
parfor (i=0; i<PROC\_NUM; i++){
for (localI[i][0]=0;localI[i][0]<STOP_ITER;localI[i][0]++){
Duplicate5(local)
global

}

}
after=clock();
printf("global time 5: %ld\n",after-before);

printf("global time 240: %ld\n",after-before);
```

The average results are as follows:

```
local time  1: 8650000
global time 1: 15460000
local time  5: 23210000
global time 5: 53490000
local time  10: 37830000
global time 10: 73220000
local time  20: 66920000
global time 20: 94690000
local time  40: 125120000
global time 40: 138540000
local time  60: 183640000
global time 60: 201320000
local time  80: 283400000
global time 80: 259060000
local time  120: 358090000
global time 120: 377640000
local time  240: 745660000
global time 240: 725460000
```

The last result where the local time exceeds the global time can be attributed to the fact that the buffered mixed local and global access uses two memory modules and by that, less contention is created. This can be explained by the fact that our Intel I7 multicore has two hardware threads on each core, when these two threads access the global memory, the access is done to the local cache.

8.8 Experimenting with the MESI's Protocol States

Not much is published about the fine implementation details of the MESI protocol
on the Core I7 machine. Specifically, one might wonder if short-circuits and "simple" logical optimizations were implemented on the tested subject machine. We can
examine a simple state transition, where a modified variable residing in a cache line,
is modified again by a different core. Theoretically, the case where a variable has
been modified by one core, and then, immediately modified by another core without
first being read, can be optimized in such a way, that no flush will be executed by
the first core and no BusRd will be done by the second core. Such optimization will
reduce the MESI protocol overhead. A minor change has been done to the remote
access penalty experiment, this time no explicit reads, only writes are done, both to
the local variable and to the global variable:

```
long flags[8][3];
/* make *remoteFlag, *localFlag reside in different
cache lines*/
long *remoteFlag = &flags[0][0];
long *localFlag = &flags[1][0];
flags[0][0]=flags[1][0]=flags[2][0]=-1;
  parblock
  { /* global access */
    for (i=0; i<STOP_ITER; i++){
      (*remoteFlag)=-i;
      progress[0][0]=i;
    }
  }:
  { /* global access */
    for (j=0; j<STOP_ITER; j++){
      (*remoteFlag)=j;
      progress[1][0]=j;
    }
  }:
  { /* local access */
    for (k=0; k<STOP_ITER; k++){
      (*localFlag)=-k;
      progress[2][0]=k;
    }
```

The experiment was conducted several times, the results are as follows: The
progress rate of the first and second threads that write to the global variable was 33–
34 % of the third thread who access the flag locally (the local thread was three times
faster than the other two). In the "remote access experiment" we have measured the
local to global access time to be 10 times faster, but, not all the "global" accesses
to memory are truly global. This is because if one thread performs two writes to a
global variable before the second thread gets to write, then the first thread has performed one global access and one local access. In the "remote access experiment"

we factored in this detail. The original progress rate of the two global threads in the "remote access experiment" was in the range of 58–87 %, a lot faster than only writing to the global variable. This finding shows that there is no optimization in only performing global writes. One reason why this kind of optimization can be hard to implement, is that the cache line is rather large, thus one thread can write to only half of the line while the other thread writes only to the second half of the cache line. In this case, if the modified cache line had not been written to the memory by the first core, the second core can not override the line, otherwise, some information will be lost.

8.9 Spawning New Threads

In here we consider the problem of measuring the overhead it takes to create a new thread, starting it, and terminate it. This is important since threads that are too short relative to this overhead usually cause a degradation rather than an improvement in performance. There are several factors that should be considered, in particular the Lazy thread mechanism of ParC implying that when possible new ParC-threads (iterations of parfor) are not explicitly generated as separate threads but are executed through regular function calls or loop iterations. For example the following parfor

```
parfor(i=0; i<1000; i++){
    //some code;
    }
```

will split the loop into $P = no\_cores$ "real" threads each executing $1000/P$ ParC threads as loop iterations. ParC also recognizes states in which this optimization can not be activated, for example

```
int flag[1000];
parfor(i=1; i<1000; i++){ flag[1]=0; }
parfor(i=0; i<1000; i++){
    //some code;
    while(flag[i]==1);
        flag[(i+1)\%1000]=0;
}
```

will generate 1000 real threads.

Knowing how much time it takes for a ParC thread to be spawned, will also reveal how much time is saved when ParC optimizes its thread generation.

Observe the following code:

```
xxx\=xxx\=xxx\= \kill
#include "time.h"
#define proc\_no 4
#define CYCLES 100000
int main(){
```

```
time_t start,stop;
long i,j,x=0;

    //warmup the thread mechanisem
    parfor (i=0;i< proc_no; i++){

    }
    time(&start);
    for (j=0; j<CYCLES; j++){
        parfor (i=0;i< proc_no; i++){

        }
    }
    time(&stop);
    printf("time to start thread %ld\n",
           (stop-start)/(double)CYCLES );

return 0;
}
```

Values of CYCLES that were used were between 100000 and 1000000. The results started from 0.3 ms per thread to 1 ms per thread with the largest CYCLE number. These results point to the fact that the average overhead for thread creation depends on the number of threads that are generated. Note that we used an initial parfor just to "warmup" the system to generate its queues and other global data-structures needed to handle the generation of new ParC threads.

In the next experiment we set to check the lazy thread mechanism. For this we made a simple change to the code above, the result was the following code:

```
    //warmup the thread mechanism
    parfor (i=0;i< proc_no; i++){

    }
    time(&start);
        for (j=0; j<1; j++){
    parfor (i=0;i<CYCLES* proc_no; i++){

        }
    }
    time(&stop);
    printf("time to start thread \%ld\n",
           (stop-start)/(double)CYCLES );
```

As expected, the results show great performance improvement, with almost no overhead for spawning new threads, as most threads are generated as lazy threads.

The experiments described in this section show that the effective overhead for spawning a thread is highly variable. The reason for this is that spawning is communication intensive, and hence depends on the loading conditions. The minimum time needed just to create a thread, start it and terminate it, is about 0.3 ms. This number grows when there is contention for the bus, either due to other threads being spawned, or due to inner computations.

8.10 Bibliographic Notes

Performance measurements of parallel programs were extensively studied, however the measuring techniques themselves have not been considered. The main idea proposed here, namely using schematic programs especially designed to isolate one parameter of the underlying parallel system has not been considered. Eggers and Katz (1989) used traces of parallel programs to evaluate how limited Bus bandwidth affects the performance of shared memory programs.

Winiecki and Bilski (2008) presented an instrumentation technique for multicores and study the outcome of the measurements for a specific type of multicore architecture. Mogul and Borg (1991) used traces of memory references and fed them to a cache simulator to compute accurate cache-hit rates over short intervals. These results are used to evaluate the harmful effect of context-switch operations to the promised locality of memory references. David et al. (2007) also considered the harmful effect of context switches on cache locality. The technique used here is basically similar to what is used in this chapter. By subtraction the overhead of executing context-switch from the overall overhead of using context-switches, David et al. (2007) obtained the overhead paid just of cache-misses due to context-switch operations. David et al. (2007) used this method to estimate the impact of processor interrupt servicing on cache misses.

Efforts were made to evaluate via simulations different hardware solutions to the cache coherence problem in multicore machines. Archibald and Baer (1986) showed that alternative approaches can limit the number of cores that can be used. The system of Wilson (1987) used simulations to show that a machine with over 100 cores can be constructed by using an extended hierarchical cache/bus architecture using a suitable multi-cache coherency protocol. Hristea et al. (1997) developed a micro benchmark suite that measures cache hierarchy performance in multicore machines.

Tools to measure performances of programs executed on multicore machines are constantly being developed. Mohr et al. (2001) designed a performance tool interface for OpenMP programs that use source-level instrumentation to allow a monitoring program to collect and display different statistics. DeRose et al. (2004) also developed tools for profiling and tracing OpenMP applications. They used these statistics to compute the overhead of temporal load-imbalances between the cores, synchronization and OS service times. Burkhart and Millen (2002) combined a set of monitoring tools to create an integrated monitoring tool for performance debugging of shared memory programs.

Studying performances of different parallel machines is a related technique where the goal is to study performances of different machines for the same given benchmark. For example, TPCC-UVa is an open-source data-base system used for global performance measurement of computer systems (Llanos, 2006). In this work, this benchmark was used to determine the effect of using multicore machines versus single-core machines. Peng et al. (2008) compared Intel Core 2 Duo, Intel Pentium D and an AMD Athlon 64—2 CPUs using different multi-threaded workloads. It is shown that different features of the memory hierarchy such as cache-to-cache communication, large L2-cache size, and fast L2 to core latency can significantly affect the performances of a multicore system.

Measurements have been used to evaluate mixed mode of programming combining both shared memory (usually OpenMP) and message-passing (usually MPI). Jost et al. (2003) studied the performance of Computational Fluid Dynamics benchmark over a cluster of SMP (Symmetric Multi-Processors) nodes using either shared memory, message passing or a combination of them. Krawezik (2003) made a comparison of MPI and three OpenMP programming styles of the NAS benchmarks. Krawezik (2003) showed that OpenMP provides competitive performance compared to MPI. Different measurements were obtained by using measurements of hardware performance counters. These counters are implemented in hardware and are used to sample hardware events such as L@/1 cache missed or number of branch miss-predictions.

References

Archibald, J., Baer, J.L.: Cache coherence protocols: Evaluation using a multiprocessor simulation model. ACM Trans. Comput. Syst. **4**(4), 273–298 (1986)

Burkhart, H., Millen, R.: Performance-measurement tools in a multiprocessor environment. IEEE Trans. Comput. **38**(5), 725–737 (2002)

David, F.M., Carlyle, J.C., Campbell, R.H.: Context switch overheads for Linux on ARM platforms. In: Proceedings of the 2007 Workshop on Experimental Computer Science, p. 3. ACM, New York (2007)

DeRose, L., Mohr, B., Seelam, S.: Profiling and tracing OpenMP applications with POMP based monitoring libraries. In: Euro-Par 2004 Parallel Processing, pp. 39–46. Springer, Berlin (2004)

Eggers, S.J., Katz, R.H.: The effect of sharing on the cache and bus performance of parallel programs. In: Proceedings of the Third International Conference on Architectural Support for Programming Languages and Operating Systems, pp. 257–270. ACM, New York (1989). ISBN 0897913000

Hristea, C., Lenoski, D., Keen, J.: Measuring memory hierarchy performance of cache-coherent multiprocessors using micro benchmarks. In: ACM/IEEE 1997 Conference Supercomputing, p. 45 (1997)

Jost, G., Jin, H., an Mey, D., Hatay, F.F.: Comparing the openmp, mpi, and hybrid programming paradigms on an smp cluster. In: Proceedings of EWOMP, vol. 3 (2003)

Krawezik, G.: Performance comparison of MPI and three OpenMP programming styles on shared memory multiprocessors. In: Proceedings of the Fifteenth Annual ACM Symposium on Parallel Algorithms and Architectures, pp. 118–127. ACM, New York (2003). ISBN 1581136617

Llanos, D.R.: TPCC-UVa: an open-source TPC-C implementation for global performance measurement of computer systems. SIGMOD Rec. **35**(4), 6–15 (2006)

Mogul, J.C., Borg, A.: The effect of context switches on cache performance. Comput. Archit. News **19**(2), 75–84 (1991)

Mohr, B., Malony, A.D., Shende, S., Wolf, F.: Design and prototype of a performance tool interface for OpenMP. J. Supercomput. **23**(1), 105–128 (2001)

Peng, L., Peir, J.K., Prakash, T.K., Staelin, C., Chen, Y.K., Koppelman, D.: Memory hierarchy performance measurement of commercial dual-core desktop processors. J. Syst. Archit. **54**(8), 816–828 (2008)

Wilson Jr., A.W.: Hierarchical cache/bus architecture for shared memory multiprocessors. In: Proceedings of the 14th Annual International Symposium on Computer Architecture, pp. 244–252. ACM, New York (1987). ISBN 0818607769

Winiecki, W., Bilski, P.: Multi-core programming approach in the real-time virtual instrumentation. In: Instrumentation and Measurement Technology Conference Proceedings, IMTC 2008, pp. 1031–1036. IEEE, New York (2008)